Sunday	Monday	Tuesday

March 2023

5 Second Week of Lent ⠀⠀V	**6** ⠀⠀V	**7** ⠀⠀V
✎ Fr. Walter J. Burghardt *Within the Word:* A Lenten Challenge in Three Verses ✎ Fr. Thomas Stegman	✙ Jean-Pierre de Caussade ✎ Eric Clayton	*[Sts. Perpetua and Felicity]* ✙ Sts. Perpetua and Felicity ✎ St. Clement of Rome
12 Third Week of Lent ⠀⠀V	**13** ⠀⠀V	**14**
✎ Sr. Melannie Svoboda *Within the Word:* Recognizing the Moment of Opportunity ✎ Catherine Upchurch	✙ Bd. Rutilio Grande ✎ Carl McColman	✙ Fannie Lou Hamer ✎ Kathy Coffey
19 Fourth Week of Lent ⠀⠀V	**20** ⠀⠀W *St. Joseph*	**21** ⠀⠀V
✎ Fr. Mark A. Villano *Within the Word:* Has God Abandoned Us? ✎ Sr. Dianne Bergant	✙ St. Cuthbert ✎ Nick Wagner	✙ St. Maria Josefa de Guerra ✎ Fr. Daniel Groody
26 Fifth Week of Lent ⠀⠀V	**27** ⠀⠀V	**28** ⠀⠀V
✎ Fr. John Meoska *Within the Word:* Lazarus, a Pivotal Figure ✎ Fr. Ronald D. Witherup	✙ St. John of Egypt ✎ Nancy Dallavalle	✙ Moses ✎ Msgr. John J. McIlhon

Key

✙ *Blessed Among Us* by Robert Ellsberg
✎ *Reflection/Within the Word* Author
[ ] *Optional Memorial*

Vestment colors:
V Violet ⠀**W** White

Wednesday	Thursday	Friday	Saturday
1 v ✝ St. Agnes of Bohemia ❧ Cardinal Basil Hume	**2** v ✝ Shahbaz Bhatti ❧ Valerie Schultz	**3** v *[St. Katharine Drexel]* ✝ Bd. Concepción Cabrera de Armida ❧ Fr. Paul Turner	**4** v *[St. Casimir]* ✝ John Wesley ❧ Christina Leaño
8 v *[St. John of God]* ✝ St. Catherine of Bologna ❧ Kathleen Norris	**9** v *[St. Frances of Rome]* ✝ St. Gregory of Nyssa ❧ Hosffman Ospino	**10** v ✝ St. Teresa Margaret Redi ❧ Mary Stommes	**11** v ✝ James Reeb ❧ Pope Francis
15 v ✝ St. Louise de Marillac ❧ Megan McKenna	**16** v ✝ Franziska Jägerstätter ❧ Sr. Ephrem Hollermann	**17** v *[St. Patrick]* ✝ Sts. Joseph of Arimathea and Nicodemus ❧ Deacon Jay Cormier	**18** v *[St. Cyril of Jerusalem]* ✝ St. Cyril of Jerusalem ❧ Sr. Irene Nowell
22 v ✝ Bd. Clemens August von Galen ❧ Daniella Zsupan-Jerome	**23** v *[St. Turibius of Mogrovejo]* ✝ St. Rebecca Ar-Rayès ❧ Michael Jordan Laskey	**24** v ✝ St. Oscar Romero ❧ Donna Barber	**25** w *Annunciation of the Lord* ✝ Ida B. Wells ❧ Michelle Francl-Donnay
29 v ✝ Marc Chagall ❧ Chiara Lubich	**30** v ✝ Thea Bowman ❧ Fr. Brendan McGuire	**31** v ✝ St. Maria Skobtsova ❧ Mary DeTurris Poust	

Give Us ThisDay®

DAILY PRAYER FOR TODAY'S CATHOLIC

Ælred Senna, OSB, *Publisher* ◆ Mary Stommes, *Editor*
Catherine Donovan, *Associate Publisher*
Regina Scaringella, OP, *Assistant Editor*
Kendra Richards Ohmann, *Publishing Assistant*
Robert Ellsberg, *"Blessed Among Us" Author*
Susan Barber, OSB, *Intercessions*
Therese L. Ratliff, *Liturgical Press Director*

Editorial Advisors

James Martin, SJ ◆ Irene Nowell, OSB
Carolyn Y. Woo ◆ Timothy Radcliffe, OP
Kathleen Norris ◆ Ronald Rolheiser, OMI

www.giveusthisday.org
Give Us This Day, Liturgical Press
PO Box 7500, Collegeville, MN 56321-7500
Customer Service: 888-259-8470, subscriptions@giveusthisday.org

© 2023 by the Order of Saint Benedict, Collegeville, Minnesota.
Printed in the United States of America.

Give Us This Day◦ (ISSN 2159-2136, print; 2166-0654, large print; 2159-2128, online) is published monthly by Liturgical Press, an apostolate of Saint John's Abbey, 2950 Saint John's Road, Collegeville, Minnesota. Rev. John Klassen, OSB, *Abbot*. For complete publication information see page 370.

CONTENTS   March 2023 ◆ Volume 13, Issue 3

The Burning Power of Love Rachelle Linner 5
Teach Us to Pray: Praying the Act of Contrition Fr. James Martin 7
The Prayer of St. Ephrem Fr. Columba Stewart 8
Prayers and Blessings 10
Prayer at Night 12
Daily Prayer 14
Order of Mass 329
Liturgy of the Word (with Holy Communion) 356
Guide to *Lectio Divina* 359
Hymns 360
About the Cover Br. Ælred Senna 369

The Burning Power of Love

Rachelle Linner

H as the Spirit led you into the desert this Lent? It is good to be there, to let God prepare you for freedom.

A Jewish interpretation of the Exodus narrative says that the children of Israel spent forty years in the desert because those who had been enslaved in Egypt had to die before the people could enter the Promised Land. Habits born under slavery were incompatible with the responsibilities of a life of freedom.

The desert is also a privileged place in Christian spirituality. It is where the monastic tradition was born, the barren wilderness where people renounced their former way of life, battled temptation, fought against afflictive thoughts, and sought to put on the mind of Christ. They faced Satan and prevailed.

If the Spirit has led you into the desert, you are blessed. You are there to meet the unknowable God. "For my thoughts are not your thoughts, nor are your ways my ways. . . . As high as the heavens are above the earth, so high are my ways above your ways and my thoughts above your thoughts" (Isa 55:8-9).

You are being led into the desert of not knowing God. Let God take away the props that support this false god you have made in your own image, the god you devised to offer an imprimatur on your words and deeds. Let God speak to your heart. Let God seduce you again.

The desert is a holy place, stark, silent, without diversions or excuses. The desert will force you to listen. The harshness of the desert brings acute knowledge of human creatureliness, your dependence on God and each other. It is not a bad thing, this admission of poverty. Your neediness is no barrier to the host who invites everyone to the feast. "All you who are thirsty, come to the water! You who have no money, come, receive grain and eat; come, without paying and without cost, drink wine and milk! . . . Heed me, and you shall eat well, you shall delight in rich fare" (Isaiah 55:1-2).

Here in the desert you will be embraced by the burning power of Love. You will be alone, but you will walk with others who are on the same journey. They are your people, your tribe. You will be with those who came before, with the saints and martyrs who watch over you on this journey. You may think you are lost, but God goes before you, a pillar of cloud in the day and a pillar of fire in the night. You will hunger and thirst, but God will provide exactly what you need, one day at a time.

Go and be filled with the holiness of the Lenten desert. Jesus accompanies you. Angels watch over you. Do not be afraid. Let God loosen the bonds that hold you captive so you can walk into the Promised Land and love as God loves: reckless and unbounded, passionate and free.

Rachelle Linner is a freelance writer, reviewer, and a spiritual director. She has a master of theological studies from Weston Jesuit School of Theology.

Teach Us to Pray
Praying the Act of Contrition
Fr. James Martin

One of the most vivid memories I have from my Catholic boyhood comes from what we used to call "CCD class" (Confraternity of Christian Doctrine, now usually called Religious Education). I was a public-school kid preparing for First Holy Communion in our local Catholic parish. One day, the Sister of St. Joseph who was teaching us "publics" took out her chalk and wrote an immense "O" on the board to begin the Act of Contrition: "O, my God, I am heartily sorry . . ."

One of the most familiar of Catholic prayers, the Act of Contrition is usually uttered by the penitent at the conclusion of the sacrament of reconciliation. But it is also a daily prayer for many. Though there are several versions of the prayer, they all express sorrow, contrition, love of God, and a "firm" amendment not to sin. Of course, we know that even after praying the Act of Contrition, we will sin again: we're human, after all. But summoning up the courage to at least try to make that amendment is a sign of God's grace in us.

The heart of the prayer, though, is about the mercy of God, "who art all good and deserving of my love." This part of the prayer is an essential reminder that while we are expressing our sorrow and contrition, God is always expressing love and forgiveness. And here, I always think of what the sacramental theologian Peter Fink, SJ, taught us in graduate school: "Confession is not about how bad you are, but how good God is."

James Martin is a Jesuit priest, editor at America *magazine, and author of many books, including* Learning to Pray: A Guide for Everyone *and* In All Seasons, For All Reasons, *a collection drawn from this column in* Give Us This Day.

The Prayer of St. Ephrem

Lord and Master of my life, do not give me a spirit of laziness
    or idle curiosity, of ambition or empty talk.

Instead, grant to me, your servant, a spirit of self-control and
    humility, of patience and love.

Yes, Lord and King, enable me to see my own failings, and
    not to judge my brother or sister, for you are blessed unto
    the ages of ages. Amen.

~

The Prayer of St. Ephrem is the great Lenten prayer of the
Byzantine-rite churches, Orthodox and Catholic. It is prayed
at least twice daily in the weekday services of Lent and used
privately as well. Although attributed to the great Syriac poet
Ephrem of Nisibis (d. 373), the prayer was composed in
Greek, probably in the fifth century, and then translated over
the centuries into the many languages of the Byzantine rite.
This broad reach recommends the prayer to us Western
Christians. Its few lines take us directly to Jesus' fundamental
imperatives: repent; be mindful of your own sins; do not
judge others.

Like all Eastern Christians, those of the Byzantine tradition express their prayer physically as well as verbally. After
each of the three verses of this prayer, they kneel and then
bend over to touch their forehead to the ground. Those who
can't make the full gesture make a deep bow. Touching the
forehead to the ground is not a gesture familiar to most of us
Latin-rite Catholics—genuflection is about as far as we get.
We associate such dramatic postures with other religions such
as Islam, not realizing that the daily prayer times of Islam
and their characteristic gestures were likely inspired by Chris-

tian practices. This takes us to another depth of universality. When we recognize our sinfulness and need for God's mercy, whatever our formal religious confession, it is natural to imitate the response of Moses before the Burning Bush or the disciples before the Transfigured Christ, falling on our faces to adore the Living God.

It is ironic that for all of our exercises, stretches, and yoga, we can be self-conscious about embodying our devotion. Those who begin to use prostrations or similar practices as they stand before an icon or recite a beloved prayer can find their prayer deepened in unexpected ways as they venture into a fuller range of expression. A friend who teaches in a Ukrainian Catholic seminary begins each class during Lent with the Prayer of St. Ephrem and its prostrations. He tells me that it changes the atmosphere of the classroom remarkably, reminding both students and teacher that they are not there to show off or to put down others, that they need not be ashamed to admit what they do not understand. I wonder how such a practice would change the atmosphere of negotiations or difficult conversations, or even our routine interactions in meetings and daily business. This Lent may be the occasion to broaden our repertoire of prayer, and not only in words.

Fr. Columba Stewart

Columba Stewart, OSB, a monk of Saint John's Abbey, is the author of Prayer and Community: The Benedictine Tradition *and* Cassian the Monk. *He is currently writing a new history of the origins of Christian monasticism.*

(Editor's note: this prayer and reflection originally appeared in the February 2013 issue of *Give Us This Day*.)

Act of Contrition

O my God,
I am heartily sorry for having offended you,
and I detest all my sins because of your just punishments,
but most of all because they offend you, my God,
who are all good and deserving of all my love.
I firmly resolve with the help of your grace
to sin no more and to avoid the near occasion of sin.
Amen.

O Cross, more worthy than cedar,
on you the life of the world was nailed,
on you Christ has triumphed:
death has destroyed death!

Glory to you, Jesus, Savior,
your cross gives us life!

Behold the tree of life
where the innocent man bears our sins
in order to reconcile earth and heaven:
Come, let us adore!

—*Days of the Lord*

Lord Jesus Christ,
Son of the living God,
have mercy on me, a sinner.

Prayer to St. Joseph

Saint Joseph,
Man of enlightening dreams
Obedient servant of God,
accompany us, with your wife, the Blessed Virgin Mary,
throughout our life
to the glory and praise of God,
now and for ever and ever.
Amen.

   —*Blessings and Prayers for Home and Family*

Forsake me not, O Lord!
My God, be not far from me!

Make haste and come to my help,
my Lord and my salvation!

   —Psalm 38:22-23

On the Solemnity of the Annunciation

God our Father,
today you give us the prophetic sign
—the Virgin has conceived Emmanuel.
May the Spirit who overshadowed Mary
come upon your Church also,
and make her the earthly sign of your love,
through Jesus, the Christ, our Lord.

   —*Proclaiming All Your Wonders*

Prayer at Night

God, come to my assistance.
Lord, make haste to help me.

EXAMINATION OF CONSCIENCE
Briefly consider your day: What did I do well? What could
I have done better? Whom did I offend? Whom did I help
or encourage?
Pray the Act of Contrition or another prayer of sorrow and
promise of amendment.

PSALM 134
O come and bless the LORD,
all you servants of the LORD,
who stand by night in the house of the LORD.
Lift up your hands to the holy place,
and bless the LORD.

May the LORD bless you from Zion,
who made both heaven and earth.

Glory to the Father . . .

SCRIPTURE   Colossians 3:12-15
Put on then, as God's chosen ones, holy and beloved,
heartfelt compassion, kindness, humility, gentleness,
and patience, bearing with one another and forgiving one
another, if one has a grievance against another; as the Lord
has forgiven you, so must you also do. And over all these
put on love, that is, the bond of perfection. And let the peace
of Christ control your hearts, the peace into which you were
also called in one body. And be thankful.

ANTIPHON

Protect us, Lord, while we are awake and safeguard us
while we sleep, that we may keep watch with Christ and
rest in peace.

CANTICLE OF SIMEON

Lord, now let your servant go in peace;
your word has been fulfilled:

my own eyes have seen the salvation
which you have prepared in the sight of every people:

a light to reveal you to the nations
and the glory of your people Israel.

Glory to the Father . . .

MARIAN ANTIPHON (or another Marian hymn, pp. 364–65)

Hail, O Mary, Queen of heaven,
Queen of all the saints and angels,
Root of Jesse, heaven's portal
Source of light of all the world.
Now rejoice, O glorious Virgin,
Blessed with beauty far surpassing
All that ever was created!
Pray for us to Christ the Lord.

BLESSING

May God grant us a peaceful night and a perfect end.
May the divine assistance be always with us and with all
    our loved ones. Amen.

Wednesday, March 1

Morning

O Lord, open my lips.
And my mouth will proclaim your praise.

(opt. hymn, pp. 360–65)

PSALM 147:12-20

O Jerusalem, glorify the LORD!
O Zion, praise your God,
who has strengthened the bars of your gates,
and has blessed your children within you;
who established peace on your borders,
and gives you your fill of finest wheat.

The Lord sends out his word to the earth;
the divine command runs swiftly.
God showers down snow like wool,
and scatters hoarfrost like ashes.

The Lord hurls down hailstones like crumbs;
before such cold, who can stand?
God sends forth a word and it melts them;
at the blowing of God's breath the waters flow.

The Lord reveals a word to Jacob;
to Israel, decrees and judgments.
God has not dealt thus with other nations,
has not taught them heaven's judgments.

Glory to the Father . . .

SCRIPTURE   1 Kings 10:1, 4, 5b-6, 9

The queen of Sheba, having heard a report of Solomon's
fame, came to test him with subtle questions. When

the queen of Sheba witnessed Solomon's great wisdom, the house he had built, . . . and the burnt offerings he offered in the house of the LORD, it took her breath away. "The report I heard in my country about your deeds and your wisdom is true," she told the king. "Blessed be the LORD, your God, who has been pleased to place you on the throne of Israel. In his enduring love for Israel, the LORD has made you king to carry out judgment and justice."

READ, PONDER, PRAY on a word or phrase from these readings or another of today's Scriptures (*Lectio Divina*, p. 359)

ANTIPHON

The queen of the south came from the ends of the earth to hear the wisdom of Solomon.

CANTICLE OF ZECHARIAH (*inside front cover*)

INTERCESSIONS

Gracious God, you lavish us with grace and gifts. In faith we pray: ℟. **Teach us your ways, O God.**

Help us to establish peace on our borders and justice for immigrants. ℟.

Strengthen your Church's response to the pain of those who have suffered abuse. ℟.

Inspire us to make choices for the good of the earth and future generations. ℟.

Our Father . . .

May God show us mercy, forgive our sin, and bring us to everlasting life through Jesus, our brother. Amen.

Blessed Among Us

St. Agnes of Bohemia
Princess and Abbess (ca. 1203–1280)

Born in Prague, Agnes was the daughter of the king of Bohemia. Despite the privileges of her station, she enjoyed no freedom to decide her own destiny. She was simply a commodity to be invested wherever she might bring the highest return for her family and its dynastic interests. Starting at the age of three, she was shipped to various kingdoms and betrothed to strangers she had never met. Through chance or providence, all these engagements came to naught. Finally, when she was to be paired with King Henry III of England, she wrote to the pope asking him to prevent the marriage on the grounds that she wished to consecrate herself to Christ. Surprisingly, Henry yielded.

What inspired Agnes's bold intention? She had been deeply affected by the arrival in Prague of the first Franciscan friars, followed shortly by the arrival of five Poor Clare sisters. In 1236, her royal life behind her, Agnes formally joined them. Agnes received a number of personal letters from St. Clare, who called Agnes her "half-self," holding her "more than any other in the greatest affection." In Bohemia alone, one hundred young girls accompanied her into the Poor Clares. She died in 1280 and was canonized in 1989.

"Place your mind before the mirror of eternity! Place your soul in the brilliance of glory! Place your heart in the figure of the divine substance! And transform your whole being into the image of the Godhead itself through contemplation."

—St. Clare to St. Agnes

The "Blessed Among Us" features each month are written by Robert Ellsberg, author of *All Saints*.

Mass
Wednesday of the First Week of Lent

ENTRANCE ANTIPHON   Cf. Psalm 25 (24):6, 2, 22

Remember your compassion, O Lord, / and your merciful love, for they are from of old. / Let not our enemies exult over us. / Redeem us, O God of Israel, from all our distress.

COLLECT

Look kindly, Lord, we pray,
on the devotion of your people,
that those who by self-denial are restrained in body
may by the fruit of good works be renewed in mind.
Through our Lord Jesus Christ, your Son,
who lives and reigns with you in the unity of the Holy Spirit,
God, for ever and ever.

A reading from the Book of the Prophet Jonah   3:1-10

The Ninevites turned from their evil way.

The word of the LORD came to Jonah a second time: "Set out for the great city of Nineveh, and announce to it the message that I will tell you." So Jonah made ready and went to Nineveh, according to the LORD's bidding. Now Nineveh was an enormously large city; it took three days to go through it. Jonah began his journey through the city, and had gone but a single day's walk announcing, "Forty days more and Nineveh shall be destroyed," when the people of Nineveh believed God; they proclaimed a fast and all of them, great and small, put on sackcloth.

When the news reached the king of Nineveh, he rose from his throne, laid aside his robe, covered himself with sackcloth, and sat in the ashes. Then he had this proclaimed throughout Nineveh, by decree of the king and his nobles:

"Neither man nor beast, neither cattle nor sheep, shall taste anything; they shall not eat, nor shall they drink water. Man and beast shall be covered with sackcloth and call loudly to God; every man shall turn from his evil way and from the violence he has in hand. Who knows, God may relent and forgive, and withhold his blazing wrath, so that we shall not perish." When God saw by their actions how they turned from their evil way, he repented of the evil that he had threatened to do to them; he did not carry it out.

The word of the Lord.

RESPONSORIAL PSALM   51:3-4, 12-13, 18-19

R̠. (19b) **A heart contrite and humbled, O God, you will not spurn.**

Have mercy on me, O God, in your goodness;
  in the greatness of your compassion wipe out my
     offense.
Thoroughly wash me from my guilt
  and of my sin cleanse me. R̠.

A clean heart create for me, O God,
  and a steadfast spirit renew within me.
Cast me not out from your presence,
  and your Holy Spirit take not from me. R̠.

For you are not pleased with sacrifices;
  should I offer a burnt offering, you would not accept it.
My sacrifice, O God, is a contrite spirit;
  a heart contrite and humbled, O God, you will not
     spurn. R̠.

GOSPEL ACCLAMATION   Joel 2:12-13
Even now, says the LORD,
return to me with your whole heart
for I am gracious and merciful.

A reading from the holy Gospel according to Luke 11:29-32

No sign will be given to this generation except the sign of Jonah.

While still more people gathered in the crowd, Jesus said to them, "This generation is an evil generation; it seeks a sign, but no sign will be given it, except the sign of Jonah. Just as Jonah became a sign to the Ninevites, so will the Son of Man be to this generation. At the judgment the queen of the south will rise with the men of this generation and she will condemn them, because she came from the ends of the earth to hear the wisdom of Solomon, and there is something greater than Solomon here. At the judgment the men of Nineveh will arise with this generation and condemn it, because at the preaching of Jonah they repented, and there is something greater than Jonah here."

The Gospel of the Lord.

PRAYER OVER THE OFFERINGS

We offer to you, O Lord,
what you have given to be dedicated to your name,
that, just as for our benefit you make these gifts a
    Sacrament,
so you may let them become for us an eternal remedy.
Through Christ our Lord.

COMMUNION ANTIPHON   Cf. Psalm 5:12

All who take refuge in you shall be glad, O Lord, / and ever cry out their joy, and you shall dwell among them.

PRAYER AFTER COMMUNION

O God, who never cease to nourish us by your Sacrament,
grant that the refreshment you give us through it
may bring us unending life.
Through Christ our Lord.

Reflection

When Love Dawns on Us

God is like a lover who loves and whose love is not returned. So God has to wait, and God waits for a change of heart in his beloved. God waits, and does not force, because to force would be to violate the law of love. God waits until the strength of his love begins to dawn on the one whom he loves and who is not yet able to return it. And God reveals himself this way, hoping that the beloved will begin to open his or her eyes and ears to what God has done.

This change of heart in the beloved, you and me, is conversion. This conversion, this change of heart, includes repentance. Repentance is not repentance for a Christian unless it includes the realization of forgiveness. If it did not, it would be shame or remorse.

But for the Christian, sorrow for our sins, a realization of our weakness, is never depressing, should never make us downcast, because if it is truly the result of the grace of God then at the same time it includes the dawning, the realization of what God's forgiveness is. So repentance for the Christian is always, paradoxically, a joyous occasion, one that leads to peace.

God, as we turn our hearts and minds to you, give us the peace of your forgiveness.

Cardinal Basil Hume, adapted from *A Turning to God*

George Basil Hume (1923–1999), OSB, Abbot of Ampleforth Abbey, was one of the most beloved religious figures in the United Kingdom.

Evening

God, come to my assistance.
Lord, make haste to help me.

(opt. hymn, pp. 360–65)

PSALM 137:1-5, 7-9
By the rivers of Babylon
there we sat and wept,
remembering Zion;
on the poplars that grew there
we hung up our harps.

For it was there that they asked us,
our captors, for songs,
our oppressors, for joy.
"Sing to us," they said,
"one of Zion's songs."

O how could we sing
the song of the LORD
on foreign soil?
If I forget you, Jerusalem,
let my right hand wither!

Remember, O LORD,
against the children of Edom
the day of Jerusalem,
when they said, "Tear it down!
Tear it down to its foundations!"

O daughter Babylon, destroyer,
blessed who repays you the payment you paid to us!
Blessed who grasps and shatters your children on the rock!

Glory to the Father . . .

SCRIPTURE   2 Peter 3:8-10

D]o not ignore this one fact, beloved, that with the Lord one day is like a thousand years and a thousand years like one day. The Lord does not delay his promise, as some regard "delay," but he is patient with you, not wishing that any should perish but that all should come to repentance. But the day of the Lord will come like a thief, and then the heavens will pass away with a mighty roar and the elements will be dissolved by fire, and the earth and everything done on it will be found out.

READ, PONDER, PRAY on a word or phrase from these readings or another of today's Scriptures (*Lectio Divina*, p. 359)

ANTIPHON
God desires that all should come to repentance and be saved.

CANTICLE OF MARY *(inside back cover)*

INTERCESSIONS
Living God, your presence is our joy. In hope we pray:
R̸. **Hear our prayer, O God.**

Strengthen our faith, and help us to bring joy to those around us. R̸.

Protect all who are homeless or endangered by drug abusers. R̸.

Shower your graces upon those who mourn, and help us to support one another in times of grief. R̸.

Our Father . . .

May God grant us the grace of repentance and lead us toward Easter joy, through Jesus and by the power of the Holy Spirit. Amen.

JO NAS

Thursday, March 2

Morning

O Lord, open my lips.
And my mouth will proclaim your praise.

PSALM 37:7-9, 37-40   (opt. hymn, pp. 360–65)

Be still before the LORD and wait in patience;
do not fret at the one who prospers,
the one who makes evil plots.

Calm your anger and forget your rage;
do not fret, it only leads to evil.
For those who do evil shall perish.
But those who hope in the LORD,
they shall inherit the land.

Mark the blameless, observe the upright;
for the peaceful a future lies in store,
but sinners shall all be destroyed,
the future of the wicked cut off.

But from the LORD comes the salvation of the righteous,
their stronghold in time of distress.
The LORD helps them and rescues them,
rescues and saves them from the wicked,
for their refuge is in God.

Glory to the Father . . .

SCRIPTURE   Judith 9:11-12, 14

Your strength is not in numbers, nor does your might
depend upon the powerful. You are God of the lowly,
helper of those of little account, supporter of the weak, protector of those in despair, savior of those without hope.

"Please, please, God of my father, God of the heritage of Israel, Master of heaven and earth, Creator of the waters, King of all you have created, hear my prayer! Make every nation and every tribe know clearly that you are God, the God of all power and might, and that there is no other who shields the people of Israel but you alone."

READ, PONDER, PRAY on a word or phrase from these readings or another of today's Scriptures (*Lectio Divina*, p. 359)

ANTIPHON
Lord, save us by your power; we have no one to help but you.

CANTICLE OF ZECHARIAH *(inside front cover)*

INTERCESSIONS
Saving God, you are our refuge. In confidence we pray:
R̃. **God of peace, hear our prayer.**

Unite efforts to end the war in Ukraine and other places that experience oppression. R̃.

Thwart the plots of those who plan destruction or injury. R̃.

Comfort and guide those who are in need of support and hope. R̃.

Our Father . . .

May almighty God bless us, protect us, and shower grace upon us, through Jesus our Savior. Amen.

Blessed Among Us

Servant of God Shahbaz Bhatti
Champion of Civil Rights, Martyr (1968–2011)

Shahbaz Bhatti was born in the Punjab region of Pakistan. As devout Catholics, his family was part of a small minority in the overwhelmingly Muslim country. From an early age, Bhatti felt a religious calling to serve both his fellow Christians and other minorities (including Hindus, Sikhs, and others) who were subjected to discrimination, persecution, and periodic outbreaks of violence. As a university student he pursued these efforts through an organization called the Christian Liberation Front.

In 2002, Bhatti convened the first meeting of the All Pakistan Minorities Alliance. As well as advancing the welfare of religious minorities, Bhatti and the Alliance undertook relief work on behalf of victims of natural disasters—thus winning widespread respect. On this basis, in 2008, he was named to a cabinet position as Federal Minister for Minority Affairs. In this office he undertook numerous efforts to promote interfaith harmony, while defending the rights of all religious minorities. At the same time, however, he challenged the gathering forces of extremism and fanaticism and drew particular opposition for his active role in challenging Pakistan's blasphemy laws. As a result, he received constant threats and spoke openly of his expectation of death and his willingness to offer his life.

On March 2, 2011, he was attacked by gunmen and killed. His cause for canonization, supported by the bishops of Pakistan, is in process.

"I know well Jesus Christ who sacrificed his life for others. I understand well the meaning of the cross. I am ready to give my life for my people."
　　　　　　　　　　　　　　　　—Servant of God Shahbaz Bhatti

Mass

Thursday of the First Week of Lent

ENTRANCE ANTIPHON   Cf. Psalm 5:2-3

To my words give ear, O Lord; give heed to my sighs. /
Attend to the sound of my cry, my King and my God.

COLLECT

Bestow on us, we pray, O Lord,
a spirit of always pondering on what is right
and of hastening to carry it out,
and, since without you we cannot exist,
may we be enabled to live according to your will.
Through our Lord Jesus Christ, your Son,
who lives and reigns with you in the unity of the Holy Spirit,
God, for ever and ever.

A reading from the Book of Esther   C:12, 14-16, 23-25

I have no protector other than you, LORD.

Queen Esther, seized with mortal anguish, had recourse
to the LORD. She lay prostrate upon the ground, together with her handmaids, from morning until evening,
and said: "God of Abraham, God of Isaac, and God of Jacob,
blessed are you. Help me, who am alone and have no help
but you, for I am taking my life in my hand. As a child I used
to hear from the books of my forefathers that you, O LORD,
always free those who are pleasing to you. Now help me,
who am alone and have no one but you, O LORD, my God.

"And now, come to help me, an orphan. Put in my mouth
persuasive words in the presence of the lion and turn his
heart to hatred for our enemy, so that he and those who are
in league with him may perish. Save us from the hand of

our enemies; turn our mourning into gladness and our sorrows into wholeness."

The word of the Lord.

RESPONSORIAL PSALM   138:1-2ab, 2cde-3, 7c-8

R℣. (3a) **Lord, on the day I called for help, you answered me.**

I will give thanks to you, O LORD, with all my heart,
   for you have heard the words of my mouth;
   in the presence of the angels I will sing your praise;
I will worship at your holy temple
   and give thanks to your name. R℣.

Because of your kindness and your truth;
   for you have made great above all things
   your name and your promise.
When I called, you answered me;
   you built up strength within me. R℣.

Your right hand saves me.
The LORD will complete what he has done for me;
   your kindness, O LORD, endures forever;
   forsake not the work of your hands. R℣.

GOSPEL ACCLAMATION   Psalm 51:12a, 14a
A clean heart create for me, O God;
give me back the joy of your salvation.

A reading from the holy Gospel according to Matthew
                                                        7:7-12

Everyone who asks, receives.

Jesus said to his disciples: "Ask and it will be given to you; seek and you will find; knock and the door will be opened to you. For everyone who asks, receives; and the one who seeks, finds; and to the one who knocks, the door will be opened. Which one of you would hand his son a stone when he asked for a loaf of bread, or a snake when he asked for a fish? If you then, who are wicked, know how to give good gifts to your children, how much more will your heavenly Father give good things to those who ask him.

"Do to others whatever you would have them do to you. This is the law and the prophets."

The Gospel of the Lord.

PRAYER OVER THE OFFERINGS

Be merciful, O Lord, to those who approach you in
    supplication,
and, accepting the oblations and prayers of your people,
turn the hearts of us all towards you.
Through Christ our Lord.

COMMUNION ANTIPHON   Matthew 7:8

Everyone who asks, receives; and the one who seeks, finds; / and to the one who knocks, the door will be opened.

PRAYER AFTER COMMUNION

We pray, O Lord our God,
that, as you have given these most sacred mysteries
to be the safeguard of our salvation,
so you may make them a healing remedy for us,
both now and in time to come.
Through Christ our Lord.

Reflection

Have a Little Faith

Leave it to a childless man to teach parents about parenting.

A new parent knows the unspoken terror of bringing the baby home. I remember thinking, "You're trusting *us* with her? We don't know what we're doing!" It was a leap of faith for the hospital staff to assume we could be adequate parents, just as we had to have faith that we could care for our daughter. We prayed for grace mightily in those first days.

Maybe that's the bottom line of faith: understanding that our only hope lies in divine assistance. The hard part is surrendering ourselves to faith. Esther's story is a dramatic and desperate representation of that recourse. Jesus directs our prayer even more simply: "Ask . . . seek . . . knock." If we have a little faith, God will answer.

Jesus delves deep into a parent's heart, assuring us that, because we know what it is to provide for our children, we already possess an intimate insight into God's love. With Jesus' comparison of giving our children "good gifts"—loaves and fishes (a manner of feeding that Jesus knows well)—rather than stones and snakes, we glimpse the parental generosity of our God.

Even if we aren't parents, if we imperfect humans can respond to another's needs, we can trust that God will respond to us. By visualizing our faith in the context of a parent's all-encompassing love, we get it: *Lord, on the day I called for help, you answered me.*

Valerie Schultz

Valerie Schultz is a freelance writer and essayist. She is author of Overdue: A Dewey Decimal System of Grace *and the recently released* A Hill of Beans: The Grace of Everyday Troubles.

Evening

God, come to my assistance.
Lord, make haste to help me.

(opt. hymn, pp. 360–65)

PSALM 145:1-9

I will extol you, my God and King,
and bless your name forever and ever.

I will bless you day after day,
and praise your name forever and ever.
The LORD is great and highly to be praised;
God's greatness cannot be measured.

Age to age shall proclaim your works,
shall declare your mighty deeds.
They will tell of your great glory and splendor,
and recount your wonderful works.

They will speak of your awesome deeds,
recount your greatness and might.
They will recall your abundant goodness,
and sing of your righteous deeds with joy.

The LORD is kind and full of compassion,
slow to anger, abounding in mercy.
How good are you, O LORD, to all,
compassionate to all your creatures.

Glory to the Father . . .

SCRIPTURE   1 John 3:21-24

Beloved, if [our] hearts do not condemn us, we have
confidence in God and receive from him whatever we
ask, because we keep his commandments and do what
pleases him. And his commandment is this: we should

believe in the name of his Son, Jesus Christ, and love one another just as he commanded us. Those who keep his commandments remain in him, and he in them, and the way we know that he remains in us is from the Spirit that he gave us.

READ, PONDER, PRAY on a word or phrase from these readings or another of today's Scriptures (*Lectio Divina*, p. 359)

ANTIPHON

Ask and it will be given to you; seek and you will find.

CANTICLE OF MARY *(inside back cover)*

INTERCESSIONS

God of splendor and might, your mercy spans the heavens and the earth. In trust we pray: ℟. God, in your wisdom, hear us.

Help us to know your love and to grow in faith. ℟.

Give patience, compassion, and joy to parents and guardians. ℟.

Guide law enforcement, detectives, and security personnel in their work. ℟.

Our Father . . .

May God bless us with courage to seek truth and to live the faith we profess, through Jesus, the Wisdom of God. Amen.

Friday, March 3

Morning

O Lord, open my lips.
And my mouth will proclaim your praise.

(opt. hymn, pp. 360–65)

PSALM 51:12-19

Create a pure heart for me, O God;
renew a steadfast spirit within me.
Do not cast me away from your presence;
take not your holy spirit from me.

Restore in me the joy of your salvation;
sustain in me a willing spirit.
I will teach transgressors your ways,
that sinners may return to you.

Rescue me from bloodshed, O God,
O God of my salvation,
and then my tongue shall ring out your righteousness.
O Lord, open my lips
and my mouth shall proclaim your praise.

For in sacrifice you take no delight;
burnt offering from me would not please you.
My sacrifice to God, a broken spirit:
a broken and humbled heart,
you will not spurn, O God.

Glory to the Father . . .

SCRIPTURE   Isaiah 44:21-23

Remember these things, Jacob, / Israel, for you are my
servant! / I formed you, a servant to me; / Israel, you

shall never be forgotten by me: / I have brushed away your offenses like a cloud, / your sins like a mist; / return to me, for I have redeemed you.

Raise a glad cry, you heavens—the LORD has acted! / Shout, you depths of the earth. / Break forth, mountains, into song, / forest, with all your trees. / For the LORD has redeemed Jacob, / shows his glory through Israel.

READ, PONDER, PRAY on a word or phrase from these readings or another of today's Scriptures (*Lectio Divina*, p. 359)

ANTIPHON
If you repent, you shall surely live.

CANTICLE OF ZECHARIAH (*inside front cover*)

INTERCESSIONS
Forgiving God, you show us the way to love. In confidence we pray: R̷. **God of salvation, receive our prayer.**

Give wisdom, compassion, and humility to those who guide nations and shape policies. R̷.

Strengthen and guide nurses, physicians, and first responders. R̷.

Help us to collaborate with one another in efforts to address climate change and violence. R̷.

Our Father . . .

May God renew in us a steadfast spirit and loving heart, by the working of the Holy Spirit, through Jesus, our brother. Amen.

Blessed Among Us

Blessed Concepción Cabrera de Armida
Mystic (1862–1937)

Concepción Cabrera de Armida, who was born in San Luis Potosí, Mexico, married at the age of twenty-two and bore nine children. When she was thirty-nine her husband died, leaving her alone to care for her children. Despite her trials, she maintained a disciplined life of prayer and enjoyed frequent mystical colloquies with Jesus and Mary. These she recorded in handwritten notes that eventually totaled 60,000 pages, resulting in 200 books. This fulfilled a message reportedly received from God: "Ask me for a long suffering life and to write a lot. . . . That's your mission on earth."

Her writings on the Eucharist, prayer, and the spiritual life were examined and viewed favorably by Church authorities. Some of them were distributed, inspiring the foundation of five apostolates of the "Work of the Cross," including religious and priestly congregations.

Conchita, as she was known, died on March 3, 1937, in Mexico City. In 2019 she became the first laywoman beatified in Mexico.

"I carry within me three lives, all very strong: family life with its multiple sorrows of a thousand kinds, that is, the life of a mother; the life of the Works of the Cross with all its sorrows and weight, which at times crushes me until I have no strength left; and the life of the spirit or interior life, which is the heaviest of all, with its highs and lows, its tempests and struggles, its light and darkness. Blessed be God for everything!"

—Blessed Concepción Cabrera de Armida

Mass

Friday of the First Week of Lent
[*St. Katharine Drexel*, opt. memorial]

ENTRANCE ANTIPHON   Cf. Psalm 25 (24):17-18
Set me free from my distress, O Lord. / See my lowliness
and suffering, / and take away all my sins.

COLLECT
Grant that your faithful, O Lord, we pray,
may be so conformed to the paschal observances,
that the bodily discipline now solemnly begun
may bear fruit in the souls of all.
Through our Lord Jesus Christ, your Son,
who lives and reigns with you in the unity of the Holy Spirit,
God, for ever and ever.

A reading from the Book of the Prophet Ezekiel 18:21-28

*Do I derive any pleasure from the death of the wicked and
not rejoice when he turns from his evil way that he may live?*

Thus says the Lord GOD: If the wicked man turns away
from all the sins he committed, if he keeps all my statutes and does what is right and just, he shall surely live, he
shall not die. None of the crimes he committed shall be
remembered against him; he shall live because of the virtue
he has practiced. Do I indeed derive any pleasure from the
death of the wicked? says the Lord GOD. Do I not rather
rejoice when he turns from his evil way that he may live?

And if the virtuous man turns from the path of virtue to
do evil, the same kind of abominable things that the wicked
man does, can he do this and still live? None of his virtuous
deeds shall be remembered, because he has broken faith
and committed sin; because of this, he shall die. You say,

"The LORD's way is not fair!" Hear now, house of Israel: Is it my way that is unfair, or rather, are not your ways unfair? When someone virtuous turns away from virtue to commit iniquity, and dies, it is because of the iniquity he committed that he must die. But if the wicked, turning from the wickedness he has committed, does what is right and just, he shall preserve his life; since he has turned away from all the sins that he committed, he shall surely live, he shall not die.

The word of the Lord.

RESPONSORIAL PSALM   130:1-2, 3-4, 5-7a, 7bc-8

R℣. (3) **If you, O Lord, mark iniquities, who can stand?**

Out of the depths I cry to you, O LORD;
    LORD, hear my voice!
Let your ears be attentive
    to my voice in supplication. R℣.

If you, O LORD, mark iniquities,
    LORD, who can stand?
But with you is forgiveness,
    that you may be revered. R℣.

I trust in the LORD;
    my soul trusts in his word.
My soul waits for the LORD
    more than sentinels wait for the dawn.
Let Israel wait for the LORD. R℣.

For with the LORD is kindness
    and with him is plenteous redemption;
And he will redeem Israel
    from all their iniquities. R℣.

Gospel Acclamation   Ezekiel 18:31
Cast away from you all the crimes you have committed,
    says the Lord,
and make for yourselves a new heart and a new spirit.

A reading from the holy Gospel according to Matthew
                                                        5:20-26
Go first and be reconciled with your brother.

J esus said to his disciples: "I tell you, unless your righteousness surpasses that of the scribes and Pharisees, you will not enter into the Kingdom of heaven.

"You have heard that it was said to your ancestors, *You shall not kill; and whoever kills will be liable to judgment.* But I say to you, whoever is angry with his brother will be liable to judgment, and whoever says to his brother, *Raqa*, will be answerable to the Sanhedrin, and whoever says, 'You fool,' will be liable to fiery Gehenna. Therefore, if you bring your gift to the altar, and there recall that your brother has anything against you, leave your gift there at the altar, go first and be reconciled with your brother, and then come and offer your gift. Settle with your opponent quickly while on the way to court. Otherwise your opponent will hand you over to the judge, and the judge will hand you over to the guard, and you will be thrown into prison. Amen, I say to you, you will not be released until you have paid the last penny."

The Gospel of the Lord.

Prayer over the Offerings
Accept the sacrificial offerings, O Lord,
by which, in your power and kindness,
you willed us to be reconciled to yourself
and our salvation to be restored.
Through Christ our Lord.

COMMUNION ANTIPHON   Ezekiel 33:11
**As I live, says the Lord, I do not desire the death of the
sinner, / but rather that he turn back and live.**

PRAYER AFTER COMMUNION
**May the holy refreshment of your Sacrament
restore us anew, O Lord,
and, cleansing us of old ways,
take us up into the mystery of salvation.
Through Christ our Lord.**

Reflection

It's On Us

God's accessible forgiveness should inspire us toward a
virtuous life, but it sometimes weakens us into greater sin.
We know we can be forgiven, we've already committed one
sin, might as well commit another.

If you think God gets frustrated with this line of thought,
today's verse before the Gospel will verify your suspicions.
"Cast away from you all the crimes you have committed, says
the LORD, and make for yourselves a new heart and a new
spirit" (Ezek 18:31).

In this verse, God does not say, "I love you," or "I forgive
you," or even "I'm here to help," as he does in so many other
places. In this verse, God does not talk about himself. God
talks about us. God does not exhort us toward a better life.
God commands it.

God can do only so much. We have to cast away our
crimes. We have to make ourselves a new heart. We have to
adopt a new spirit. God only points the way.

This verse from Ezekiel prepares for a Gospel in which Jesus says that our righteousness must surpass "that of the scribes and Pharisees" (Matt 5:20). The same Gospel acclamation appears twice more during Lent: Tuesday of the Second Week, where later in Matthew Jesus again criticizes "the scribes and Pharisees" (23:1-12); and Saturday of the Fifth Week, when religious leaders plot to take Jesus' life (John 11:45-56).

On this Friday of Lent, we abstain from meat to show our repentance. But we must take a further step: cast our crimes away to make for ourselves a new heart.

Fr. Paul Turner

Paul Turner is the pastor of the Cathedral of the Immaculate Conception in Kansas City, Missouri. He is the author of numerous books and is coeditor of the Liturgy and Life Study Bible.

Evening

God, come to my assistance.
Lord, make haste to help me.

(opt. hymn, pp. 360–65)

PSALM 119:9-16
How shall a youth remain pure on life's way?
By obeying your word.
I seek you with all my heart;
let me not stray from your commands.

I treasure your word in my heart,
lest I sin against you.
Blest are you, O LORD;
teach me your statutes.

With my lips have I recounted
all the decrees of your mouth.
I rejoice in the way of your precepts,
as though all riches were mine.

I will ponder your precepts,
and consider your paths.
I take delight in your statutes;
I will not forget your word.

Glory to the Father . . .

SCRIPTURE   Romans 2:1-4
Y]ou are without excuse, every one of you who passes
judgment. For by the standard by which you judge
another you condemn yourself, since you, the judge, do the
very same things. We know that the judgment of God on
those who do such things is true. Do you suppose, then,
you who judge those who engage in such things and yet do

them yourself, that you will escape the judgment of God?
Or do you hold his priceless kindness, forbearance, and
patience in low esteem, unaware that the kindness of God
would lead you to repentance?

READ, PONDER, PRAY on a word or phrase from these readings or
another of today's Scriptures (*Lectio Divina*, p. 359)

ANTIPHON
Be reconciled to one another.

CANTICLE OF MARY (*inside back cover*)

INTERCESSIONS
Reconciling God, you are wise beyond all time. In hope
we pray: R℣. **God, in your loving-kindness, hear our
prayer.**

Inspire us to care for the earth and to foster greater
hospitality in our communities. R℣.

Advance efforts to relieve those who suffer the effects of
natural or human-made disasters. R℣.

Give unending life to those who have died with their
hope fixed on you. R℣.

Our Father . . .

May the Word of God be always on our lips and in our
hearts, by the grace of God and the power of the Holy
Spirit. Amen.

Saturday, March 4

Morning

O Lord, open my lips.
And my mouth will proclaim your praise.

(opt. hymn, pp. 360–65)

PSALM 124

"If the LORD had not been on our side,"
let Israel say—
"If the LORD had not been on our side
when people rose against us,
then would they have swallowed us alive
when their anger was kindled.

"Then would the waters have engulfed us,
the torrent gone over us;
over our head would have swept
the raging waters."

Blest be the LORD who did not give us
as prey to their teeth!
Our life, like a bird, has escaped
from the snare of the fowler.

Indeed, the snare has been broken,
and we have escaped.
Our help is in the name of the LORD,
who made heaven and earth.

Glory to the Father . . .

SCRIPTURE   Leviticus 19:2, 33-34
Speak to the whole Israelite community and tell them:
Be holy, for I, the LORD your God, am holy.

When an alien resides with you in your land, do not mistreat such a one. You shall treat the alien who resides with you no differently than the natives born among you; you shall love the alien as yourself; for you too were once aliens in the land of Egypt. I, the LORD, am your God.

READ, PONDER, PRAY on a word or phrase from these readings or another of today's Scriptures (*Lectio Divina*, p. 359)

ANTIPHON
Love your enemies, and pray for those who persecute you.

CANTICLE OF ZECHARIAH *(inside front cover)*

INTERCESSIONS
Loving God, you made us and we belong to you. In faith we pray: R̶. **Lead us to greater love, O God.**

Help us to forgive those who have trespassed against us. R̶.

Give us grace to ask for forgiveness and to be reconciled with one another. R̶.

Heal the wounds of division and the scars of abuse. R̶.

Our Father . . .

May the Spirit of God light our way and guard us in peace. Amen.

Blessed Among Us

John Wesley
Founder, Methodism (1703–1791)

John Wesley, the son of devout Anglicans, received holy orders following his studies at Oxford. Rather than serve in a parish, Wesley felt called to become a missionary preacher. He tried this out in Georgia, but his efforts were singularly unfruitful, and he was virtually booted out of the colony.

In 1738 he returned to England with a sense of failure—a feeling that he, "who went to America to convert others, was never really converted to God." The turning point came during a mission on Aldersgate Street in London where, as he said, he suddenly "felt my heart strangely warmed." He found his voice as an evangelist and preacher, imparting to the crowds—particularly the poor and working class who flocked to his sermons—a conviction that the essence of Christianity was love. On his preaching tours he covered the length and breadth of England. "The whole world is my parish," he liked to say.

The spirit of Methodism, as it became known, combined an affective piety with earnest morality. Wesley himself was an ardent opponent of slavery and a champion of prison reform. Though he separated from the Anglican Church, he was a proponent of what would later be termed ecumenism. In meeting other Christians his first question was not about doctrine but only this: "Is thine heart right, as my heart is with thy heart? . . . If it be, give me thy hand."

Wesley died on March 2, 1791.

"How far is love, even with many wrong opinions, to be preferred before truth itself without love? We may die without the knowledge of many truths and yet be carried into Abraham's bosom. But if we die without love, what will knowledge avail?"

—John Wesley

Mass
Saturday of the First Week of Lent
[*St. Casimir*, opt. memorial]

ENTRANCE ANTIPHON   Cf. Psalm 19 (18):8

The law of the Lord is perfect; it revives the soul. / The decrees of the Lord are steadfast; they give wisdom to the simple.

COLLECT

Turn our hearts to you, eternal Father,
and grant that, seeking always the one thing necessary
and carrying out works of charity,
we may be dedicated to your worship.
Through our Lord Jesus Christ, your Son,
who lives and reigns with you in the unity of the Holy Spirit,
God, for ever and ever.

A reading from the Book of Deuteronomy   26:16-19

You will be a people sacred to the LORD God.

Moses spoke to the people, saying: "This day the LORD, your God, commands you to observe these statutes and decrees. Be careful, then, to observe them with all your heart and with all your soul. Today you are making this agreement with the LORD: he is to be your God and you are to walk in his ways and observe his statutes, commandments and decrees, and to hearken to his voice. And today the LORD is making this agreement with you: you are to be a people peculiarly his own, as he promised you; and provided you keep all his commandments, he will then raise you high in praise and renown and glory above all other nations he has made, and you will be a people sacred to the LORD, your God, as he promised."

The word of the Lord.

RESPONSORIAL PSALM   119:1-2, 4-5, 7-8
℟. (1b) **Blessed are they who follow the law of the Lord!**

Blessed are they whose way is blameless,
  who walk in the law of the LORD.
Blessed are they who observe his decrees,
  who seek him with all their heart. ℟.

You have commanded that your precepts
  be diligently kept.
Oh, that I might be firm in the ways
  of keeping your statutes! ℟.

I will give you thanks with an upright heart,
  when I have learned your just ordinances.
I will keep your statutes;
  do not utterly forsake me. ℟.

GOSPEL ACCLAMATION   2 Corinthians 6:2b
Behold, now is a very acceptable time;
behold, now is the day of salvation.

A reading from the holy Gospel according to Matthew
                                    5:43-48

Be perfect, just as your heavenly Father is perfect.

Jesus said to his disciples: "You have heard that it was
said, *You shall love your neighbor and hate your enemy.*
But I say to you, love your enemies, and pray for those who
persecute you, that you may be children of your heavenly
Father, for he makes his sun rise on the bad and the good,
and causes rain to fall on the just and the unjust. For if you
love those who love you, what recompense will you have?
Do not the tax collectors do the same? And if you greet your
brothers and sisters only, what is unusual about that? Do

not the pagans do the same? So be perfect, just as your heavenly Father is perfect."
The Gospel of the Lord.

PRAYER OVER THE OFFERINGS
May these blessed mysteries
by which we are restored, O Lord, we pray,
make us worthy of the gift they bestow.
Through Christ our Lord.

COMMUNION ANTIPHON   Matthew 5:48
Be perfect, as your heavenly Father is perfect, says the Lord.

PRAYER AFTER COMMUNION
Show unceasing favor, O Lord,
to those you refresh with this divine mystery,
and accompany with salutary consolations
those you have imbued with heavenly teaching.
Through Christ our Lord.

Reflection

Two Hands

The Dalai Lama once spoke about compassion to a packed audience in a California university. He shared that the fear he felt when Chinese soldiers captured Tibet was not fear of physical pain. "I feared I would lose compassion for my captors."

What would it look like if we too feared losing compassion for those who harmed us? If we took Jesus' command to love our enemies seriously?

Many years ago I was introduced to a practice called the two hands of nonviolence. It is a both-and approach to difficult, even harmful people.

One hand is lifted at the wrist, palm facing outward. This "stop" gesture acknowledges how I refuse to accept any harm or sin that another might be doing. I might even actively resist the other, calling for justice where there might be none. This hand sets appropriate boundaries.

The second hand is extended horizontally, palm facing upward. With this gesture I acknowledge that despite whatever harm the other may have caused, I will not shut them out of my heart. This open palm says, "I will love you, even if I don't condone your actions."

Both-And. Loving the sinner and hating the sin. Perhaps if we, like the Dalai Lama, were aware of what hating another does to our hearts and our relationship with God, we too might fear losing compassion for another.

May we have a healthy fear of forgetting who each and every person is—our kin, also beloved by God.

Christina Leaño

Christina Leaño is a retreat and spiritual director and staff member of the Laudato Si' Movement. Her interest lies in the intersection of contemplative spirituality and social and ecological justice.
www.christinaleano.net.

Evening

God, come to my assistance.
Lord, make haste to help me.

(opt. hymn, pp. 360–65)

PSALM 81:2-4, 6c-11
Sing joyfully to God our strength,
shout in triumph to the God of Jacob.
Raise a song and sound the timbrel,
the sweet-sounding lyre with the harp;
blow the trumpet at the new moon,
when the moon is full, on our feast.

A voice I did not know said to me:
"I freed your shoulder from the burden;
your hands were freed from the builder's basket.
You called in distress and I delivered you.

"I answered, concealed in the thunder;
at the waters of Meribah I tested you.
Listen, my people, as I warn you.
O Israel, if only you would heed!

"Let there be no strange god among you,
nor shall you worship a foreign god.
I am the LORD your God,
who brought you up from the land of Egypt.
Open wide your mouth, and I will fill it."

Glory to the Father . . .

SCRIPTURE   Romans 8:31-34
What then shall we say to this? If God is for us, who
can be against us? He who did not spare his own Son
but handed him over for us all, how will he not also give us

everything else along with him? Who will bring a charge against God's chosen ones? It is God who acquits us. Who will condemn? It is Christ [Jesus] who died, rather, was raised, who also is at the right hand of God, who indeed intercedes for us.

READ, PONDER, PRAY on a word or phrase from these readings or another of today's Scriptures (*Lectio Divina*, p. 359)

ANTIPHON
Today the Lord chooses you to be his own people.

CANTICLE OF MARY *(inside back cover)*

INTERCESSIONS
Liberating God, you freed our ancestors from slavery in Egypt. In hope we pray: R̸. **Holy God, hear our prayer.**

Advance efforts to aid immigrants and refugees and those who live in poverty. R̸.

Inspire negotiations for peace among nations, and give perseverance and support to peacemakers. R̸.

Help us to bolster and sustain assistance to women in crisis pregnancies. R̸.

Our Father . . .

May God free us from every bondage of sin, and lead us to walk in newness of life through Jesus, our redeemer. Amen.

Pet... ...h an...
...he was transfigured before...

...ling white, such as no fuller on earth could bleach them. Then Elijah
...em along with Moses, and they were conversing with Jesus. Then Pet...
...s in reply, "Rabbi, it is good that we are here! Let us make three tents
...one for Moses, and one for Elijah." He hardly knew what to say, they...
...fied. Then a cloud came, casting a shadow over them; then from...
... a voice, "This is my beloved Son. Listen to him." Suddenly, looking...

Sunday, March 5

Morning

O Lord, open my lips.
And my mouth will proclaim your praise.

(opt. hymn, pp. 360–65)

PSALM 150:1b-6a
Praise God in the holy temple;
praise the Lord in the mighty firmament.
Praise God for powerful deeds;
for boundless grandeur, praise God.

O praise the Lord with sound of trumpet;
give praise with lute and harp.
Praise God with timbrel and dance;
give praise with strings and pipes.

O praise God with resounding cymbals;
give praise with clashing of cymbals.
Let everything that breathes praise the LORD!

Glory to the Father . . .

SCRIPTURE   1 Kings 19:9b-12

[T]he word of the LORD came to him: Why are you here, Elijah? He answered: "I have been most zealous for the LORD, the God of hosts, but the Israelites have forsaken your covenant. They have destroyed your altars and murdered your prophets by the sword. I alone remain, and they seek to take my life." Then the LORD said: Go out and stand on the mountain before the LORD; the LORD will pass by. There was a strong and violent wind rending the mountains and

Transfiguration of Jesus by Lucinda Naylor.

crushing rocks before the LORD—but the LORD was not in the wind; after the wind, an earthquake—but the LORD was not in the earthquake; after the earthquake, fire—but the LORD was not in the fire; after the fire, a light silent sound.

READ, PONDER, PRAY on a word or phrase from these readings or another of today's Scriptures (*Lectio Divina*, p. 359)

ANTIPHON

From the cloud a voice said, "This is my beloved Son."

CANTICLE OF ZECHARIAH *(inside front cover)*

INTERCESSIONS

God of mystery and grace, you are forever with us. In joy we pray: R/. **Delight our hearts, O God.**

Transfigure your Church into a beacon of light and a place of welcome for all people. R/.

Strengthen faith and courage in catechumens and all who seek to deepen their relationship with Jesus and the Church. R/.

Redeem us from violence, and help us to end all wars. R/.

Our Father . . .

May God deepen in us the gifts of faith, hope, and love, and strengthen us to embrace the paschal mystery with eyes fixed on the light of Christ. Amen.

Mass
Second Sunday of Lent

ENTRANCE ANTIPHON   Cf. Psalm 27 (26):8-9

Of you my heart has spoken: Seek his face. / It is your face, O Lord, that I seek; / hide not your face from me.

Or: Cf. Psalm 25 (24):6, 2, 22

Remember your compassion, O Lord, / and your merciful love, for they are from of old. / Let not our enemies exult over us. / Redeem us, O God of Israel, from all our distress.

(The Gloria is omitted.)

COLLECT

O God, who have commanded us
to listen to your beloved Son,
be pleased, we pray,
to nourish us inwardly by your word,
that, with spiritual sight made pure,
we may rejoice to behold your glory.
Through our Lord Jesus Christ, your Son,
who lives and reigns with you in the unity of the Holy Spirit,
God, for ever and ever.

A reading from the Book of Genesis 12:1-4a

The call of Abraham, the father of God's people.

The LORD said to Abram: "Go forth from the land of your kinsfolk and from your father's house to a land that I will show you.

"I will make of you a great nation, / and I will bless you; / I will make your name great, / so that you will be a blessing. / I will bless those who bless you / and curse those who

curse you. / All the communities of the earth / shall find blessing in you." / Abram went as the LORD directed him.
The word of the Lord.

RESPONSORIAL PSALM   33:4-5, 18-19, 20, 22
R̶/. (22) **Lord, let your mercy be on us, as we place our trust in you.**

Upright is the word of the LORD,
   and all his works are trustworthy.
He loves justice and right;
   of the kindness of the LORD the earth is full. R̶/.

See, the eyes of the LORD are upon those who fear him,
   upon those who hope for his kindness,
to deliver them from death
   and preserve them in spite of famine. R̶/.

Our soul waits for the LORD,
   who is our help and our shield.
May your kindness, O LORD, be upon us
   who have put our hope in you. R̶/.

A reading from the second Letter of Saint Paul to Timothy   1:8b-10
> *God has saved us and called us to be holy.*

Beloved: Bear your share of hardship for the gospel with the strength that comes from God.

He saved us and called us to a holy life, not according to our works but according to his own design and the grace bestowed on us in Christ Jesus before time began, but now made manifest through the appearance of our savior Christ Jesus, who destroyed death and brought life and immortality to light through the gospel.
The word of the Lord.

GOSPEL ACCLAMATION   Cf. Matthew 17:5

From the shining cloud the Father's voice is heard:
This is my beloved Son, listen to him.

A reading from the holy Gospel according to Matthew
17:1-9

Jesus' face shone like the sun.

Jesus took Peter, James, and John his brother, and led them up a high mountain by themselves. And he was transfigured before them; his face shone like the sun and his clothes became white as light. And behold, Moses and Elijah appeared to them, conversing with him. Then Peter said to Jesus in reply, "Lord, it is good that we are here. If you wish, I will make three tents here, one for you, one for Moses, and one for Elijah." While he was still speaking, behold, a bright cloud cast a shadow over them, then from the cloud came a voice that said, "This is my beloved Son, with whom I am well pleased; listen to him." When the disciples heard this, they fell prostrate and were very much afraid. But Jesus came and touched them, saying, "Rise, and do not be afraid." And when the disciples raised their eyes, they saw no one else but Jesus alone.

As they were coming down from the mountain, Jesus charged them, "Do not tell the vision to anyone until the Son of Man has been raised from the dead."

The Gospel of the Lord.

CREED (p. 332)

PRAYER OVER THE OFFERINGS

May this sacrifice, O Lord, we pray,
cleanse us of our faults
and sanctify your faithful in body and mind
for the celebration of the paschal festivities.
Through Christ our Lord.

Communion Antiphon   Matthew 17:5
This is my beloved Son, with whom I am well pleased; /
listen to him.

Prayer after Communion
As we receive these glorious mysteries,
we make thanksgiving to you, O Lord,
for allowing us while still on earth
to be partakers even now of the things of heaven.
Through Christ our Lord.

Reflection

A Greater Risk

*This is my beloved Son, with whom I am well pleased;
listen to him.*

The thrilling fact is, this Jesus who speaks to you is not a
character out of a dead past. . . . Listening to Scripture in
the liturgy is not the same as reading Augustine's *Confessions*
. . . not the same as hearing a Shakespeare sonnet or Handel's
Messiah. When the New Testament is read to you, Jesus himself speaks to you. Now. Here is the risen Christ, incompa-
rably alive, opening up to you the meaning of what you are
hearing, as he did to the desolate disciples on the road to
Emmaus. And as you listen, you too can exclaim as they
exclaimed: Did not our hearts burn within us while he talked
to us . . . while he opened to us the scriptures?" (Lk 24:32).
But for that, your hearts have to be open. You have to say,
with Samuel of old, "Speak, Lord, for thy servant heareth"
(1 Sam 3:9, 10).

But again, there is something distinctive here. Listening to
Jesus is not the same as listening to others. The same intensity,

yes, the same openness; but a greater risk. When the Father told Peter, James, and John "Listen to him," he was saying "Obey him; do what he tells you; follow him." To listen to Jesus is to be his disciple, to listen the way Abraham listened to the Lord and left his "country and kindred and [his] father's house" (Gen 12:1-4). Is this how you let Scripture speak to you? Are you saying "Speak, Lord, for thy servant heareth," or do you really mean, as the [Christian] ethicist Paul Ramsey rephrased it, "Speak, Lord, and thy servant will think it over"?

If you really listen to Jesus in the proclaimed word, you have a fair chance of hearing him in your everyday life. Not a vision, I assure you, but Jesus speaking in your heart as truly as anyone you love profoundly speaks to your heart.

Fr. Walter J. Burghardt, *Sir, We Would Like to See Jesus*

Walter J. Burghardt, SJ, spent much of his career as a scholar of Church history and theology. He was a spellbinding preacher whose powerful calls for social justice and understanding influenced generations of priests and pastors.

Evening

God, come to my assistance.
Lord, make haste to help me.

(opt. hymn, pp. 360–65)

PSALM 123
To you have I lifted up my eyes,
you who dwell in the heavens.

Behold, like the eyes of slaves
on the hand of their lords,
like the eyes of a servant
on the hand of her mistress,
so our eyes are on the LORD our God,
till mercy be shown us.

Have mercy on us, LORD, have mercy.
We are filled with contempt.
Indeed, all too full is our soul
with the scorn of the arrogant,
the disdain of the proud.

Glory to the Father . . .

SCRIPTURE   Hebrews 12:18-24

You have not approached that which could be touched
and a blazing fire and gloomy darkness and storm and
a trumpet blast and a voice speaking words such that those
who heard begged that no message be further addressed to
them, for they could not bear to hear the command: "If even
an animal touches the mountain, it shall be stoned." Indeed,
so fearful was the spectacle that Moses said, "I am terrified
and trembling." No, you have approached Mount Zion and
the city of the living God, the heavenly Jerusalem, and
countless angels in festal gathering, and the assembly of the

firstborn enrolled in heaven, and God the judge of all, and the spirits of the just made perfect, and Jesus, the mediator of a new covenant, and the sprinkled blood that speaks more eloquently than that of Abel.

READ, PONDER, PRAY on a word or phrase from these readings or another of today's Scriptures (*Lectio Divina*, p. 359)

ANTIPHON
Jesus was transfigured before them; his face shone like the sun.

CANTICLE OF MARY *(inside back cover)*

INTERCESSIONS
Merciful God of our ancestors, in Jesus you give us a glimpse of your light. In faith we pray: ℟. **Let us behold your glory, O God.**

Open our eyes to the beauty of the natural world, and lead us to wonder and praise. ℟.

Renew hope in those who wait for the return of a loved one or an answer to prayer. ℟.

Break through the darkness of racism, prejudice, and hatred, and lead all people to experience the right to dignity, equality, and respect. ℟.

Our Father . . .

May God be gracious to us, bless us with peace, and lead us by the light of Christ. Amen.

Within the Word

A Lenten Challenge in Three Verses

Monday's short Gospel reading is long on challenges for many, if not all, of us. Jesus exhorts his followers not to judge or condemn. He is not referring to the condemnation of such things as violence and injustice, which *should* be named and condemned. Rather, he's urging us to stop judging and condemning one another, our fellow human beings created in God's image and likeness.

Why the prohibition against judging and condemning others? Because these are *divine* prerogatives, not ours. Only God knows what lies in the hearts of people, which is the basis of judgment. It is helpful to recall what we were reminded of on Ash Wednesday: that we ourselves are dust, and to dust we shall return. Another reason not to judge and condemn one another is that each one of us stands in need of God's mercy and forgiveness. Moreover, we have a tendency to judge and condemn in others what we dislike—consciously or unconsciously—in ourselves. Yet another reason to forego judging and condemning others is that we often do so behind their backs, in conversation with others. The more charitable, albeit difficult, thing to do is to directly confront those whose attitudes and behaviors should be challenged—but to do so with humility and love, what the tradition calls "fraternal correction." So, let's leave judgment and condemnation in the hands of God.

At the same time, Jesus insists, there are two ways in which we *must* be like God: forgiving others and being generous to those in need. Indeed, Luke's Gospel is chock full of instances where Jesus extols mercy to sinners (think of his parable of the Prodigal Son) and lauds compassionate generosity (think of the Good Samaritan). Forgiveness of sins and generosity are grounded in God's mercy. Hence, the opening exhortation to be merciful as our heavenly Father is merciful.

It is surely no accident that in Luke's version of the Lord's Prayer (11:2-4), the two central petitions pertain to generosity and forgiveness. When we pray for our daily bread, we remind ourselves that we are totally dependent upon God for all that we have and are. Daily acknowledgment of our dependence on God not only reminds us of our creaturely identity; it also bolsters our trust in and gratitude to God for all the blessings in our lives. Gratitude tends to beget generosity within us toward others. Indeed, as today's Gospel conveys, God is never outdone in bestowing generous love. We have many good reasons to give generously.

And we have many good reasons to *forgive*. To pray for forgiveness is to acknowledge our sinfulness. The mark of a person who has truly appropriated this divine gift is the ability and willingness to forgive others. Indeed, in Luke's version of the Lord's Prayer, we pray that God forgive us, *for* we are committed to forgiving those who trespass against us. Matthew's version of the Lord's Prayer adds another important nuance: we ask to be forgiven *as* we forgive others (Matt 6:12). If divine generosity begets our gratitude and willingness to share with others, so God's compassionate mercy begets our ability and willingness to extend forgiveness to others.

The challenge presented by Monday's Gospel thus entails our individual growth as Jesus' followers and our participation in the ushering in of God's reign. We are, after all, on this Lenten journey together.

—Fr. Thomas Stegman

Thomas Stegman, SJ, is professor of New Testament at the Boston College School of Theology and Ministry.

Monday, March 6

Morning

O Lord, open my lips.
And my mouth will proclaim your praise.

(opt. hymn, pp. 360–65)

PSALM 20:2-6, 8-10

May the LORD answer you in time of trial;
may the name of Jacob's God protect you,
sending you help from the holy place,
and giving you support from Zion.

May God remember all your offerings,
receive your sacrifice with favor,
give you your heart's desire,
and fulfill every one of your plans.

May we ring out our joy at your victory,
and raise banners in the name of our God.
May the LORD grant all your prayers.

Some put their trust in chariots or horses,
but we in the name of the LORD, our God.
They will collapse and fall,
but we shall rise up and hold firm.
Grant salvation to the king, O LORD,
give answer on the day we call.

Glory to the Father . . .

SCRIPTURE   Amos 7:1-6

This is what the Lord GOD showed me: He was forming
a locust swarm when the late growth began to come
up (the late growth after the king's mowing). When they
had finished eating the grass in the land, I said: / Forgive,

O Lord God! / Who will raise up Jacob? / He is so small! / The LORD relented concerning this. "This shall not be," said the Lord God.

This is what the Lord God showed me: He was summoning a rain of fire. It had devoured the great abyss and was consuming the fields. Then I said: / Cease, O Lord God! / Who will raise up Jacob? / He is so small! / The LORD relented concerning this. "This also shall not be," said the Lord God.

READ, PONDER, PRAY on a word or phrase from these readings or another of today's Scriptures (*Lectio Divina*, p. 359)

ANTIPHON
Yours, O Lord, are compassion and forgiveness.

CANTICLE OF ZECHARIAH *(inside front cover)*

INTERCESSIONS
God of salvation, you are worthy of all praise and glory. In trust we pray: R̸. **O God, set us free.**

Heal divisions among Christians, and help us to live as one body in Christ. R̸.

Prosper efforts to address gun violence, hate crimes, and domestic abuse. R̸.

Release those who are unjustly imprisoned or enslaved by human trafficking. R̸.

Our Father . . .

May God be gracious to us, keep us in peace, and lead us along the everlasting way, through Jesus, the light of the world. Amen.

Blessed Among Us

Jean-Pierre de Caussade
Jesuit and Spiritual Director (1675–1751)

Little is known of this French Jesuit, whose priestly life was spent in a series of relatively obscure assignments. For one year he served as spiritual director to a community of Visitation nuns. To them he addressed a series of letters and conferences, published a century after his death as *Abandonment to Divine Providence*. It was quickly recognized as a spiritual classic, and on this work his reputation rests.

The theme of the book is easily summarized. In brief, it outlines the path to holiness that lies in the performance of our everyday tasks and duties. Every moment is given to us from God and thus bears the stamp of God's will for us. When we "accept what we cannot avoid and endure with love and resignation things which could cause us weariness and disgust," we are following the path to sanctification.

Among the key words in Caussade's work are "the present moment." It is even possible, he claims, to speak of "the sacrament of the present moment." Just as Christ, in the Eucharist, is visible to the eyes of faith, so to the faithful Christian it should be evident that God's will is truly present, though disguised, in what otherwise might be dismissed as the ordinary and everyday. "Every moment we live through," he wrote, "is like an ambassador who declares the will of God." By living in this spirit of mindfulness and abandonment, our own lives become holy texts, a "living gospel." Fr. de Caussade died on March 6, 1751.

"The Holy Spirit writes no more Gospels except in our hearts. . . . We, if we are holy, are the paper; our sufferings . . . are the ink. The workings of the Holy Spirit are his pen, and with it he writes a living gospel."
　　　　　　　　　　　　　　　　　—Jean-Pierre de Caussade, SJ

Mass
Monday of the Second Week of Lent

ENTRANCE ANTIPHON   Cf. Psalm 26 (25):11-12

**Redeem me, O Lord, and have mercy on me. / My foot
stands on level ground; / I will bless the Lord in the
assembly.**

COLLECT

O God, who have taught us
to chasten our bodies
for the healing of our souls,
enable us, we pray,
to abstain from all sins,
and strengthen our hearts
to carry out your loving commands.
Through our Lord Jesus Christ, your Son,
who lives and reigns with you in the unity of the Holy Spirit,
God, for ever and ever.

A reading from the Book of the Prophet Daniel   9:4b-10

We have sinned, been wicked and done evil.

ord, great and awesome God, you who keep your merciful
covenant toward those who love you and observe your
commandments! We have sinned, been wicked and done
evil; we have rebelled and departed from your commandments and your laws. We have not obeyed your servants the
prophets, who spoke in your name to our kings, our princes,
our fathers, and all the people of the land. Justice, O Lord,
is on your side; we are shamefaced even to this day: we, the
men of Judah, the residents of Jerusalem, and all Israel, near
and far, in all the countries to which you have scattered them
because of their treachery toward you. O LORD, we are
shamefaced, like our kings, our princes, and our fathers, for

having sinned against you. But yours, O Lord, our God, are compassion and forgiveness! Yet we rebelled against you and paid no heed to your command, O Lord, our God, to live by the law you gave us through your servants the prophets."
The word of the Lord.

RESPONSORIAL PSALM   79:8, 9, 11 and 13
Ry. (see 103:10a) **Lord, do not deal with us according to our sins.**

Remember not against us the iniquities of the past;
    may your compassion quickly come to us,
    for we are brought very low. Ry.

Help us, O God our savior,
    because of the glory of your name;
Deliver us and pardon our sins
    for your name's sake. Ry.

Let the prisoners' sighing come before you;
    with your great power free those doomed to death.
Then we, your people and the sheep of your pasture,
    will give thanks to you forever;
    through all generations we will declare your praise. Ry.

GOSPEL ACCLAMATION   See John 6:63c, 68c
Your words, Lord, are Spirit and life;
you have the words of everlasting life.

A reading from the holy Gospel according to Luke   6:36-38
Forgive and you will be forgiven.

Jesus said to his disciples: "Be merciful, just as your Father is merciful.

"Stop judging and you will not be judged. Stop condemning and you will not be condemned. Forgive and you will be forgiven. Give and gifts will be given to you; a good measure, packed together, shaken down, and overflowing, will be poured into your lap. For the measure with which you measure will in return be measured out to you."

The Gospel of the Lord.

PRAYER OVER THE OFFERINGS
Accept in your goodness these our prayers, O Lord,
and set free from worldly attractions
those you allow to serve the heavenly mysteries.
Through Christ our Lord.

COMMUNION ANTIPHON   Luke 6:36
Be merciful, as your Father is merciful, says the Lord.

PRAYER AFTER COMMUNION
May this Communion, O Lord,
cleanse us of wrongdoing
and make us heirs to the joy of heaven.
Through Christ our Lord.

Reflection

And That Is That

Be merciful, just as your Father is merciful.

I imagine this passage being read to my daughters. How might they react? Was their father—their experience of a father, *me*—merciful?

Not always.

My wife's silent glare said as much as we drove along. I was in the middle of a long-winded monologue, reprimanding my four-year-old for her lack of gratitude for a certain gift. How her ingratitude hurt others, how her behavior upset those close to her. I was really laying it on, and I had inevitably crossed a line.

Hours later, I called my daughter aside, tail between my legs. My guilt was palpable, and I was prepared to atone. "I'm really sorry," I began. "When we were in the car, I shouldn't have . . ."

"It's okay, Daddy. You didn't mean it." Then: A big hug. A smile.

"Thank you," I stammered.

And that was that.

When hearing today's reading from the book of Daniel, we might be tempted to beat our chests in shame, to list our many sins, to go on and on about how far we've fallen. We're sinners, wicked and evil.

But in the Gospel, we see something different: No judgment. A desire to give generously—to *forgive* generously— and be about God's work. To trust that the compassion we show others will be shown to us.

Why? It's a circle of loving-kindness. Maybe my daughter just reflects back to me the love I show her. I hope so! Even at her very young age, she recognizes the virtuous circle of forgiveness and mercy.

Love one another. Forgive one another. And do so generously—as God does, our God who delights in us and has no interest in keeping score.

Eric Clayton

Eric Clayton is deputy director for communications at the Jesuit Conference of Canada and the United States. He is the author of Cannonball Moments: Telling Your Story, Deepening Your Faith. *Learn more at* ericclaytonwrites.com.

Evening

God, come to my assistance.
Lord, make haste to help me.

(opt. hymn, pp. 360–65)

PSALM 17:1-7
O LORD, hear a cause that is just,
pay heed to my cry.
Turn your ear to my prayer:
no deceit is on my lips.
From you may my justice come forth.
Your eyes discern what is upright.

Search my heart and visit me by night.
Test me by fire, and you will find no wrong in me.

My mouth does not transgress as others do;
on account of the words of your lips,
I have avoided the paths of the violent.

I kept my steps firmly in your paths.
My feet have never faltered.

To you I call; for you will surely heed me, O God.
Turn your ear to me; hear my words.
Display your faithful love,
you who deliver from their foes
those who trust in your right hand.

Glory to the Father . . .

SCRIPTURE   1 John 3:11-16
T]his is the message you have heard from the beginning:
we should love one another, unlike Cain who belonged
to the evil one and slaughtered his brother. Why did he
slaughter him? Because his own works were evil, and those

of his brother righteous. Do not be amazed, [then,] . . . if the world hates you. We know that we have passed from death to life because we love our brothers. Whoever does not love remains in death. Everyone who hates his brother is a murderer, and you know that no murderer has eternal life remaining in him. The way we came to know love was that he laid down his life for us; so we ought to lay down our lives for our brothers.

READ, PONDER, PRAY on a word or phrase from these readings or another of today's Scriptures (*Lectio Divina*, p. 359)

ANTIPHON
Be merciful, just as your Father is merciful.

CANTICLE OF MARY *(inside back cover)*

INTERCESSIONS
Forgiving God, you are all-merciful. With gratitude for your gifts we pray: R℣. **God, come to our assistance.**

For those who generously share their time, talents, and material gifts, we pray: R℣.

For those who work through the night in hospitals, care facilities, and prisons, we pray: R℣.

For those who struggle with addiction and for their loved ones, we pray: R℣.

Our Father . . .

May the peace of Christ reign in our hearts, now and always. Amen.

Tuesday, March 7

Morning

O Lord, open my lips.
And my mouth will proclaim your praise.

(opt. hymn, pp. 360–65)

PSALM 84:2-8

How lovely is your dwelling place,
O LORD of hosts.
My soul is longing and yearning
for the courts of the LORD.
My heart and my flesh cry out
to the living God.

Even the sparrow finds a home,
and the swallow a nest for herself
in which she sets her young, at your altars,
O LORD of hosts, my king and my God.

Blessed are they who dwell in your house,
forever singing your praise.
Blessed the people whose strength is in you,
whose hearts are set on the pilgrimage.

As they go through the Baca Valley,
they make it a place of springs;
the autumn rain covers it with pools.
They walk with ever-growing strength;
the God of gods will appear in Zion.

Glory to the Father . . .

SCRIPTURE   Deuteronomy 10:12, 17-19

Now, therefore, Israel, what does the LORD, your God,
ask of you but to fear the LORD, your God, to follow in

all his ways, to love and serve the LORD, your God, with your whole heart and with your whole being. For the LORD, your God, is the God of gods, the Lord of lords, the great God, mighty and awesome, who has no favorites, accepts no bribes, who executes justice for the orphan and the widow, and loves the resident alien, giving them food and clothing. So you too should love the resident alien, for that is what you were in the land of Egypt.

READ, PONDER, PRAY on a word or phrase from these readings or another of today's Scriptures (*Lectio Divina*, p. 359)

ANTIPHON
Make justice your aim: hear the orphan's plea, defend the widow.

CANTICLE OF ZECHARIAH (*inside front cover*)

INTERCESSIONS
Cosmic God, your mercies are renewed each morning. In trust we pray: R⁊. We wait for you, O God.

Give discernment and support to those who are discerning a call to the priesthood, diaconate, or religious life. R⁊.

Protect and free those who are surrounded by political conflict, drug trafficking, and violence. R⁊.

Sustain patience and hope in those who are undergoing treatment for cancer, rehabilitation, or therapy. R⁊.

Our Father . . .

May God embolden us to live the Gospel of Jesus with joy and peace, through the power of the Holy Spirit. Amen.

Blessed Among Us

Saints Perpetua and Felicity
Martyrs (d. 203)

"The Passion of Perpetua and Felicity," an account of the martyrdom of a prosperous young woman and her servant in Carthage, is one of the most powerful and poignant documents of the early Church. Perpetua, the mother of a newborn son, was twenty-two when she was arrested with her pregnant servant Felicity for violating a prohibition against conversion to Christianity. This account of these two young mothers stands in contrast to the numerous accounts of "virgin martyrs." "The Passion," written largely in the voice of Perpetua herself, depicts the struggle of a woman to claim her own identity and vocation against the claims of society. In her reply to the consul, who appeals to her status as wife, daughter, and mother, one senses that in Christ she has found the power and freedom to name herself and the courage to accept the consequences: "I am a Christian."

In a series of prophetic visions, Perpetua is comforted by the assurance that her fate is ordained and her brief suffering will lead to eternal reward. After entrusting her infant son to safe hands, she receives the grace to bear whatever may come. Felicity, meanwhile, goes into premature labor in her prison cell and is able to hand over her newborn daughter to Christian friends. The next day the prisoners went forth from the darkness of their cell into the glaring amphitheater, "as it were to heaven, cheerful and bright of countenance." Stripped before the jeering crowd, they were exposed to wild beasts and put to the sword.

"For this cause came we willingly unto this, that our liberty might not be obscured. For this cause have we devoted our lives."

—St. Perpetua

Mass
Tuesday of the Second Week of Lent
[*Saints Perpetua and Felicity*, opt. memorial]

ENTRANCE ANTIPHON   Cf. Psalm 13 (12):4-5

Give light to my eyes lest I fall asleep in death, / lest my
enemy say: I have overcome him.

COLLECT

Guard your Church, we pray, O Lord, in your unceasing
    mercy,
and, since without you mortal humanity is sure to fall,
may we be kept by your constant helps from all harm
and directed to all that brings salvation.
Through our Lord Jesus Christ, your Son,
who lives and reigns with you in the unity of the Holy Spirit,
God, for ever and ever.

A reading from the Book of the Prophet Isaiah 1:10, 16-20

Learn to do good; make justice your aim.

Hear the word of the LORD, / princes of Sodom! / Listen
to the instruction of our God, / people of Gomorrah!

Wash yourselves clean! / Put away your misdeeds from
before my eyes; / cease doing evil; learn to do good. / Make
justice your aim: redress the wronged, / hear the orphan's
plea, defend the widow.

Come now, let us set things right, / says the LORD: /
Though your sins be like scarlet, / they may become white
as snow; / Though they be crimson red, / they may become
white as wool. / If you are willing, and obey, / you shall eat
the good things of the land; / But if you refuse and resist, /
the sword shall consume you: / for the mouth of the LORD
has spoken!

The word of the Lord.

RESPONSORIAL PSALM 50:8-9, 16bc-17, 21 and 23

R℣. (23b) **To the upright I will show the saving power of God.**

"Not for your sacrifices do I rebuke you,
for your burnt offerings are before me always.
I take from your house no bullock,
no goats out of your fold." R℣.

"Why do you recite my statutes,
and profess my covenant with your mouth,
Though you hate discipline
and cast my words behind you?" R℣.

"When you do these things, shall I be deaf to it?
Or do you think that I am like yourself?
I will correct you by drawing them up before your eyes.
He that offers praise as a sacrifice glorifies me;
and to him that goes the right way I will show the
salvation of God." R℣.

GOSPEL ACCLAMATION Ezekiel 18:31

Cast away from you all the crimes you have committed,
says the LORD,
and make for yourselves a new heart and a new spirit.

A reading from the holy Gospel according to Matthew

23:1-12

They preach but they do not practice.

Jesus spoke to the crowds and to his disciples, saying, "The scribes and the Pharisees have taken their seat on the chair of Moses. Therefore, do and observe all things whatsoever they tell you, but do not follow their example. For they preach but they do not practice. They tie up heavy burdens hard to carry and lay them on people's shoulders, but they will not lift a finger to move them. All their works are performed to be seen. They widen their phylacteries and lengthen their tassels. They love places of honor at banquets, seats of honor in synagogues, greetings in marketplaces, and the salutation 'Rabbi.' As for you, do not be called 'Rabbi.' You have but one teacher, and you are all brothers. Call no one on earth your father; you have but one Father in heaven. Do not be called 'Master'; you have but one master, the Christ. The greatest among you must be your servant. Whoever exalts himself will be humbled; but whoever humbles himself will be exalted."

The Gospel of the Lord.

PRAYER OVER THE OFFERINGS
Be pleased to work your sanctification within us
by means of these mysteries, O Lord,
and by it may we be cleansed of earthly faults
and led to the gifts of heaven.
Through Christ our Lord.

COMMUNION ANTIPHON   Psalm 9:2-3
I will recount all your wonders. / I will rejoice in you and be glad, / and sing psalms to your name, O Most High.

PRAYER AFTER COMMUNION
May the refreshment of this sacred table,
O Lord, we pray,
bring us an increase in devoutness of life
and the constant help of your work of conciliation.
Through Christ our Lord.

Reflection

Let Us Set Things Right

Under the inspiration of the Holy Spirit, the ministers of God's grace have spoken of repentance; indeed, the Master of the whole universe himself spoke of repentance with an oath: *As I live,* says the Lord, *I do not wish the death of the sinner but his repentance* [Ezek 33:11]. He added this evidence of his goodness: *House of Israel, repent of your wickedness. . . . If their sins should reach from earth to heaven, if they are brighter than scarlet and blacker than sackcloth, you need only turn to me with your whole heart and say, "Father," and I will listen to you as to a holy people.*

In other words, God wanted all his beloved ones to have the opportunity to repent and he confirmed this desire by his own almighty will. That is why we should obey his sovereign and glorious will and prayerfully entreat his mercy and kindness. We should be suppliant before him and turn to his compassion, rejecting empty works and quarreling and jealousy which only lead to death. . . .

. . . [L]et us hasten toward the goal of peace, set before us from the beginning. Let us keep our eyes firmly fixed on the Father and Creator of the whole universe, and hold fast to his splendid and transcendent gifts of peace and all his blessings.

St. Clement of Rome, from a letter in *The Liturgy of the Hours*

Clement of Rome was the fourth pope, serving in the final years of the first century (92–99).

Evening

God, come to my assistance.
Lord, make haste to help me.

(opt. hymn, pp. 360–65)

PSALM 119:89-96

Forever is your word, O LORD,
standing firm in the heavens.
From age to age is your truth;
like the earth, it stands firm.

Your judgments endure to this day,
for all things are your servants.
Had your law not been my delight,
I would have died in my affliction.

I will never forget your precepts,
for with them you give me life.
Save me, I am yours,
for I seek your precepts.

Though the wicked lie in wait to destroy me,
yet I ponder your decrees.
I have seen that all perfection has an end,
but your command is boundless.

Glory to the Father . . .

SCRIPTURE   1 John 3:17-20, 23

If someone who has worldly means sees a brother in need
and refuses him compassion, how can the love of God
remain in him? Children, let us love not in word or speech
but in deed and truth.

   [Now] this is how we shall know that we belong to the
truth and reassure our hearts before him in whatever our
hearts condemn, for God is greater than our hearts and

knows everything. And his commandment is this: we should believe in the name of his Son, Jesus Christ, and love one another just as he commanded us.

READ, PONDER, PRAY on a word or phrase from these readings or another of today's Scriptures (*Lectio Divina*, p. 359)

ANTIPHON
The greatest among you must be your servant.

CANTICLE OF MARY *(inside back cover)*

INTERCESSIONS
Creating God, by your Spirit you fashion our hearts anew. In hope we pray: R̷. **God of life, hear our prayer.**

Renew the vitality of those who experience burnout, exhaustion, or deep disappointment. R̷.

Help us to extend and expand services for those who suffer mental illness. R̷.

Increase our love of learning and desire for you. R̷.

Our Father . . .

May God answer our prayers and deliver us from every affliction, through Jesus, our redeemer. Amen.

Wednesday, March 8

Morning

O Lord, open my lips.
And my mouth will proclaim your praise.

(opt. hymn, pp. 360–65)

PSALM 59:2-6, 17-18

Rescue me, God, from my foes;
protect me from those who attack me.
O rescue me from those who do evil,
and save me from those who are bloodthirsty.

See, they lie in wait for my life;
the strong band together against me.
For no offense, no sin of mine, O LORD,
for no guilt of mine they rush to take their stand.

Awake! Come to meet me, and see!
LORD God of hosts, you are Israel's God.
Rouse yourself and punish the nations;
show no mercy to evil traitors.

As for me, I will sing of your strength,
and acclaim your faithful love in the morning,
for you have been my stronghold,
a refuge in the day of my distress.

O my Strength, to you I will sing praise,
for you, O God, are my stronghold,
the God who shows me faithful love.

Glory to the Father . . .

SCRIPTURE   Jeremiah 38:4-6

[T]he princes said to the king, "This man ought to be put
to death. He is weakening the resolve of the soldiers

left in this city and of all the people, by saying such things to them; he is not seeking the welfare of our people, but their ruin." King Zedekiah answered: "He is in your hands," for the king could do nothing with them. And so they took Jeremiah and threw him into the cistern of Prince Malchiah, in the court of the guard, letting him down by rope. There was no water in the cistern, only mud, and Jeremiah sank down into the mud.

READ, PONDER, PRAY on a word or phrase from these readings or another of today's Scriptures (*Lectio Divina*, p. 359)

ANTIPHON

Must good be repaid with evil, that they should dig a pit to take my life?

CANTICLE OF ZECHARIAH *(inside front cover)*

INTERCESSIONS

Generous God, you create us in your image and likeness. On this International Women's Day we pray: ℟. **God, in your love, hear our prayer.**

Heal women who suffer from discrimination, abuse, and violation of their dignity. ℟.

Advance efforts to establish equality for women worldwide. ℟.

Raise up women to lead us toward greater peace, unity, and celebration of diversity. ℟.

Our Father . . .

May God give us the courage to be the hands and heart of Christ in our daily encounters, by the power of the Holy Spirit. Amen.

Blessed Among Us

St. Catherine of Bologna
Abbess and Mystic (1413–1463)

St. Catherine was born of a noble family in Bologna and raised in luxury. Yet at fourteen she persuaded her family to let her join a community of Franciscan tertiaries. From an early age she had experienced visions of Jesus, "who would enter into her soul like a radiant sunshine to establish there the profoundest peace." But there were also demonic thoughts that sometimes plunged her into despair. Through constant prayer she vanquished such doubts, and one night during the Christmas vigil she was rewarded by an encounter with the Blessed Mother, who offered her the great privilege of holding her infant Son. "I leave you to picture the joy of this poor creature," she wrote, "when she found herself holding the Son of the eternal Father in her arms."

After some years, Catherine was directed to take charge of a convent of Poor Clares in Bologna. Her reputed gifts of healing and prophecy—as well as her deep kindness—attracted many novices. Whenever she had to correct a young sister, she would insist on sharing her punishment. When one of the novices was tempted to leave, Catherine pledged to take her place in purgatory until the end of time if only she would remain. (The novice stayed.)

She died on March 9, 1463. Among her last instructions, she said, "If you would have all, you must give all." Apart from several books, Catherine left behind a number of hymns and paintings. She is honored as a patron of artists.

"It means little to wear a worn habit and walk with bowed head; to be truly humble one has to know how to bear humiliation. It is the touchstone of Christian discipleship."

—St. Catherine of Bologna

Mass

Wednesday of the Second Week of Lent
[*St. John of God*, opt. memorial]

ENTRANCE ANTIPHON   Cf. Psalm 38 (37):22-23

**Forsake me not, O Lord! My God, be not far from me! /
Make haste and come to my help, O Lord, my strong
salvation!**

COLLECT

**Keep your family, O Lord,
schooled always in good works,
and so comfort them with your protection here
as to lead them graciously to gifts on high.
Through our Lord Jesus Christ, your Son,
who lives and reigns with you in the unity of the Holy Spirit,
God, for ever and ever.**

A reading from the Book of the Prophet Jeremiah   18:18-20

Come, let us persecute him.

The people of Judah and the citizens of Jerusalem said,
"Come, let us contrive a plot against Jeremiah. It will
not mean the loss of instruction from the priests, nor of
counsel from the wise, nor of messages from the prophets.
And so, let us destroy him by his own tongue; let us carefully
note his every word."

Heed me, O LORD, / and listen to what my adversaries
say. / Must good be repaid with evil / that they should dig
a pit to take my life? / Remember that I stood before you /
to speak in their behalf, / to turn away your wrath from
them.

The word of the Lord.

RESPONSORIAL PSALM   31:5-6, 14, 15-16

R℞. (17b) **Save me, O Lord, in your kindness.**

You will free me from the snare they set for me,
  for you are my refuge.
Into your hands I commend my spirit;
  you will redeem me, O LORD, O faithful God. R℞.

I hear the whispers of the crowd,
  that frighten me from every side,
as they consult together against me,
  plotting to take my life. R℞.

But my trust is in you, O LORD;
  I say, "You are my God."
In your hands is my destiny; rescue me
  from the clutches of my enemies and my persecutors. R℞.

GOSPEL ACCLAMATION   John 8:12

I am the light of the world, says the Lord;
whoever follows me will have the light of life.

A reading from the holy Gospel according to Matthew
                                        20:17-28

They will condemn the Son of Man to death.

As Jesus was going up to Jerusalem, he took the Twelve disciples aside by themselves, and said to them on the way, "Behold, we are going up to Jerusalem, and the Son of Man will be handed over to the chief priests and the scribes, and they will condemn him to death, and hand him over to the Gentiles to be mocked and scourged and crucified, and he will be raised on the third day."

Then the mother of the sons of Zebedee approached Jesus with her sons and did him homage, wishing to ask him for something. He said to her, "What do you wish?" She answered him, "Command that these two sons of mine sit, one at your right and the other at your left, in your kingdom." Jesus said in reply, "You do not know what you are asking. Can you drink the chalice that I am going to drink?" They said to him, "We can." He replied, "My chalice you will indeed drink, but to sit at my right and at my left, this is not mine to give but is for those for whom it has been prepared by my Father." When the ten heard this, they became indignant at the two brothers. But Jesus summoned them and said, "You know that the rulers of the Gentiles lord it over them, and the great ones make their authority over them felt. But it shall not be so among you. Rather, whoever wishes to be great among you shall be your servant; whoever wishes to be first among you shall be your slave. Just so, the Son of Man did not come to be served but to serve and to give his life as a ransom for many."

The Gospel of the Lord.

PRAYER OVER THE OFFERINGS
Look with favor, Lord,
on the sacrificial gifts we offer you,
and by this holy exchange
undo the bonds of our sins.
Through Christ our Lord.

COMMUNION ANTIPHON   Matthew 20:28
The Son of Man did not come to be served but to serve, /
and to give his life as a ransom for many.

PRAYER AFTER COMMUNION
Grant, we pray, O Lord our God,
that what you have given us as the pledge of immortality
may work for our eternal salvation.
Through Christ our Lord.

Reflection

A Prophet's Call

Today's reading from Jeremiah brings two adages to mind: that even paranoids have real enemies, and that no good deed goes unpunished. It's probably unfair to label Jeremiah as paranoid. Prophets don't answer God's call in order to be liked, and Jeremiah's task is especially dire: he must foretell Jerusalem's destruction and the exile of its people to Babylon. No wonder the religious and political leaders of his day were outraged and plotted to kill him.

Although his enemies aim to use every word he says against him, Jeremiah has faith that the words he speaks have been given to him by God. It's the pain of betrayal that truly hurts. He had once pleaded with God on behalf of these people, seeking mercy rather than punishment, and now addresses God directly, asking, "Must good be repaid with evil?"

We find our answer in the Gospel, with Jesus exemplifying his own prophetic role. He's been healing the sick and bringing good news of God's forgiveness of sins—and for this, those he has loved and served will betray, condemn, and crucify him. But Jesus does not doubt that God's grace is at work even here, and that his sacrifice will allow his followers to better understand what centuries later Dietrich Bonhoeffer termed "the cost of discipleship." We're reminded that in large ways and small, we're all meant to be "friends of God and prophets" (Wis 7:27), called to accept the burden of giving our lives in the service of others.

Kathleen Norris

Kathleen Norris is an oblate of St. Benedict and the author of many books, including The Cloister Walk *and* Acedia and Me.

Evening

God, come to my assistance.
Lord, make haste to help me.

(opt. hymn, pp. 360–65)

PSALM 66:1-9

Cry out with joy to God, all the earth;
O sing to the glory of God's name.
O render glorious praise.
Say to God, "How awesome your deeds!

Because of the greatness of your strength,
your enemies cower before you.
Before you all the earth shall bow down,
shall sing to you, sing to your name!"

Come and see the works of God:
awesome deeds among the children of Adam.
God turned the sea into dry land;
they passed through the river on foot.

There did we rejoice in the Lord,
who rules forever with might,
whose eyes keep watch on the nations:
let rebels not exalt themselves.

O peoples, bless our God;
let our voice of praise resound,
to the God who gave life to our souls
and kept our feet from stumbling.

Glory to the Father . . .

SCRIPTURE   James 3:13-18

Who among you is wise and understanding? Let him show his works by a good life in the humility that comes from wisdom. But if you have bitter jealousy and selfish ambition in your hearts, do not boast and be false to the truth. Wisdom of this kind does not come down from above but is earthly, unspiritual, demonic. For where jealousy and selfish ambition exist, there is disorder and every foul practice. But the wisdom from above is first of all pure, then peaceable, gentle, compliant, full of mercy and good fruits, without inconstancy or insincerity. And the fruit of righteousness is sown in peace for those who cultivate peace.

READ, PONDER, PRAY on a word or phrase from these readings or another of today's Scriptures (*Lectio Divina*, p. 359)

ANTIPHON
Whoever wishes to be great among you shall be your servant.

CANTICLE OF MARY *(inside back cover)*

INTERCESSIONS
God of heaven and earth, all creation sings to your name. In joy we pray: R7. **Teach us your ways, O God.**

Help us to advance dialogue and collaboration among clergy, religious, and laity in your Church. R7.

Renew the minds and hearts of those who are in prison, and radiate your love through prison employees. R7.

Strengthen and support caregivers and hospice workers. R7.

Our Father . . .

May God give life to our souls and keep our feet from stumbling, through Jesus, our peace. Amen.

Thursday, March 9

Morning

O Lord, open my lips.
And my mouth will proclaim your praise.

(opt. hymn, pp. 360–65)

PSALM 9:2-9

I will praise you, LORD, with all my heart;
all your wonders I will recount.
I will rejoice in you and be glad,
and sing psalms to your name, O Most High.

See how my enemies turn back,
how they stumble and perish before you.
You upheld the justice of my cause;
you sat enthroned, judging with righteousness.

You have rebuked the nations, destroyed the wicked;
you have wiped out their name forever and ever.
The foe is destroyed, eternally ruined.
You uprooted their cities; their memory has perished.

But the LORD sits enthroned forever,
and has set up a throne for judgment.
God will judge the world with righteousness,
and will govern the peoples with equity.

Glory to the Father . . .

SCRIPTURE   Proverbs 3:5-12

Trust in the LORD with all your heart, / on your own
intelligence do not rely; / In all your ways be mindful
of him, / and he will make straight your paths. / Do not be
wise in your own eyes, / fear the LORD and turn away from

evil; / This will mean health for your flesh / and vigor for your bones. / Honor the LORD with your wealth, / with first fruits of all your produce; / Then will your barns be filled with plenty, / with new wine your vats will overflow. / The discipline of the LORD, my son, do not spurn; / do not disdain his reproof; / For whom the LORD loves he reproves, / as a father, the son he favors.

READ, PONDER, PRAY on a word or phrase from these readings or another of today's Scriptures (*Lectio Divina*, p. 359)

ANTIPHON
Happy are those who trust in the Lord.

CANTICLE OF ZECHARIAH *(inside front cover)*

INTERCESSIONS
Holy God, you judge the world with righteousness.
In hope we pray: R̥. **God, in your justice, give us life.**

Help your Church to grow in understanding of the call to be Eucharist for the world. R̥.

Relieve those who suffer from famine, hunger, or lack of clean water and air. R̥.

Gather into your loving embrace those who suffer the death of a loved one to violence. R̥.

Our Father . . .

May God grant us salvation and prosper the work of our hands and hearts, through Christ our saving hope. Amen.

Blessed Among Us

St. Gregory of Nyssa
Bishop (ca. 330–ca. 395)

St. Gregory was one of ten children born in Cappadocia to a remarkable family. (Both of his parents, his sister, and two brothers were canonized as saints.) At first Gregory pursued a secular path, studying philosophy in Athens. But eventually he was persuaded to renounce "the ignoble glory" of secular knowledge and to seek ordination. In 372 he was named bishop of the small outpost of Nyssa. It was a time of bitter rivalry between orthodox bishops and the proponents of Arianism, a heresy that denied the full divinity of Christ.

The contest was pursued by means fair and foul. Gregory's enemies at one point had him arrested and sent into exile, before he was restored to his see in 378. Through his prolific writing, preaching, and contributions at the Council of Constantinople (381), Gregory emerged as one of the most effective champions of orthodoxy. He helped provide the language that affirmed the unity of being among the Persons of the Trinity, while also defending the divine and human wills in Christ.

Aside from doctrinal questions, Gregory was highly influential in the area of mystical theology. He prepared many texts on the theme of the soul's journey to union with God, including a "Life of Moses," which presents the story of Moses, his communion with God in the burning bush, and his wanderings in the desert as a symbolic account of the spiritual life. For Gregory, the purpose of prayer was to withdraw the soul from sin so that in its original purity it might serve as a mirror of the divine glory.

"If, by life rightly led, you wash away the mud that has been put on your heart, the Godlike beauty will again shine out in you."

—St. Gregory of Nyssa

Mass

Thursday of the Second Week of Lent
[*St. Frances of Rome*, opt. memorial]

ENTRANCE ANTIPHON   Cf. Psalm 139 (138):23-24

Test me, O God, and know my thoughts. / See that my
path is not wicked, / and lead me in the way everlasting.

COLLECT

O God, who delight in innocence and restore it,
direct the hearts of your servants to yourself,
that, caught up in the fire of your Spirit,
we may be found steadfast in faith
and effective in works.
Through our Lord Jesus Christ, your Son,
who lives and reigns with you in the unity of the Holy Spirit,
God, for ever and ever.

A reading from the Book of the Prophet Jeremiah 17:5-10

A curse on those who trust in mortals;
a blessing on those who trust in the Lord God.

Thus says the LORD: / Cursed is the man who trusts in
human beings, / who seeks his strength in flesh, /
whose heart turns away from the LORD. / He is like a barren
bush in the desert / that enjoys no change of season, / But
stands in a lava waste, / a salt and empty earth. / Blessed is
the man who trusts in the LORD, / whose hope is the LORD.
/ He is like a tree planted beside the waters / that stretches
out its roots to the stream: / It fears not the heat when it
comes, / its leaves stay green; / In the year of drought it
shows no distress, / but still bears fruit. / More tortuous
than all else is the human heart, / beyond remedy; who can
understand it? / I, the LORD, alone probe the mind / and

test the heart, / To reward everyone according to his ways,
/ according to the merit of his deeds.
The word of the Lord.

RESPONSORIAL PSALM   1:1-2, 3, 4 and 6
℟. (40:5a) **Blessed are they who hope in the Lord.**

Blessed the man who follows not
    the counsel of the wicked
Nor walks in the way of sinners,
    nor sits in the company of the insolent,
But delights in the law of the LORD
    and meditates on his law day and night. ℟.

He is like a tree
    planted near running water,
That yields its fruit in due season,
    and whose leaves never fade.
    Whatever he does, prospers. ℟.

Not so, the wicked, not so;
    they are like chaff which the wind drives away.
For the LORD watches over the way of the just,
    but the way of the wicked vanishes. ℟.

GOSPEL ACCLAMATION   See Luke 8:15
Blessed are they who have kept the word with a generous
    heart / and yield a harvest through perseverance.

A reading from the holy Gospel according to Luke 16:19-31

Good things came to you and bad things to Lazarus;
    now he is comforted while you are in agony.

Jesus said to the Pharisees: "There was a rich man who
dressed in purple garments and fine linen and dined
sumptuously each day. And lying at his door was a poor man

named Lazarus, covered with sores, who would gladly have eaten his fill of the scraps that fell from the rich man's table. Dogs even used to come and lick his sores. When the poor man died, he was carried away by angels to the bosom of Abraham. The rich man also died and was buried, and from the netherworld, where he was in torment, he raised his eyes and saw Abraham far off and Lazarus at his side. And he cried out, 'Father Abraham, have pity on me. Send Lazarus to dip the tip of his finger in water and cool my tongue, for I am suffering torment in these flames.' Abraham replied, 'My child, remember that you received what was good during your lifetime while Lazarus likewise received what was bad; but now he is comforted here, whereas you are tormented. Moreover, between us and you a great chasm is established to prevent anyone from crossing who might wish to go from our side to yours or from your side to ours.' He said, 'Then I beg you, father, send him to my father's house, for I have five brothers, so that he may warn them, lest they too come to this place of torment.' But Abraham replied, 'They have Moses and the prophets. Let them listen to them.' He said, 'Oh no, father Abraham, but if someone from the dead goes to them, they will repent.' Then Abraham said, 'If they will not listen to Moses and the prophets, neither will they be persuaded if someone should rise from the dead.'"

The Gospel of the Lord.

PRAYER OVER THE OFFERINGS

By this present sacrifice, we pray, O Lord,
sanctify our observance,
that what Lenten discipline outwardly declares
it may inwardly bring about.
Through Christ our Lord.

COMMUNION ANTIPHON   Psalm 119 (118):1
**Blessed are those whose way is blameless, / who walk in
the law of the Lord.**

PRAYER AFTER COMMUNION
**May this sacrifice, O God,
remain active in its effects
and work ever more strongly within us.
Through Christ our Lord.**

Reflection

Tomorrow's Justice Today

At the heart of Christianity is the conviction that tomorrow
holds the promise of being better than today. Such is the hope
that sustains us when the sun sets at the end of each day.
Whether or not today may be deemed good, or almost good,
tomorrow is pregnant with possibility.

This positive attitude toward tomorrow is grounded in
what God reveals to humanity through Jesus Christ. Our final
destiny is to dwell in the eternal presence of God. Rich or
poor, young or old, famous or not, to be in God is our ultimate vocation.

There is, however, a slippery slope ingrained in this talk
about the future. Many Christians throughout history have
fallen into the trap of conformism, failing to ask critical questions about the status quo that prevents countless people from
flourishing. Others are too comfortable justifying the unjus-
tifiable, even when it is contradictory to our faith and values.
Both groups fall short of their prophetical potential by taking
for granted a better tomorrow.

Talk about the future must take seriously the question of justice. If our hope for a better future is dismissive of the unjust conditions of the present, then we have not understood the message of Jesus.

Eternal life in God is a gift that we can embrace or refuse. It is a gift that begins in the here and now of our lives, and receiving it in fullness involves considerations about our existence as a whole.

We can listen to Jesus' wisdom on how life decisions, just and unjust, play a role in defining our ultimate relationship with God. Or we can listen to other voices. The choice is ours.

Hosffman Ospino

Hosffman Ospino is associate professor of theology and education at Boston College's School of Theology and Ministry.

Evening

God, come to my assistance.
Lord, make haste to help me.

(opt. hymn, pp. 360–65)

PSALM 132:1-10

O LORD, remember David
and all the hardships he endured,
the oath he swore to the LORD,
his vow to the Strong One of Jacob.

"I will not enter the house where I dwell,
nor go to the bed where I rest;
I will give no sleep to my eyes,
to my eyelids I will give no slumber,
till I find a place for the LORD,
a dwelling for the Strong One of Jacob."

We heard of it at Ephrata;
we found it in the plains of Yearim.
"Let us go to the place of God's dwelling;
let us bow down at God's footstool."

Go up, LORD, to the place of your rest,
you and the ark of your strength.
Your priests shall be clothed with righteousness;
your faithful shall ring out their joy.
For the sake of David your servant,
do not reject your anointed.

Glory to the Father . . .

SCRIPTURE   1 Corinthians 12:12, 24b-27

As a body is one though it has many parts, and all the parts of the body, though many, are one body, so also Christ.

God has so constructed the body as to give greater honor to a part that is without it, so that there may be no division in the body, but that the parts may have the same concern for one another. If [one] part suffers, all the parts suffer with it; if one part is honored, all the parts share its joy.

Now you are Christ's body, and individually parts of it.

READ, PONDER, PRAY on a word or phrase from these readings or another of today's Scriptures (*Lectio Divina*, p. 359)

ANTIPHON

If one member of Christ's body suffers, all the members suffer.

CANTICLE OF MARY *(inside back cover)*

INTERCESSIONS

God of unity and peace, you call us to be one body in Christ. Relying on your grace, we pray: ℟. Merciful God, hear our prayer.

Direct our religious and civic leaders to lead with righteousness and justice. ℟.

Give peace to those whose earthly pilgrimage is nearing the end. ℟.

Prosper advances in medical research for disease treatment and control. ℟.

Our Father . . .

May God prepare and open our hearts to receive the Lord with trust, and renew us by the Gospel, through the power of the Holy Spirit. Amen.

Friday, March 10

Morning

O Lord, open my lips.
And my mouth will proclaim your praise.

(opt. hymn, pp. 360–65)

PSALM 90:1-4, 14-17
O Lord, you have been our refuge,
from generation to generation.
Before the mountains were born,
or the earth or the world were brought forth,
you are God, from age to age.

You turn human beings back to dust,
and say, "Return, O children of Adam."
To your eyes a thousand years
are like yesterday, come and gone,
or like a watch in the night.

At dawn, fill us with your faithful love;
we shall exult and rejoice all our days.
Give us joy for the days of our affliction,
for the years when we looked upon evil.

Let your deed be seen by your servants,
and your glorious power by their children.
Let the favor of the LORD our God be upon us;
give success to the work of our hands.
O give success to the work of our hands.

Glory to the Father . . .

SCRIPTURE   Genesis 4:8-10
Cain said to his brother Abel, "Let us go out in the field."
When they were in the field, Cain attacked his brother

Abel and killed him. Then the LORD asked Cain, Where is your brother Abel? He answered, "I do not know. Am I my brother's keeper?" God then said: What have you done? Your brother's blood cries out to me from the ground!

READ, PONDER, PRAY on a word or phrase from these readings or another of today's Scriptures (*Lectio Divina*, p. 359)

ANTIPHON

We are all brothers and sisters in Christ.

CANTICLE OF ZECHARIAH *(inside front cover)*

INTERCESSIONS

God, our refuge, at dawn you fill us with your faithful love. We humbly pray: R∕. **God, teach us your hidden wisdom.**

Give joy and inspiration to theological thinkers and doers. R∕.

Animate our faith, hope, and creativity in difficult or challenging circumstances. R∕.

Embolden leaders to use their position and gifts for the common good. R∕.

Our Father . . .

May God bless us with the peace of Christ that surpasses all understanding, and enrich our lives with every gift of the Spirit. Amen.

Blessed Among Us

St. Teresa Margaret Redi
Carmelite (1747–1770)

St. Teresa Margaret Redi, who lived six short years in the Carmelite convent of Florence before her death at twenty-two, has been compared to the later, and better-known, St. Thérèse of Lisieux. Born to a noble family in Tuscany, Teresa was educated in a convent in Florence before determining that she was called to the Carmelites. Though her father tried desperately to dissuade her, he eventually relented, convinced of the genuineness of her vocation.

As a novice Teresa eagerly embraced the ascetic discipline of the rule—while comprehending that God desired love and not merely outward obedience. For the sake of love, she was willing to exceed anything required of her. As she wrote, "Nothing will seem difficult when we realize that the loved one wants only love for love. He has given himself completely to us; let us give him our whole heart and we shall live in joy."

After taking her vows, Sr. Teresa served as infirmarian—delighting in the opportunity to care for her ailing sisters, even when, unbeknownst to them, she had her own private sufferings. On Pentecost 1767 she was struck deeply by the verse, "God is love." Afterward, in every action, every form of service, every act of devotion, she endeavored to return God's love. The power of this intention took a toll. After a sudden illness, she died of peritonitis on March 7, 1770. She was canonized in 1934.

"Love does not want a divided heart; he wants all or nothing."

—St. Teresa Margaret Redi

Mass

Friday of the Second Week of Lent

ENTRANCE ANTIPHON   Cf. Psalm 31 (30):2, 5

In you, O Lord, I put my trust, let me never be put to shame; / release me from the snare they have hidden for me, / for you indeed are my refuge.

COLLECT

Grant, we pray, almighty God,
that, purifying us by the sacred practice of penance,
you may lead us in sincerity of heart
to attain the holy things to come.
Through our Lord Jesus Christ, your Son,
who lives and reigns with you in the unity of the Holy Spirit,
God, for ever and ever.

A reading from the Book of Genesis   37:3-4, 12-13a, 17b-28a

Here comes the man of dreams; let us kill him.

Israel loved Joseph best of all his sons, for he was the child of his old age; and he had made him a long tunic. When his brothers saw that their father loved him best of all his sons, they hated him so much that they would not even greet him.

One day, when his brothers had gone to pasture their father's flocks at Shechem, Israel said to Joseph, "Your brothers, you know, are tending our flocks at Shechem. Get ready; I will send you to them."

So Joseph went after his brothers and caught up with them in Dothan. They noticed him from a distance, and before he came up to them, they plotted to kill him. They said to one another: "Here comes that master dreamer! Come on, let us kill him and throw him into one of the cisterns here; we could say that a wild beast devoured him. We shall then see what comes of his dreams."

When Reuben heard this, he tried to save him from their hands, saying, "We must not take his life. Instead of shedding blood," he continued, "just throw him into that cistern there in the desert; but do not kill him outright." His purpose was to rescue him from their hands and return him to his father. So when Joseph came up to them, they stripped him of the long tunic he had on; then they took him and threw him into the cistern, which was empty and dry.

They then sat down to their meal. Looking up, they saw a caravan of Ishmaelites coming from Gilead, their camels laden with gum, balm and resin to be taken down to Egypt. Judah said to his brothers: "What is to be gained by killing our brother and concealing his blood? Rather, let us sell him to these Ishmaelites, instead of doing away with him ourselves. After all, he is our brother, our own flesh." His brothers agreed. They sold Joseph to the Ishmaelites for twenty pieces of silver.

The word of the Lord.

RESPONSORIAL PSALM   105:16-17, 18-19, 20-21

R℣. (5a) **Remember the marvels the Lord has done.**

When the LORD called down a famine on the land
    and ruined the crop that sustained them,
He sent a man before them,
    Joseph, sold as a slave. R℣.

They had weighed him down with fetters,
    and he was bound with chains,
Till his prediction came to pass
    and the word of the LORD proved him true. R℣.

The king sent and released him,
    the ruler of the peoples set him free.
He made him lord of his house
    and ruler of all his possessions. R℣.

Gospel Acclamation   John 3:16

God so loved the world that he gave his only-begotten Son;
so that everyone who believes in him might have eternal life.

A reading from the holy Gospel according to Matthew

21:33-43, 45-46

This is the heir; let us kill him.

Jesus said to the chief priests and the elders of the people:
"Hear another parable. There was a landowner who
planted a vineyard, put a hedge around it, dug a wine press
in it, and built a tower. Then he leased it to tenants and went
on a journey. When vintage time drew near, he sent his
servants to the tenants to obtain his produce. But the tenants
seized the servants and one they beat, another they killed,
and a third they stoned. Again he sent other servants, more
numerous than the first ones, but they treated them in the
same way. Finally, he sent his son to them, thinking, 'They
will respect my son.' But when the tenants saw the son, they
said to one another, 'This is the heir. Come, let us kill him
and acquire his inheritance.' They seized him, threw him
out of the vineyard, and killed him. What will the owner
of the vineyard do to those tenants when he comes?" They
answered him, "He will put those wretched men to a
wretched death and lease his vineyard to other tenants who
will give him the produce at the proper times." Jesus said
to them, "Did you never read in the Scriptures: / *The stone
that the builders rejected / has become the cornerstone; / by
the Lord has this been done, / and it is wonderful in our eyes?
/* Therefore, I say to you, the Kingdom of God will be taken
away from you and given to a people that will produce its
fruit." When the chief priests and the Pharisees heard his
parables, they knew that he was speaking about them. And
although they were attempting to arrest him, they feared
the crowds, for they regarded him as a prophet.

The Gospel of the Lord.

Prayer over the Offerings

**May your merciful grace prepare your servants, O God,
for the worthy celebration of these mysteries,
and lead them to it by a devout way of life.
Through Christ our Lord.**

Communion Antiphon   1 John 4:10

God loved us, and sent his Son / as expiation for our sins.

Prayer after Communion

**Having received this pledge of eternal salvation,
we pray, O Lord,
that we may set our course so well
as to attain the redemption you promise.
Through Christ our Lord.**

Reflection

Picture It

It's a remarkable photo—twelve Hernandez-Perez siblings, all born to the same mother and father, ranging in age from 76 to 97. Last fall, they won the Guinness World Record for the combined age of living siblings. There's a picture worth over a thousand years! More remarkably, the family says, "There was never a falling-out between us siblings. We all always help and support each other."

The family photo of Joseph and his eleven brothers—and his sister, Dinah, who most often is not pictured—is more complicated. One dad, four moms, thirteen kids. Joseph's mother, Rachel, died giving birth to his baby brother. She would have been out of the picture by the time Joseph's stepbrothers threw him in a cistern and then sold him into slavery. We know how the saga goes: from falling-out to family reunion. But it took many years for that to happen, and untold suffering all around, making the eventual reunification of Joseph and his brothers—and his father—even more wondrous. Imagine that photo op. Caption contest, anyone? How about this: *Remember the marvels the Lord has done!*

Perhaps because I have fourteen siblings, I marvel over these family stories. While I'd guess the Hernandez-Perez siblings have had a tussle or two along the way, I believe they are there for each other in every joy and sorrow. That's my experience too. But I also understand Joseph and his brothers. After all, we had a cistern in my first childhood home! To be sure, none of our squabbles were so fierce that the cistern ever came into play. But we have other stories, one of them illustrated by a six-year-old . . .

There were "only" twelve of us kids when one of my brothers was assigned a typical first-grade art project: draw a picture of your family (panoramic, if need be!). When his teacher looked at the portrait and saw a mom and a dad and eleven kids of various sizes, she thought my brother had miscounted. Or gotten tired of it all and just decided to be done. "Aren't there twelve kids in your family?" she asked. It depends who you ask and on what day. He'd left out an older sibling "on purpose" because they'd had a falling out. He didn't like him and was sure nobody else would miss him either!

Alas, my mother was not a saver of such first-grade treasures, but the story is lesson enough. Somehow, by the grace of God and with good parenting, we grew up not leaving anyone out of the picture. We can line up for a family photo in a flash—it's a learned skill—stand shoulder-to-shoulder and mean it.

We are all God's children—all of us drawn together by the love that gives us birth and sustains us. It's a remarkable portrait. What caption will we give it?

Mary Stommes

Mary Stommes is an oblate of St. Benedict and the editor of Give Us This Day.

Evening

God, come to my assistance.
Lord, make haste to help me.

(opt. hymn, pp. 360–65)

PSALM 102:2-3, 24-29
Hear my prayer, O LORD,
and let my cry come to you.
Do not hide your face from me
in the day of my distress.
Turn your ear towards me;
on the day when I call,
speedily answer me.

The Lord has broken my strength in midcourse,
and has shortened my days.
I say: "My God, do not take me away
before half of my days are complete,
you, whose days last from age to age.

Long ago you founded the earth,
and the heavens are the work of your hands.
They will perish but you will remain.
They will all wear out like a garment.
You will change them like clothes, and they change.
But you are the same, and your years do not end."

The children of your servants shall dwell untroubled,
and their descendants established before you.

Glory to the Father . . .

SCRIPTURE   Acts 7:9-15a
The patriarchs, jealous of Joseph, sold him into slavery
in Egypt; but God was with him and rescued him from
all his afflictions. He granted him favor and wisdom before

Pharaoh, the king of Egypt, who put him in charge of Egypt and [of] his entire household. Then a famine and great affliction struck all Egypt and Canaan, and our ancestors could find no food; but when Jacob heard that there was grain in Egypt, he sent our ancestors there a first time. The second time, Joseph made himself known to his brothers, and Joseph's family became known to Pharaoh. Then Joseph sent for his father Jacob, inviting him and his whole clan, seventy-five persons; and Jacob went down to Egypt."

READ, PONDER, PRAY on a word or phrase from these readings or another of today's Scriptures (*Lectio Divina*, p. 359)

ANTIPHON

God sent Joseph ahead of Israel to save them from destruction.

CANTICLE OF MARY *(inside back cover)*

INTERCESSIONS

Compassionate God, you never forsake us. In company with our faithful ancestors we pray: R̖. **Hear us, O God.**

Help us to extend hospitality to refugees and all who are fleeing from danger. R̖.

Spread your healing balm upon those who are brokenhearted or sad. R̖.

Give peace to the dying and those who wait beside them. R̖.

Our Father . . .

May God favor us with peace and keep us from harm, through Jesus, the son of Joseph and Mary. Amen.

Saturday, March 11

Morning

O Lord, open my lips.
And my mouth will proclaim your praise.

(opt. hymn, pp. 360–65)

PSALM 50:1-2, 7-9, 14-15

The God of gods, the LORD,
has spoken and summoned the earth,
from the rising of the sun to its setting.
Out of Zion, the perfection of beauty,
God is shining forth.

"Listen, my people, I will speak;
Israel, I will testify against you,
for I am God, your God.

"I do not rebuke you for your sacrifices;
your offerings are always before me.
I do not take more bullocks from your farms,
nor goats from among your herds.

"Give your praise as a sacrifice to God,
and fulfill your vows to the Most High.
Then call on me in the day of distress.
I will deliver you and you shall honor me."

Glory to the Father . . .

SCRIPTURE   Isaiah 55:6-9

Seek the LORD while he may be found, / call upon him
while he is near. / Let the wicked forsake their way, /
and sinners their thoughts; / Let them turn to the LORD to
find mercy; / to our God, who is generous in forgiving. /

For my thoughts are not your thoughts, / nor are your ways my ways—oracle of the Lord. / For as the heavens are higher than the earth, / so are my ways higher than your ways, / my thoughts higher than your thoughts.

READ, PONDER, PRAY on a word or phrase from these readings or another of today's Scriptures (*Lectio Divina*, p. 359)

ANTIPHON

Who is there like you, the God who removes guilt and pardons sin?

CANTICLE OF ZECHARIAH *(inside front cover)*

INTERCESSIONS

God of abundant pardon, you are slow to anger and rich in love. With trust in your compassion we pray: R̸. Have mercy on us, O God.

Teach us to be quick to admit our transgressions and to be patient with ourselves and one another. R̸.

Bring peace and calm to those who are overstimulated, overworked, or overwhelmed. R̸.

Unite people of faith in efforts to integrate healing practices that address systemic racism. R̸.

Our Father . . .

May God bless us with peace, and lead us to know the tenderness and care of Jesus, the Good Shepherd. Amen.

Blessed Among Us

James Reeb
Civil Rights Martyr (1927–1965)

Reverend James Reeb, a white Unitarian minister, had long been committed to racial justice. He was among the first of hundreds of northern clergy who responded to a call for volunteers from the civil rights movement to plan a march from Selma to Montgomery, Alabama. A previous effort, on March 7, had been blocked by mounted state troopers who charged the marchers with whips and clubs as they tried to cross the Edmund Pettus Bridge in Selma—a day known as Bloody Sunday.

Leaving his wife and four children in Boston, Reeb arrived in Selma two days later on March 9. His stay was short. That very night, as he and two other ministers left a diner, they were accosted by a gang of white men with clubs. One of them struck Reeb in the head, cracking his skull. He died two days later.

President Johnson invoked Reverend Reeb in his speech before a joint session of Congress: "At times history and fate meet in a single time in a single place to shape a turning point in man's unending search for freedom. . . . So it was last week in Selma, Alabama."

Soon after, Congress passed the Voting Rights Act. Later that year, three men charged with Reeb's murder were acquitted by an all-white jury.

"James Reeb symbolizes the forces of good will in our nation. He demonstrated the conscience of the nation. He was an attorney for the defense of the innocent in the court of world opinion. He was a witness to the truth that men of different races and classes might live, eat, and work together as brothers."

—Martin Luther King Jr.

Mass

Saturday of the Second Week of Lent

ENTRANCE ANTIPHON   Psalm 145 (144):8-9

The Lord is kind and full of compassion, slow to anger,
abounding in mercy. / How good is the Lord to all,
compassionate to all his creatures.

COLLECT

O God, who grant us by glorious healing remedies while
    still on earth
to be partakers of the things of heaven,
guide us, we pray, through this present life
and bring us to that light in which you dwell.
Through our Lord Jesus Christ, your Son,
who lives and reigns with you in the unity of the Holy Spirit,
God, for ever and ever.

A reading from the Book of the Prophet Micah

7:14-15, 18-20

God will cast our sins into the depths of the sea.

Shepherd your people with your staff, / the flock of your
inheritance, / That dwells apart in a woodland, / in the
midst of Carmel. / Let them feed in Bashan and Gilead, /
as in the days of old; / As in the days when you came from
the land of Egypt, / show us wonderful signs.

Who is there like you, the God who removes guilt / and
pardons sin for the remnant of his inheritance; / Who does
not persist in anger forever, / but delights rather in clem-
ency, / And will again have compassion on us, / treading
underfoot our guilt? / You will cast into the depths of the
sea all our sins; / You will show faithfulness to Jacob, / and

grace to Abraham, / As you have sworn to our fathers / from days of old.

The word of the Lord.

RESPONSORIAL PSALM 103:1-2, 3-4, 9-10, 11-12
℟. (8a) **The Lord is kind and merciful.**

Bless the LORD, O my soul;
  and all my being, bless his holy name.
Bless the LORD, O my soul,
  and forget not all his benefits. ℟.

He pardons all your iniquities,
  he heals all your ills.
He redeems your life from destruction,
  he crowns you with kindness and compassion. ℟.

He will not always chide,
  nor does he keep his wrath forever.
Not according to our sins does he deal with us,
  nor does he requite us according to our crimes. ℟.

For as the heavens are high above the earth,
  so surpassing is his kindness toward those who fear him.
As far as the east is from the west,
  so far has he put our transgressions from us. ℟.

GOSPEL ACCLAMATION   Luke 15:18
I will get up and go to my father and shall say to him,
Father, I have sinned against heaven and against you.

A reading from the holy Gospel according to Luke
15:1-3, 11-32
Your brother was dead and has come to life.

Tax collectors and sinners were all drawing near to listen to Jesus, but the Pharisees and scribes began to complain, saying, "This man welcomes sinners and eats with them." So to them Jesus addressed this parable. "A man had two sons, and the younger son said to his father, 'Father, give me the share of your estate that should come to me.' So the father divided the property between them. After a few days, the younger son collected all his belongings and set off to a distant country where he squandered his inheritance on a life of dissipation. When he had freely spent everything, a severe famine struck that country, and he found himself in dire need. So he hired himself out to one of the local citizens who sent him to his farm to tend the swine. And he longed to eat his fill of the pods on which the swine fed, but nobody gave him any. Coming to his senses he thought, 'How many of my father's hired workers have more than enough food to eat, but here am I, dying from hunger. I shall get up and go to my father and I shall say to him, "Father, I have sinned against heaven and against you. I no longer deserve to be called your son; treat me as you would treat one of your hired workers."' So he got up and went back to his father. While he was still a long way off, his father caught sight of him, and was filled with compassion. He ran to his son, embraced him and kissed him. His son said to him, 'Father, I have sinned against heaven and against you; I no longer deserve to be called your son.' But his father ordered his servants, 'Quickly, bring the finest robe and put it on him; put a ring on his finger and sandals on his feet. Take the fattened calf and slaughter it. Then let us celebrate with a feast, because this son of mine was dead, and has come to life again; he was lost, and has been found.' Then the celebration began. Now the older son had been out in the field and, on his way back, as he neared the house, he heard the sound of music and dancing. He called one of the servants and asked what this might mean. The servant said to him, 'Your brother has returned and your father has slaughtered the fattened calf because he has him back safe and sound.' He became angry, and when he refused to enter the house, his father came out and pleaded with him. He said to his father in reply, 'Look, all these years I served you and not once did I disobey your orders; yet you never gave me even a young goat to feast on with my friends. But when your son returns who swallowed up your property with prostitutes, for him you slaughter the fattened calf.' He said to him, 'My son, you are here with me always; everything I have is yours. But now we must celebrate and rejoice, because your brother was dead and has come to life again; he was lost and has been found.'"

The Gospel of the Lord.

PRAYER OVER THE OFFERINGS
Through these sacred gifts, we pray, O Lord,
may our redemption yield its fruits,
restraining us from unruly desires
and leading us onward to the gifts of salvation.
Through Christ our Lord.

COMMUNION ANTIPHON   Luke 15:32
You must rejoice, my son, / for your brother was dead
and has come to life; / he was lost and is found.

PRAYER AFTER COMMUNION
May your divine Sacrament, O Lord, which we have
    received,
fill the inner depths of our heart
and, by its working mightily within us,
make us partakers of its grace.
Through Christ our Lord.

Reflection

The Logic of Mercy

The poor father! One son went away, and the other was never close to him! The suffering of the father is like the suffering of God, the suffering of Jesus when we distance ourselves from him, either because we go far away or because we are nearby without being close.

The elder son needs mercy too. The righteous, those who believe they are righteous, are also in need of mercy. This son represents us when we wonder whether it is worth all the trouble if we get nothing in return. Jesus reminds us that one does not stay in the house of the Father for a reward but because one has the dignity of being children who share responsibility. There is no "bargaining" with God, but rather following in the footsteps of Jesus who gave himself on the Cross without measure.

"Son, you are always with me, and all that is mine is yours. It was fitting to make merry and be glad" (vv. 31-32). The father speaks like this to the older son. His logic is that of mercy! The younger son thought he deserved punishment for his sins, the elder son was waiting for a recompense for his service. The two brothers don't speak to one another, they live in different ways, but they both reason according to a logic that is foreign to Jesus: if you do good, you get a prize; if you do evil you are punished. This is not Jesus' logic, it's not! This logic is reversed by the words of the father: "It was fitting to make merry and be glad, for this your brother was dead, and is alive; he was lost, and is found" (v. 32). . . .

The sons can decide whether to join in the joy of the father or to reject it. They must ask themselves what they really want and what their vision is for their life. The parable is left open-ended: we do not know what the older son decided to do.

And this is an incentive for us. This Gospel passage teaches us that we all need to enter the House of the Father and to share in his joy, in his feast of mercy. . . . Brothers and sisters, let us open our hearts, in order to be "merciful like the Father"!

— Pope Francis, General Audience, May 11, 2016

Jorge Mario Bergoglio, SJ, was the archbishop of Buenos Aires from 1998 until his election as pope in 2013. Pope Francis has proclaimed a Gospel of joy and peace, of care for the poor and for the earth, "our common home."

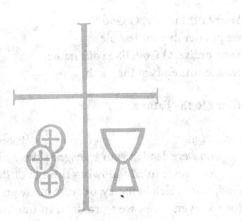

Evening

God, come to my assistance.
Lord, make haste to help me.

(opt. hymn, pp. 360–65)

PSALM 48:2-4, 9-11ab

Great is the LORD and highly to be praised
in the city of our God,
whose holy mountain rises in beauty,
the joy of all the earth.

Mount Zion, in the heart of the North,
the city of the Mighty King!
God, in the midst of her citadels,
is shown to be her stronghold.

As we have heard, so we have seen
in the city of our God,
in the city of the LORD of hosts,
which God establishes forever.

Your faithful love, O God,
we ponder in your temple.
Your praise, O God, like your name,
reaches the ends of the earth.

Glory to the Father . . .

SCRIPTURE   Ephesians 2:1-2a, 4-7

You were dead in your transgressions and sins in which
you once lived following the age of this world. But
God, who is rich in mercy, because of the great love he had
for us, even when we were dead in our transgressions,
brought us to life with Christ (by grace you have been
saved), raised us up with him, and seated us with him in

the heavens in Christ Jesus, that in the ages to come he might show the immeasurable riches of his grace in his kindness to us in Christ Jesus.

READ, PONDER, PRAY on a word or phrase from these readings or another of today's Scriptures (*Lectio Divina*, p. 359)

ANTIPHON
Father, I have sinned against heaven and against you.

CANTICLE OF MARY *(inside back cover)*

INTERCESSIONS
Reconciling God, you forgive our sins and entrust us with the message of reconciliation. In hope we pray:
R̸. God, be with us.

Prosper negotiations for peace among warring countries. R̸.

Heal families separated by misunderstanding, injury, or pride. R̸.

Give peace and absolution to the dying, and fulfill your promise of eternal life. R̸.

Our Father . . .

May God bless us, be gracious to us, and keep us in peace. Amen.

Sunday, March 12

Morning

O Lord, open my lips.
And my mouth will proclaim your praise.

(opt. hymn, pp. 360–65)

PSALM 118:24-29

This is the day the LORD has made;
let us rejoice in it and be glad.

We beseech you, O LORD, grant salvation;
We beseech you, O LORD, grant success.
Blest is he who comes
in the name of the LORD.
We bless you from the house of the LORD;
the LORD is God, and has given us light.

Go forward in procession with branches,
as far as the horns of the altar.
You are my God, I thank you.
My God, I praise you.
Give thanks to the LORD, who is good,
whose faithful love endures forever.

Glory to the Father . . .

SCRIPTURE   Sirach 24:19-23

Come to me, all who desire me, / and be filled with my fruits. / You will remember me as sweeter than honey, / better to have than the honeycomb. / Those who eat of me will hunger still, / those who drink of me will thirst for more. / Whoever obeys me will not be put to shame, / and those who serve me will never go astray."

Jesus and the Samaritan Woman at the Well, gold leaf, paint, and etching on glass, ca. 1420, German.

All this is the book of the covenant of the Most High God, / the Law which Moses commanded us / as a heritage for the community of Jacob.

READ, PONDER, PRAY on a word or phrase from these readings or another of today's Scriptures (*Lectio Divina*, p. 359)

ANTIPHON
The water I shall give will become a spring of water welling up to eternal life.

CANTICLE OF ZECHARIAH *(inside front cover)*

INTERCESSIONS
Loving God, in Jesus you offered friendship and new life to the Samaritan woman. In hope we pray: R7. **Give us new life in you, O God.**

Inspire us to reach out to the homebound and to those who feel alienated from the Church. R7.

Strengthen the faith and perseverance of those who are preparing for baptism or confirmation. R7.

Inspire us to find creative and effective practices to ensure clean water for all of creation. R7.

Our Father . . .

May God strengthen us in faith, hope, and love, by the power of the Holy Spirit. Amen.

Mass

Third Sunday of Lent

ENTRANCE ANTIPHON   Cf. Psalm 25 (24):15-16

My eyes are always on the Lord, / for he rescues my feet
from the snare. / Turn to me and have mercy on me, / for
I am alone and poor.

Or: Cf. Ezekiel 36:23-26

When I prove my holiness among you, / I will gather you
from all the foreign lands; / and I will pour clean water
upon you / and cleanse you from all your impurities, /
and I will give you a new spirit, says the Lord.

(The Gloria is omitted.)

COLLECT

O God, author of every mercy and of all goodness,
who in fasting, prayer and almsgiving
have shown us a remedy for sin,
look graciously on this confession of our lowliness,
that we, who are bowed down by our conscience,
may always be lifted up by your mercy.
Through our Lord Jesus Christ, your Son,
who lives and reigns with you in the unity of the Holy Spirit,
God, for ever and ever.

A reading from the Book of Exodus   17:3-7

Give us water, so that we may drink.

In those days, in their thirst for water, the people grumbled
against Moses, saying, "Why did you ever make us leave
Egypt? Was it just to have us die here of thirst with our
children and our livestock?" So Moses cried out to the LORD,

"What shall I do with this people? A little more and they will stone me!" The Lord answered Moses, "Go over there in front of the people, along with some of the elders of Israel, holding in your hand, as you go, the staff with which you struck the river. I will be standing there in front of you on the rock in Horeb. Strike the rock, and the water will flow from it for the people to drink." This Moses did, in the presence of the elders of Israel. The place was called Massah and Meribah, because the Israelites quarreled there and tested the Lord, saying, "Is the Lord in our midst or not?"

The word of the Lord.

RESPONSORIAL PSALM   95:1-2, 6-7, 8-9

R̦. (8) **If today you hear his voice, harden not your hearts.**

Come, let us sing joyfully to the Lord;
    let us acclaim the Rock of our salvation.
Let us come into his presence with thanksgiving;
    let us joyfully sing psalms to him. R̦.

Come, let us bow down in worship;
    let us kneel before the Lord who made us.
For he is our God,
    and we are the people he shepherds, the flock he
        guides. R̦.

Oh, that today you would hear his voice:
    "Harden not your hearts as at Meribah,
    as in the day of Massah in the desert,
Where your fathers tempted me;
    they tested me though they had seen my works." R̦.

A reading from the Letter of Saint Paul to the Romans
5:1-2, 5-8

The love of God has been poured into our hearts
through the Holy Spirit that has been given to us.

Brothers and sisters: Since we have been justified by faith, we have peace with God through our Lord Jesus Christ, through whom we have gained access by faith to this grace in which we stand, and we boast in hope of the glory of God.

And hope does not disappoint, because the love of God has been poured out into our hearts through the Holy Spirit who has been given to us. For Christ, while we were still helpless, died at the appointed time for the ungodly. Indeed, only with difficulty does one die for a just person, though perhaps for a good person one might even find courage to die. But God proves his love for us in that while we were still sinners Christ died for us.

The word of the Lord.

GOSPEL ACCLAMATION   Cf. John 4:42, 15
Lord, you are truly the Savior of the world;
give me living water, that I may never thirst again.

A reading from the holy Gospel according to John
4:5-42 (Shorter Form [ ], 4:5-15, 19b-26, 39a, 40-42)

The water that I shall give will become a spring of eternal life.

Jesus came to a town of Samaria called Sychar, near the plot of land that Jacob had given to his son Joseph. Jacob's well was there. Jesus, tired from his journey, sat down there at the well. It was about noon.

A woman of Samaria came to draw water. Jesus said to her, "Give me a drink." His disciples had gone into the town to buy food. The Samaritan woman said to him, "How can you, a Jew, ask me, a Samaritan woman, for a drink?"—For Jews use nothing in common with Samaritans.—Jesus answered and said to her, "If you knew the gift of God and who is saying to you, 'Give me a drink,' you would have asked him and he would have given you living water." The woman said to him, "Sir, you do not even have a bucket and the cistern is deep; where then can you get this living water? Are you greater than our father Jacob, who gave us this cistern and drank from it himself with his children and his flocks?" Jesus answered and said to her, "Everyone who drinks this water will be thirsty again; but whoever drinks the water I shall give will never thirst; the water I shall give will become in him a spring of water welling up to eternal life." The woman said to him, "Sir, give me this water, so that I may not be thirsty or have to keep coming here to draw water."]

Jesus said to her, "Go call your husband and come back." The woman answered and said to him, "I do not have a husband." Jesus answered her, "You are right in saying, 'I do not have a husband.' For you have had five husbands, and the one you have now is not your husband. What you have said is true." The woman said to him, "Sir, [I can see that you are a prophet. Our ancestors worshiped on this mountain; but you people say that the place to worship is in Jerusalem." Jesus said to her, "Believe me, woman, the hour is coming when you will worship the Father neither on this mountain nor in Jerusalem. You people worship what you do not understand; we worship what we understand, because salvation is from the Jews. But the hour is coming, and is now here, when true worshipers will worship the Father in Spirit and truth; and indeed the Father seeks such people to worship him. God is Spirit, and those who worship him must worship in Spirit and truth." The woman said to him, "I know that the Messiah is coming, the one called the Christ; when he comes, he will tell us everything." Jesus said to her, "I am he, the one (who is) speaking with you."]

At that moment his disciples returned, and were amazed that he was talking with a woman, but still no one said, "What are you looking for?" or "Why are you talking with her?" The woman left her water jar and went into the town and said to the people, "Come see a man who told me everything I have done. Could he possibly be the Christ?" They went out of the town and came to him. Meanwhile, the disciples urged him, "Rabbi, eat." But he said to them, "I have food to eat of which you do not know." So the disciples said to one another, "Could someone have brought him something to eat?" Jesus said to them, "My food is to do the will of the one who sent me and to finish his work. Do you not say, 'In four months the harvest will be here'? I tell you, look up and see the fields ripe for the harvest. The reaper is already receiving payment and gathering crops for eternal life, so that the sower and reaper can rejoice together. For here the saying is verified that 'One sows and another reaps.' I sent you to reap what you have not worked for; others have done the work, and you are sharing the fruits of their work."

[Many of the Samaritans of that town began to believe in him] because of the word of the woman who testified, "He told me everything I have done." [When the Samaritans came to him, they invited him to stay with them; and he stayed there two days. Many more began to believe in him because of his word, and they said to the woman, "We no longer believe because of your word; for we have heard for ourselves, and we know that this is truly the savior of the world."]

The Gospel of the Lord.

CREED (p. 332)

PRAYER OVER THE OFFERINGS
Be pleased, O Lord, with these sacrificial offerings,
and grant that we who beseech pardon for our own sins,
may take care to forgive our neighbor.
Through Christ our Lord.

COMMUNION ANTIPHON   John 4:13-14
For anyone who drinks it, says the Lord, / the water I
shall give will become in him / a spring welling up to
eternal life.

PRAYER AFTER COMMUNION
As we receive the pledge
of things yet hidden in heaven
and are nourished while still on earth
with the Bread that comes from on high,
we humbly entreat you, O Lord,
that what is being brought about in us in mystery
may come to true completion.
Through Christ our Lord.

Reflection

An Open Letter to the Woman at the Well

Dear Sister,

Thank you! Thank you for coming to the well that day to perform a routine boring chore: drawing water. Woman's work. You remind me that I too can encounter Divinity in the ordinary tasks of daily life.

Thank you for not running away that day. For daring to speak with this stranger—a man and a Jew, no less! Your gutsiness encourages me to risk speaking with individuals very different from myself.

Thank you for giving in to your curiosity. I sometimes think only the big virtues matter in life: faith, hope, and love. But even little curiosities can sneak into my life and set me up for an encounter with God.

Thank you for your messy life. Out of shame (I'm guessing) you tried to hide your five husbands (plus your current lover) from Jesus. But Jesus' response to you tells me that I don't need a perfectly ordered life to engage with him.

Thank you for leaving your water jar at the well and running into town to share the news of this stranger. That left-behind jar is a sure sign that your encounter with Jesus has altered your priorities.

Thank you for your enthusiasm. The fact that so many townspeople came to meet Jesus—simply because of your witness—underscores the importance of enthusiasm in my own life of faith.

And finally, I sense that Jesus was irresistibly drawn to your openness, genuineness, and spunk. Well, so am I! And so I say again: thank you, sister, thank you!

.... Sr. Melannie Svoboda

Melannie Svoboda, a Sister of Notre Dame from Chardon, Ohio, writes and gives talks and retreats. Her latest book is The Grace of Beauty: Its Mystery, Power, and Delight in Daily Life. *Visit her blog, "Sunflower Seeds," at www.melanniesvobodasnd.org.*

Evening

God, come to my assistance.
Lord, make haste to help me.

(opt. hymn, pp. 360–65)

PSALM 144:9-15

To you, O God, will I sing a new song;
I will play on the ten-stringed harp
to you who give kings their victory,
who redeemed your servant David,
from the evil sword.

Rescue me, free me from the hands of foreign foes,
whose mouths speak lies,
whose right hands are raised in perjury.

Let our sons then flourish like saplings,
grown tall and strong from their youth;
our daughters graceful as columns,
as though they were carved for a palace.

Let our barns be filled to overflowing
with crops of every kind;
our sheep increasing by thousands,
tens of thousands in our fields,
our cattle heavy with young.

No ruined wall, no exile,
no sound of weeping in our streets.
Blessed the people of whom this is true;
blessed the people whose God is the LORD!

Glory to the Father . . .

SCRIPTURE   Revelation 22:1-5

Then the angel showed me the river of life-giving water,
sparkling like crystal, flowing from the throne of God

and of the Lamb down the middle of its street. On either side of the river grew the tree of life that produces fruit twelve times a year, once each month; the leaves of the trees serve as medicine for the nations. Nothing accursed will be found there anymore. The throne of God and of the Lamb will be in it, and his servants will worship him. They will look upon his face, and his name will be on their foreheads. Night will be no more, nor will they need light from lamp or sun, for the Lord God shall give them light, and they shall reign forever and ever.

READ, PONDER, PRAY on a word or phrase from these readings or another of today's Scriptures (*Lectio Divina*, p. 359)

ANTIPHON
Whoever drinks the water I give will never thirst.

CANTICLE OF MARY (*inside back cover*)

INTERCESSIONS
Creating God, you are our delight, and Jesus is your new song. In joy we pray: R⁊. Give us life-giving water, O God.

Console those who suffer trauma because of war, oppression, abuse, or disaster. R⁊.

Spread your healing balm upon those who grieve and mourn. R⁊.

Give wisdom and courage to farmers, and grant clement weather for planting and harvesting. R⁊.

Our Father . . .

May the love of God, the peace of Christ, and the communion of the Holy Spirit be with us and remain with us forever. Amen.

Within the Word

Recognizing the Moment of Opportunity

On the Third Sunday of Lent, as people in many parishes are preparing to come into full communion with the Church, we hear the compelling story of what is popularly known as "The Woman at the Well" (John 4:4-42). In reality, there is more to the scene than a woman at a well. There is surprise, hope, and truth, with the well as a fitting image for the depths of what Jesus is offering in the encounter.

In this lengthiest conversation between Jesus and anyone in the New Testament, we are witnessing the in-breaking of the kingdom of God in the life of a woman on the fringes of society. In her, the promise of her dignity before God and the offer of salvation will blossom. Because of her, the reality of God's kingdom will come to be known throughout the region of Samaria.

This scene in Samaria speaks to us about how Jesus recognizes, and then uses, the moment of opportunity. Many of us see time as only chronological (from the Greek *chronos*); events occur in sequence, time is measurable and oriented to accomplishing tasks. But the Greeks had another term for time (*kairos*) that seems to be more in tune with the ministry of Jesus. *Kairos* is about the quality of moments rather than their quantity; it is about looking for meaningful opportunities. In the context of faith, we might think of these moments as grace filled.

The woman comes to the well for water; Jesus offers her living water, piquing her curiosity. The woman comes at an odd time, perhaps to avoid being seen; Jesus sees her for who she is and offers her recognition. The woman points out the generations of animosity between her people (Samaritans) and his people (Jews); Jesus persists in speaking with her. The woman knows her religious tradition; Jesus honors her by entering into intelligent dialogue. The woman professes hope for a coming Messiah; Jesus reveals his identity to her.

The encounter is transformative, with Jesus and the woman both entering into a moment of opportunity, a *kairos* moment. As we discover in the conversation between the woman and Jesus, she has a bit of a reputation in her community, perhaps the very thing that causes her to come in the heat of the day to draw water from the well. Only three verses out of thirty-nine deal with her living situation, indicating that Jesus is more concerned with sharing the Good News than with calling out her sin or demanding her repentance. He sees that the moment is ripe for transformation.

Most Jewish travelers during the time of Jesus would have skirted Samaria by taking the route along the edge of the Jordan River. Some suggest Jesus chose the quickest route by going through Samaria. Interestingly, however, Jesus does not seem to be in a hurry because after the events unfold, he accepts the invitation to stay in Samaria for another two days. One message from this story in John's Gospel is that Jesus skirts prejudices rather than skirting outcasts. By doing so, his actions overturn long-held mistrust, and his message becomes truly revolutionary.

—Cackie Upchurch

Catherine (Cackie) Upchurch is the former director of Little Rock Scripture Study, general editor of the Little Rock Catholic Study Bible, *and the author of several volumes in the* Alive in the Word *series, including* Easter, Season of Realized Hope.

Monday, March 13

Morning

O Lord, open my lips.
And my mouth will proclaim your praise.

(opt. hymn, pp. 360–65)

PSALM 65:6-11

With wondrous deliverance you answer us,
O God our savior.
You are the hope of all the earth,
and of far distant seas.

You establish the mountains with your strength;
you are girded with power.
You still the roaring of the seas,
the roaring of their waves,
and the tumult of the peoples.

Distant peoples stand in awe
at your wondrous deeds.
The lands of sunrise and sunset
you fill with your joy.

You visit the earth, give it water;
you fill it with riches.
God's ever-flowing river brims over
to prepare the grain.

And thus it is you who prepare it:
you drench its furrows;
you level it, soften it with showers;
you bless its growth.

Glory to the Father . . .

SCRIPTURE   Ezekiel 36:25-28

will sprinkle clean water over you to make you clean; from
all your impurities and from all your idols I will cleanse
you. I will give you a new heart, and a new spirit I will put
within you. I will remove the heart of stone from your flesh
and give you a heart of flesh. I will put my spirit within you
so that you walk in my statutes, observe my ordinances, and
keep them. You will live in the land I gave to your ancestors;
you will be my people, and I will be your God.

READ, PONDER, PRAY on a word or phrase from these readings or
another of today's Scriptures (*Lectio Divina*, p. 359)

ANTIPHON
There is no God in all the earth except the God of Israel.

CANTICLE OF ZECHARIAH (*inside front cover*)

INTERCESSIONS
God our savior, you are the hope of all the earth. In
confidence we pray: R̥. **God, in your wisdom, hear our
prayer.**

Make your Church a sign of your inclusive love
and unity. R̥.

Give us clarity of vision so we may recognize Christ in
one another. R̥.

Increase awareness of the trials and needs of pregnant
women, and protect mother and child from harm. R̥.

Our Father . . .

May the Lord strengthen us in faith and answer our
prayers according to God's immeasurable love for every
person and all creation. Amen.

Blessed Among Us

Blessed Rutilio Grande
Jesuit Martyr of El Salvador (1928–1977)

Born into a poor family in El Salvador, Rutilio Grande entered the Jesuits at seventeen. His early years as a priest were undistinguished, but in the mid-1960s he experienced a second conversion, acquiring a new sense of vocation. Rather than set an example of perfection, he determined, the role of the priest was to offer an example of self-sacrifice and loving service.

Increasingly, he exemplified a new Church in El Salvador, committed to awakening in the poor a sense of their dignity and rights. His reputation as a "radical," an enemy of the system, took root. Under pressure, he resigned as director of social action projects for the seminary and took up a post as pastor of the small town of Aguilares. There he established a vigorous social ministry. Once again, his sermons became infamous among the town's elite. In one he proclaimed that if Jesus Christ were to come to El Salvador he would be condemned as a dangerous rabble-rouser and crucified again. "God forbid," he proclaimed, "that I be one of the crucifiers."

On March 12, 1977, his van was sprayed with gunfire, killing him as well as an old peasant and a teenage boy traveling with him. His death marked a turning point for El Salvador—the first but not the last time a priest would face violence. His death deeply touched the new archbishop, Oscar Romero, prompting his own journey on the road to Calvary.

Grande was beatified in 2022, joined, significantly, by the two companions, Manuel Solórzano and Nelson Rutilio Lemus, who died beside him.

"Very soon the Bible won't be allowed to cross our borders. We'll get only the bindings, because all the pages are subversive."

—Blessed Rutilio Grande

Mass
Monday of the Third Week of Lent *

* The following readings may be used on any Lenten day this week,
   especially in Years B and C when the Gospel of the Samaritan woman
   is not read on the Third Sunday of Lent: Exod 17:1-7; John 4:5-42.

ENTRANCE ANTIPHON   Psalm 84 (83):3

My soul is longing and yearning for the courts of the
Lord. / My heart and my flesh cry out to the living God.

COLLECT

May your unfailing compassion, O Lord,
cleanse and protect your Church,
and, since without you she cannot stand secure,
may she be always governed by your grace.
Through our Lord Jesus Christ, your Son,
who lives and reigns with you in the unity of the Holy Spirit,
God, for ever and ever.

A reading from the second Book of Kings   5:1-15ab

*There were many people with leprosy in Israel, but none were
made clean, except Naaman the Syrian (Luke 4:27).*

Naaman, the army commander of the king of Aram, was
highly esteemed and respected by his master, for
through him the LORD had brought victory to Aram. But
valiant as he was, the man was a leper. Now the Arameans
had captured in a raid on the land of Israel a little girl, who
became the servant of Naaman's wife. "If only my master
would present himself to the prophet in Samaria," she said
to her mistress, "he would cure him of his leprosy." Naaman
went and told his lord just what the slave girl from the land
of Israel had said. "Go," said the king of Aram. "I will send
along a letter to the king of Israel." So Naaman set out,
taking along ten silver talents, six thousand gold pieces, and

ten festal garments. To the king of Israel he brought the letter, which read: "With this letter I am sending my servant Naaman to you, that you may cure him of his leprosy."

When he read the letter, the king of Israel tore his garments and exclaimed: "Am I a god with power over life and death, that this man should send someone to me to be cured of leprosy? Take note! You can see he is only looking for a quarrel with me!" When Elisha, the man of God, heard that the king of Israel had torn his garments, he sent word to the king: "Why have you torn your garments? Let him come to me and find out that there is a prophet in Israel."

Naaman came with his horses and chariots and stopped at the door of Elisha's house. The prophet sent him the message: "Go and wash seven times in the Jordan, and your flesh will heal, and you will be clean." But Naaman went away angry, saying, "I thought that he would surely come out and stand there to invoke the LORD his God, and would move his hand over the spot, and thus cure the leprosy. Are not the rivers of Damascus, the Abana and the Pharpar, better than all the waters of Israel? Could I not wash in them and be cleansed?" With this, he turned about in anger and left.

But his servants came up and reasoned with him. "My father," they said, "if the prophet had told you to do something extraordinary, would you not have done it? All the more now, since he said to you, 'Wash and be clean,' should you do as he said." So Naaman went down and plunged into the Jordan seven times at the word of the man of God. His flesh became again like the flesh of a little child, and he was clean.

He returned with his whole retinue to the man of God. On his arrival he stood before him and said, "Now I know that there is no God in all the earth, except in Israel."

The word of the Lord.

RESPONSORIAL PSALM   42:2, 3; 43:3, 4

R̟. (see 42:3) **Athirst is my soul for the living God. When shall I go and behold the face of God?**

As the hind longs for the running waters,
  so my soul longs for you, O God. R̟.

Athirst is my soul for God, the living God.
  When shall I go and behold the face of God? R̟.

Send forth your light and your fidelity;
  they shall lead me on
And bring me to your holy mountain,
  to your dwelling-place. R̟.

Then will I go in to the altar of God,
  the God of my gladness and joy;
Then will I give you thanks upon the harp,
  O God, my God! R̟.

GOSPEL ACCLAMATION   See Psalm 130:5, 7

I hope in the LORD, I trust in his word;
with him there is kindness and plenteous redemption.

A reading from the holy Gospel according to Luke   4:24-30

Like Elijah and Elisha, Jesus was sent not only to the Jews.

Jesus said to the people in the synagogue at Nazareth: "Amen, I say to you, no prophet is accepted in his own native place. Indeed, I tell you, there were many widows in Israel in the days of Elijah when the sky was closed for three and a half years and a severe famine spread over the entire land. It was to none of these that Elijah was sent, but only to a widow in Zarephath in the land of Sidon. Again, there were many lepers in Israel during the time of Elisha the prophet; yet not one of them was cleansed, but only Naaman the Syrian." When the people in the synagogue heard this,

they were all filled with fury. They rose up, drove him out of the town, and led him to the brow of the hill on which their town had been built, to hurl him down headlong. But he passed through the midst of them and went away.
The Gospel of the Lord.

PRAYER OVER THE OFFERINGS
May what we offer you, O Lord,
in token of our service,
be transformed by you into the sacrament of salvation.
Through Christ our Lord.

COMMUNION ANTIPHON   Psalm 117 (116):1, 2
O praise the Lord, all you nations, / for his merciful love towards us is great.

PRAYER AFTER COMMUNION
May communion in this your Sacrament,
we pray, O Lord,
bring with it purification and the unity that is your gift.
Through Christ our Lord.

Reflection

Open to the Blessing

I admire doctors who, as part of their job, sometimes have to deliver very unwelcome news to those in their care. My daughter passed away at age twenty-nine after a lifelong battle with polycystic kidney disease. Her doctors had helped her manage a complex illness involving her kidneys, liver, and spleen—but as her options narrowed, the news often wasn't good. Although caring and kind, Rhiannon's doctors were matter-of-fact about the challenges she faced and the likely outcome the future held. How hard it is, I marveled, to tell someone news they do not want to hear.

The proverb "Don't shoot the messenger" cautions against the normal human tendency to get angry at those who bring bad news, even if they are not in any way responsible. Today's Gospel shows that even Jesus knew what it was like to get blamed for a message no one wants to receive.

Why did the crowd get angry? Jesus had merely pointed to the mystery of God's unexplainable ways. Why would God bless a foreigner like Naaman while so many people in Israel received no cure for their illness? Jesus challenged his own neighbors and friends to open their eyes to see the miracle in their midst. But their anger—and preconceived notions—got in the way.

We cannot control God's blessings; to trust God means learning to accept that prayers don't always get answered the way we want. May today's Gospel story remind us to keep our eyes, ears, and minds open for blessings that can come in unexpected and surprising ways.

Carl McColman

Carl McColman is the author numerous books, including Unteachable Lessons *and* Eternal Heart. *He blogs about contemplative living at* www.anamchara.com.

Evening

God, come to my assistance.
Lord, make haste to help me.

(opt. hymn, pp. 360–65)

PSALM 7:2-8, 18
O LORD, my God, I take refuge in you.
Save and rescue me from all my pursuers,
lest like a lion they tear me apart,
and drag me off with no one to rescue me.

If I have done this, O LORD, my God,
if there is wrong on my hands,
if I have paid back evil for good,
or plundered my foe without cause:

Then let my foes pursue my soul and seize me,
let them trample my life to the ground,
and lay my honor in the dust.

O LORD, rise up in your anger;
be exalted in your fury toward my foes.
Awake for me the justice you have ordered.
Let the company of peoples gather round you,
as you take your seat above them on high.

I thank the LORD for divine righteousness,
and sing to the name of the LORD, the Most High.

Glory to the Father . . .

SCRIPTURE   Romans 3:21-26
N]ow the righteousness of God has been manifested
apart from the law, though testified to by the law and
the prophets, the righteousness of God through faith in
Jesus Christ for all who believe. For there is no distinction;

all have sinned and are deprived of the glory of God. They are justified freely by his grace through the redemption in Christ Jesus, whom God set forth as an expiation, through faith, by his blood, to prove his righteousness because of the forgiveness of sins previously committed, through the forbearance of God—to prove his righteousness in the present time, that he might be righteous and justify the one who has faith in Jesus.

READ, PONDER, PRAY on a word or phrase from these readings or another of today's Scriptures (*Lectio Divina*, p. 359)

ANTIPHON
There is no distinction between Jew and Greek; the same Lord is Lord of all.

CANTICLE OF MARY (*inside back cover*)

INTERCESSIONS
Righteous God, you are our refuge and our strength.
In hope we pray: R̖. Keep us safe, O God.

Inspire detectives, security personnel, and intelligence officers. R̖.

Prosper efforts to capture drug cartels, and protect citizens surrounded by corrupt officials. R̖.

Guard those who suffer mental illness, financial stress, or abuse. R̖.

Our Father . . .

May God bless us with steadfast faith, unwavering hope, and love that casts out all fear, through Jesus, our brother. Amen.

Tuesday, March 14

Morning

O Lord, open my lips.
And my mouth will proclaim your praise.

(opt. hymn, pp. 360–65)

PSALM 18:2-3, 7-8, 17-20

I love you, LORD, my strength;
O LORD, my rock, my fortress, my savior;
my God, my rock where I take refuge;
my shield, my saving strength, my stronghold.

In my anguish I called to the LORD;
I cried to my God for help.
In the heavenly temple my voice was heard;
my crying reached God's ears.

The earth then reeled and rocked;
the mountains were shaken to their base,
quaking at the anger of God.

From on high God reached down and seized me,
drew me forth from the mighty waters,
and saved me from my powerful foe,
from my enemies, whose strength I could not match.

They assailed me in the day of my misfortune,
but the LORD was my strong support,
bringing me out to a place of freedom,
saving me, indeed, with delight.

Glory to the Father . . .

SCRIPTURE   Zechariah 1:4-6

D o not be like your ancestors to whom the earlier
prophets proclaimed: Thus says the LORD of hosts:

Turn from your evil ways and from your wicked deeds. But they did not listen or pay attention to me—oracle of the LORD.—Your ancestors, where are they? And the prophets, can they live forever? But my words and my statutes, with which I charged my servants the prophets, did these not overtake your ancestors? Then they repented and admitted: "Just as the LORD of hosts intended to treat us according to our ways and deeds, so the LORD has done."

READ, PONDER, PRAY on a word or phrase from these readings or another of today's Scriptures (*Lectio Divina*, p. 359)

ANTIPHON
Lord, do not take your mercy from us.

CANTICLE OF ZECHARIAH *(inside front cover)*

INTERCESSIONS
God, our rock, you are our strong support. Relying on your grace, we pray: R̿. **God, help us.**

Lead us to return wholeheartedly to you, and renew us by your living Word. R̿.

Encourage those who experience a call to the single life, and strengthen your Church's outreach to those who embrace this vocation. R̿.

Enlighten all people to show respect for the dignity of the elderly. R̿.

Our Father . . .

May God bless us with peace, and guide us with wisdom's clear light, through Jesus, our strength. Amen.

Blessed Among Us

Fannie Lou Hamer
Civil Rights Leader (1917–1977)

Until 1962, the life of Fannie Lou Hamer was little different from that of her parents or other poor Black women in the Mississippi Delta. One of twenty children, she was educated to the fourth grade and then fell into the life of sharecropping. Her life changed after attending a civil rights rally when she decided to register to vote, an action, at the time, that literally courted death. As a result, she and her family were evicted from their home. She took this as a sign to work full time as a field secretary for the Student Nonviolent Coordinating Committee, quickly rising to a position of leadership.

In 1963 she was arrested while trying to desegregate a bus terminal in Charleston, South Carolina. In jail she was savagely beaten, emerging with a damaged kidney and permanently impaired eyesight. In 1964 she led a "Freedom Delegation" from Mississippi to the Democratic National Convention in Atlantic City. "I am sick and tired of being sick and tired," she proclaimed. Though the delegation was evicted by the party bosses, Hamer touched the conscience of the nation with her eloquent account of the oppression of Blacks in the segregated South and their nonviolent struggle to affirm their dignity and human rights.

She continued in that struggle, battling injustice, war, and poverty, sustained by her deep faith in the God of the oppressed. "If I fall," she said, "I will fall five-feet four-inches forward in the fight for freedom." She died on March 14, 1977.

"I feel sorry for anybody that could let hate wrap them up. Ain't no such thing as I can hate anybody and hope to see God's face."

—Fannie Lou Hamer

Mass

Tuesday of the Third Week of Lent

ENTRANCE ANTIPHON   Cf. Psalm 17 (16):6, 8

To you I call, for you will surely heed me, O God; / turn
your ear to me; hear my words. / Guard me as the apple
of your eye; / in the shadow of your wings protect me.

COLLECT

May your grace not forsake us, O Lord, we pray,
but make us dedicated to your holy service
and at all times obtain for us your help.
Through our Lord Jesus Christ, your Son,
who lives and reigns with you in the unity of the Holy Spirit,
God, for ever and ever.

A reading from the Book of the Prophet Daniel 3:25, 34-43

We ask you to receive us with humble and contrite hearts.

Azariah stood up in the fire and prayed aloud: / "For
your name's sake, O Lord, do not deliver us up forever,
/ or make void your covenant. / Do not take away your
mercy from us, / for the sake of Abraham, your beloved, /
Isaac your servant, and Israel your holy one, / To whom you
promised to multiply their offspring / like the stars of
heaven, / or the sand on the shore of the sea. / For we are
reduced, O Lord, beyond any other nation, / brought low
everywhere in the world this day / because of our sins. / We
have in our day no prince, prophet, or leader, / no burnt
offering, sacrifice, oblation, or incense, / no place to offer
first fruits, to find favor with you. / But with contrite heart
and humble spirit / let us be received; / As though it were
burnt offerings of rams and bullocks, / or thousands of fat
lambs, / So let our sacrifice be in your presence today / as
we follow you unreservedly; / for those who trust in you

cannot be put to shame. / And now we follow you with our whole heart, / we fear you and we pray to you. / Do not let us be put to shame, / but deal with us in your kindness and great mercy. / Deliver us by your wonders, / and bring glory to your name, O Lord."

The word of the Lord.

RESPONSORIAL PSALM   25:4-5ab, 6 and 7bc, 8-9

R/. (6a) **Remember your mercies, O Lord.**

Your ways, O LORD, make known to me;
   teach me your paths,
Guide me in your truth and teach me,
   for you are God my savior. R/.

Remember that your compassion, O LORD,
   and your kindness are from of old.
In your kindness remember me,
   because of your goodness, O LORD. R/.

Good and upright is the LORD;
   thus he shows sinners the way.
He guides the humble to justice,
   he teaches the humble his way. R/.

GOSPEL ACCLAMATION   Joel 2:12-13
Even now, says the LORD,
return to me with your whole heart;
for I am gracious and merciful.

A reading from the holy Gospel according to Matthew
18:21-35

> *Unless each of you forgives your brother and sister,*
> *the Father will not forgive you.*

Peter approached Jesus and asked him, "Lord, if my brother sins against me, how often must I forgive him?

As many as seven times?" Jesus answered, "I say to you, not seven times but seventy-seven times. That is why the Kingdom of heaven may be likened to a king who decided to settle accounts with his servants. When he began the accounting, a debtor was brought before him who owed him a huge amount. Since he had no way of paying it back, his master ordered him to be sold, along with his wife, his children, and all his property, in payment of the debt. At that, the servant fell down, did him homage, and said, 'Be patient with me, and I will pay you back in full.' Moved with compassion the master of that servant let him go and forgave him the loan. When that servant had left, he found one of his fellow servants who owed him a much smaller amount. He seized him and started to choke him, demanding, 'Pay back what you owe.' Falling to his knees, his fellow servant begged him, 'Be patient with me, and I will pay you back.' But he refused. Instead, he had him put in prison until he paid back the debt. Now when his fellow servants saw what had happened, they were deeply disturbed, and went to their master and reported the whole affair. His master summoned him and said to him, 'You wicked servant! I forgave you your entire debt because you begged me to. Should you not have had pity on your fellow servant, as I had pity on you?' Then in anger his master handed him over to the torturers until he should pay back the whole debt. So will my heavenly Father do to you, unless each of you forgives your brother from your heart."

The Gospel of the Lord.

PRAYER OVER THE OFFERINGS
Grant us, O Lord, we pray,
that this saving sacrifice may cleanse us of our faults
and become an oblation
pleasing to your almighty power.
Through Christ our Lord.

Communion Antiphon   Cf. Psalm 15 (14):1-2

Lord, who may abide in your tent, / and dwell on your holy mountain? / Whoever walks without fault and does what is just.

Prayer after Communion

**May the holy partaking of this mystery
give us life, O Lord, we pray,
and grant us both pardon and protection.
Through Christ our Lord.**

Reflection

Feet to the Fire

Interesting inversion in today's Scriptures, balanced like a sculpted vase.

In Daniel, Azariah prays from a furnace, a setting which would make some of us slightly self-obsessed. With no human rituals left, he asks for the balm of God's mercy. He focuses on God's wonders—and when he's delivered (3:52-90), Azariah sings praise to stars, showers, wind, dew, lightning, frost, snow, clouds, hills, rivers, seas, birds, even "fire and heat" (v. 66). What could've destroyed, instead transforms.

The mystery of Matthew's unforgiving servant is how the debtors are supposed to pay during their torture or imprisonment. Even more intriguing is wondering why the servant who was spared enslavement turns viciously on one who owes him less. We're astonished by the bodacious compassion of the king and marvel that someone could pivot so blatantly from forgiveness to destruction.

But the deeper, more painful question is, how often do *we*? We receive gifts we never thought we'd have: relationships, homes, recoveries, work, travel. At the time, we shudder or shout, weep or kiss the ground, so overwhelmed with joy and disbelief. But like petulant children the week after Christmas, we're soon "habituated," whining for more. We've been forgiven far more than we could ever list, so we cringe to remember how we've exaggerated and harassed the slightest debt owed us.

When we're roasting in the fire of guilt or blame, high time to redirect focus: to shining seas; a forest canopy; the layered persimmon, crimson, and fuchsia tones of sunset; the cleansing crash of waterfall. Azariah got that right—nothing like God's creation to guide our feet into ways of peace.

Kathy Coffey

Kathy Coffey is a mother of four, a speaker and retreat leader. An award-winning writer, she is author of When the Saints Came Marching In *and* More Hidden Women of the Gospels. *For more information, see her website:* kathyjcoffey.com.

Evening

God, come to my assistance.
Lord, make haste to help me.

(opt. hymn, pp. 360–65)

(opt. hymn, pp. 360–65)

PSALM 119:137-144

You are righteous, O LORD;
your judgments are upright.
You have imposed your decrees with righteousness,
and with utter fidelity.

I am consumed with zeal,
for my foes forget your word.
Your promise has been thoroughly tested,
and it is cherished by your servant.

Although I am young and despised,
I do not forget your precepts.
Your righteousness is righteous forever,
and your law is truth.

Though anguish and distress have found me,
your commands are my delight.
Your decrees are forever just;
give me insight, and I shall live.

Glory to the Father . . .

SCRIPTURE   2 Corinthians 7:8-11a

E]ven if I saddened you by my letter, I do not regret it;
and if I did regret it ([for] I see that that letter saddened
you, if only for a while), I rejoice now, not because you were
saddened, but because you were saddened into repentance;
for you were saddened in a godly way, so that you did not
suffer loss in anything because of us. For godly sorrow pro-

duces a salutary repentance without regret, but worldly sorrow produces death. For behold what earnestness this godly sorrow has produced for you.

READ, PONDER, PRAY on a word or phrase from these readings or another of today's Scriptures (*Lectio Divina*, p. 359)

ANTIPHON
Lord, deal with us in your great mercy.

CANTICLE OF MARY *(inside back cover)*

INTERCESSIONS
Just God, your judgments are right and true. In hope we pray: R̥. God, in your justice, heed our prayer.

Free us from illusions and the accumulation of excess. R̥.

Inspire efforts to share the earth's food and water resources with all people, particularly those living in poverty. R̥.

Prosper efforts to ensure excellence in education for every child. R̥.

Our Father . . .

May we prefer nothing to the love of Christ, and may he bring us together to everlasting life. Amen.

Wednesday, March 15

Morning

O Lord, open my lips.
And my mouth will proclaim your praise.

(opt. hymn, pp. 360–65)

PSALM 86:1-8
Turn your ear, O LORD, and answer me,
for I am poor and needy.
Preserve my soul, for I am faithful;
save the servant who trusts in you, my God.

Have mercy on me, O Lord,
for I cry to you all the day long.
Gladden the soul of your servant,
for I lift up my soul to you, O Lord.

O Lord, you are good and forgiving,
full of mercy to all who call to you.
Give ear, O LORD, to my prayer,
and attend to my voice in supplication.

In the day of distress, I will call to you,
and surely you will answer me.
Among the gods there is none like you, O Lord,
nor works to compare with yours.

Glory to the Father . . .

SCRIPTURE   Proverbs 4:1-7
Hear, O children, a father's instruction, / be attentive,
that you may gain understanding! / Yes, excellent ad-
vice I give you; / my teaching do not forsake. / When I was
my father's child, / tender, the darling of my mother, / He

taught me and said to me: / "Let your heart hold fast my words: / keep my commands, and live! / Get wisdom, get understanding! / Do not forget or turn aside from the words of my mouth. / Do not forsake her, and she will preserve you; / love her, and she will safeguard you; / The beginning of wisdom is: get wisdom; / whatever else you get, get understanding."

READ, PONDER, PRAY on a word or phrase from these readings or another of today's Scriptures (*Lectio Divina*, p. 359)

ANTIPHON
Teach God's wonderful deeds to your children and your children's children.

CANTICLE OF ZECHARIAH *(inside front cover)*

INTERCESSIONS
Ever-living God, your words are spirit and life. In hope we pray: R̥. Have mercy on us, O God.

Help us to reflect on our Lenten commitments in light of Gospel love. R̥.

Attend to the cries of parents with children who are sick, missing, or deeply troubled. R̥.

Support married couples who experience struggle in their relationship. R̥.

Our Father . . .

May God gladden our hearts and answer our prayers, through Jesus, our hope for redemption. Amen.

Blessed Among Us

St. Louise de Marillac
Cofounder, Daughters of Charity (1591–1660)

Following the death of her father when she was fifteen, Louise de Marillac agreed to marry a wealthy courtier in the household of the French queen. She was a happy wife and mother, but when her husband died she vowed she would devote the rest of her life to the service of God. After some years searching for her vocation, she was introduced to Fr. Vincent de Paul, who became her spiritual director and with whom she went on to form one of the great partnerships in the history of religious life.

Monsieur Vincent, as he was called, was widely known for the extraordinary range of his charitable projects. These included a circle of aristocratic ladies who joined him to work in the Parisian slums among the sick and destitute. Louise committed herself to this work. But soon they formed the notion of a community of women completely committed to loving service among the poor. Thus were born the Daughters of Charity. Rome's recognition of a congregation of women living outside an enclosed convent and engaged in apostolic work in the world was a novel achievement. In their spiritual formation the sisters were constantly reminded that the poor were their masters. She admonished her sisters to be "diligent in serving the poor . . . to love the poor, honor them, my children, as you would honor Christ himself."

Louise died on March 15, 1660, followed six months later by Vincent. By the time of her canonization in 1934, the Daughters of Charity numbered more than 50,000 worldwide.

"[A Daughter of Charity] is well aware that we are leaving God for God if we leave one of our spiritual exercises for the service of the poor."

—St. Louise de Marillac

Mass

Wednesday of the Third Week of Lent

ENTRANCE ANTIPHON   Cf. Psalm 119 (118):133

Let my steps be guided by your promise; may evil never rule me.

COLLECT

Grant, we pray, O Lord,
that, schooled through Lenten observance
and nourished by your word,
through holy restraint
we may be devoted to you with all our heart
and be ever united in prayer.
Through our Lord Jesus Christ, your Son,
who lives and reigns with you in the unity of the Holy Spirit,
God, for ever and ever.

A reading from the Book of Deuteronomy   4:1, 5-9

Keep the commandments and your work will be complete.

Moses spoke to the people and said: "Now, Israel, hear the statutes and decrees which I am teaching you to observe, that you may live, and may enter in and take possession of the land which the LORD, the God of your fathers, is giving you. Therefore, I teach you the statutes and decrees as the LORD, my God, has commanded me, that you may observe them in the land you are entering to occupy. Observe them carefully, for thus will you give evidence of your wisdom and intelligence to the nations, who will hear of all these statutes and say, 'This great nation is truly a wise and intelligent people.' For what great nation is there that has gods so close to it as the LORD, our God, is to us whenever we call upon him? Or what great nation has statutes and decrees that are as just as this whole law which I am setting before you today?

"However, take care and be earnestly on your guard not to forget the things which your own eyes have seen, nor let them slip from your memory as long as you live, but teach them to your children and to your children's children."

The word of the Lord.

RESPONSORIAL PSALM   147:12-13, 15-16, 19-20

R⍨. (12a) **Praise the Lord, Jerusalem.**

Glorify the LORD, O Jerusalem;
    praise your God, O Zion.
For he has strengthened the bars of your gates;
    he has blessed your children within you. R⍨.

He sends forth his command to the earth;
    swiftly runs his word!
He spreads snow like wool;
    frost he strews like ashes. R⍨.

He has proclaimed his word to Jacob,
    his statutes and his ordinances to Israel.
He has not done thus for any other nation;
    his ordinances he has not made known to them. R⍨.

GOSPEL ACCLAMATION   See John 6:63c, 68c
Your words, Lord, are Spirit and life;
you have the words of everlasting life.

A reading from the holy Gospel according to Matthew
5:17-19

Whoever keeps and teaches the law will be called great.

Jesus said to his disciples: "Do not think that I have come to abolish the law or the prophets. I have come not to abolish but to fulfill. Amen, I say to you, until heaven and earth pass away, not the smallest letter or the smallest part of a letter will pass from the law, until all things have taken place. Therefore, whoever breaks one of the least of these commandments and teaches others to do so will be called least in the Kingdom of heaven. But whoever obeys and teaches these commandments will be called greatest in the Kingdom of heaven."

The Gospel of the Lord.

PRAYER OVER THE OFFERINGS
Accept, O Lord, we pray, the prayers of your people
along with these sacrificial offerings,
and defend those who celebrate your mysteries
from every kind of danger.
Through Christ our Lord.

COMMUNION ANTIPHON   Cf. Psalm 16 (15):11
You will show me the path of life, / the fullness of joy in
your presence, O Lord.

PRAYER AFTER COMMUNION
May the heavenly banquet, at which we have been fed,
sanctify us, O Lord,
and, cleansing us of all errors,
make us worthy of your promises from on high.
Through Christ our Lord.

Reflection

From One Generation to the Next

Adhering to even the smallest letter of the Law cannot be done alone. This kind of obedience, of holiness, assumes that we live in a community bound to Jesus. This community echoes the people of God in the desert learning to be free, to live in trust daily, practicing hope and relying on the providence of God for even food, water, direction, and survival. If we are to know our God, then we must learn together, travel together, pray together, and support one another. We go home together, or we don't go at all. We are all part of one another. We are called to listen, to hear together, so that we can turn to others and provide affirmation, confirmation, and encouragement. Clarity, steadfastness, obedience, and strength come from unity, from community.

We begin by loving the Law, and then together searching out what the smallest jot and letter of the law demands of us individually and together. . . . For instance, "Thou shalt not kill" can be interpreted to apply only to our own family, clan, tribe, or nation. But the smallest letter reminds us that not only are we not to kill anyone—friend, neighbor, stranger, wrongdoer, or enemy—but we are to protect those most in need from danger, disease, violence, misuse of power, those caught in the webs of hatred, nationalism, racism, and poverty. We are to resist destruction and violence with nonviolence, with meekness and forgiveness and courage, offering creative and imaginative hope to the powerless. Obeying the least letter of the Law reveals that we are intent on honoring God publicly in all human beings, situations, and nations, intent on letting the Spirit of God define what is to be practiced and taught from one generation to the next. Lived thus, the Law deepens our humanity and extends the power of God into all areas of life.

Megan McKenna, *Lent: Reflections and Stories on the Daily Readings*

Megan McKenna is an author, theologian, storyteller, and lecturer. She has taught at a number of schools, including Fordham University and the Washington Theological Union.

Evening

God, come to my assistance.
Lord, make haste to help me.

(opt. hymn, pp. 360–65)

Psalm 42:2-6

Like the deer that yearns for running streams,
so my soul is yearning for you, my God.

My soul is thirsting for God, the living God;
when can I enter and appear before the face of God?

My tears have become my bread,
by day, by night,
as they say to me all the day long,
"Where is your God?"

These things will I remember as I pour out my soul:
for I would go to the place of your wondrous tent,
all the way to the house of God,
amid cries of gladness and thanksgiving,
the throng keeping joyful festival.

Why are you cast down, my soul;
why groan within me?
Hope in God, whom I will praise yet again,
my saving presence and my God.

Glory to the Father . . .

Scripture   2 Timothy 4:1-5

charge you in the presence of God and of Christ Jesus,
who will judge the living and the dead, and by his appear-
ing and his kingly power: proclaim the word; be persistent
whether it is convenient or inconvenient; convince, repri-
mand, encourage through all patience and teaching. For

the time will come when people will not tolerate sound doctrine but, following their own desires and insatiable curiosity, will accumulate teachers and will stop listening to the truth and will be diverted to myths. But you, be self-possessed in all circumstances; put up with hardship; perform the work of an evangelist; fulfill your ministry.

READ, PONDER, PRAY on a word or phrase from these readings or another of today's Scriptures (*Lectio Divina*, p. 359)

ANTIPHON
Whoever teaches these commandments will be called greatest in God's kingdom.

CANTICLE OF MARY (*inside back cover*)

INTERCESSIONS
God of our longing, you are our saving presence. With praise in our hearts we pray: R̶. Save us, O God.

Strengthen us to learn from one another and to bear with one another's weaknesses in love and patience. R̶.

Fill our minds and hearts with your saving Word. R̶.

Welcome into your everlasting glory all who have died. R̶.

Our Father . . .

May God strengthen us for every good work and word, through Jesus and by the power of the Holy Spirit. Amen.

Thursday, March 16

Morning

O Lord, open my lips.
And my mouth will proclaim your praise.

(opt. hymn, pp. 360–65)

PSALM 119:25-32

My soul holds fast to the dust;
revive me by your word.
I declared my ways and you answered me;
teach me your statutes.

Make me grasp the way of your precepts,
and I will ponder your wonders.
My soul pines away with grief;
by your word raise me up.

Keep me from the way of falsehood;
grant me mercy by your law.
I have chosen the way of faithfulness;
your decrees I have upheld.

I cling to your decrees, O LORD;
let me not be put to shame.
I will run the way of your commands;
you open wide my heart.

Glory to the Father . . .

SCRIPTURE   Deuteronomy 28:1-2, 9-10a

Now, if you diligently obey the voice of the LORD, your God, carefully observing all his commandments which I give you today, the LORD, your God, will set you high above all the nations of the earth. All these blessings will come upon you and overwhelm you when you obey the voice of the Lᴏʀᴅ, your God.

The Lᴏʀᴅ will establish you as a holy people, as he swore to you, if you keep the commandments of the Lᴏʀᴅ, your God, and walk in his ways. All the peoples of the earth will see that the name of the Lᴏʀᴅ is proclaimed over you.

Rᴇᴀᴅ, Pᴏɴᴅᴇʀ, Pʀᴀʏ on a word or phrase from these readings or another of today's Scriptures (*Lectio Divina*, p. 359)

Aɴᴛɪᴘʜᴏɴ
Listen to my voice: I will be your God and you will be my people.

Cᴀɴᴛɪᴄʟᴇ ᴏғ Zᴇᴄʜᴀʀɪᴀʜ *(inside front cover)*

Iɴᴛᴇʀᴄᴇssɪᴏɴs
Benevolent God, your goodness is unending. In faith we pray: R̸. **Open our hearts, O God.**

Strengthen our faith, and enliven us to practice works of charity each day. R̸.

Deepen your Church's commitment to those who live in poverty or are treated unjustly. R̸.

Pour your life-giving Word into homilists, catechists, retreat masters, theologians, and spiritual writers. R̸.

Our Father . . .

May God bless us with listening hearts and generous spirits, through Jesus, the way, the truth, and the life. Amen.

Blessed Among Us

Franziska Jägerstätter
Wife and Mother (1913–2013)

On August 9, 1943, Franz Jägerstätter, an Austrian farmer and devout Catholic, was beheaded by the Nazis for refusing to serve in Hitler's army. Having determined that the Nazis were a demonic force, he believed it would endanger his soul to take the military oath. Neighbors thought him mad—or at least a religious fanatic. His pastor and even his bishop tried to dissuade him. The one person who stood by his side was his wife Franziska. Naturally, she would have preferred not to lose her husband, the father of their three daughters. But she honored his conscience and did nothing to dissuade him from his path.

The letters Franz and his wife exchanged after his arrest reflect their deep love for one another. "Dearly beloved husband," Franziska's letters begin. Trying her best to spare Franz the details of her own difficulties, she hoped for the best, while constantly expressing her submission to God's will. After learning of his death, she wrote, "I have lost a good husband and exemplary father for my children. . . . However, the loving God had ordained things to be otherwise, and our beautiful union was lost. I already look forward to our reunion in heaven where no war can any longer separate us."

While the war lasted, Franziska suffered scorn from her neighbors as the widow of a traitor. Local embarrassment about Franz's witness endured for many years. But Franziska lived to see his memory gradually honored, and finally, in 2007, to attend the ceremony of his beatification. She died on March 16, 2013, shortly after her hundredth birthday.

"It was a long Good Friday. But I feel I am closer to Easter now."

—Franziska Jägerstätter

Mass

Thursday of the Third Week of Lent

ENTRANCE ANTIPHON

I am the salvation of the people, says the Lord. / Should
they cry to me in any distress, / I will hear them, and I will
be their Lord for ever.

COLLECT

We implore your majesty most humbly, O Lord,
that, as the feast of our salvation draws ever closer,
so we may press forward all the more eagerly
towards the worthy celebration of the Paschal Mystery.
Through our Lord Jesus Christ, your Son,
who lives and reigns with you in the unity of the Holy Spirit,
God, for ever and ever.

A reading from the Book of the Prophet Jeremiah   7:23-28

This is the nation that will not listen to the voice of the LORD God.

Thus says the LORD: This is what I commanded my
people: Listen to my voice; then I will be your God and
you shall be my people. Walk in all the ways that I command
you, so that you may prosper.

But they obeyed not, nor did they pay heed. They walked
in the hardness of their evil hearts and turned their backs,
not their faces, to me. From the day that your fathers left
the land of Egypt even to this day, I have sent you untiringly
all my servants the prophets. Yet they have not obeyed me
nor paid heed; they have stiffened their necks and done
worse than their fathers. When you speak all these words
to them, they will not listen to you either; when you call to
them, they will not answer you. Say to them: This is the
nation that does not listen to the voice of the LORD, its God,

or take correction. Faithfulness has disappeared; the word itself is banished from their speech.

The word of the Lord.

RESPONSORIAL PSALM 95:1-2, 6-7, 8-9

℞. (8) **If today you hear his voice, harden not your hearts.**

Come, let us sing joyfully to the LORD;
    let us acclaim the Rock of our salvation.
Let us come into his presence with thanksgiving;
    let us joyfully sing psalms to him. ℞.

Come, let us bow down in worship;
    let us kneel before the LORD who made us.
For he is our God,
    and we are the people he shepherds, the flock he
        guides. ℞.

Oh, that today you would hear his voice:
    "Harden not your hearts as at Meribah,
    as in the day of Massah in the desert,
Where your fathers tempted me;
    they tested me though they had seen my works." ℞.

GOSPEL ACCLAMATION Joel 2:12-13

Even now, says the LORD,
return to me with your whole heart,
for I am gracious and merciful.

A reading from the holy Gospel according to Luke 11:14-23

Whoever is not with me is against me.

Jesus was driving out a demon that was mute, and when the demon had gone out, the mute man spoke and the crowds were amazed. Some of them said, "By the power of Beelzebul, the prince of demons, he drives out demons." Others, to test him, asked him for a sign from heaven. But he knew their thoughts and said to them, "Every kingdom divided against itself will be laid waste and house will fall against house. And if Satan is divided against himself, how will his kingdom stand? For you say that it is by Beelzebul that I drive out demons. If I, then, drive out demons by Beelzebul, by whom do your own people drive them out? Therefore they will be your judges. But if it is by the finger of God that I drive out demons, then the Kingdom of God has come upon you. When a strong man fully armed guards his palace, his possessions are safe. But when one stronger than he attacks and overcomes him, he takes away the armor on which he relied and distributes the spoils. Whoever is not with me is against me, and whoever does not gather with me scatters."

The Gospel of the Lord.

PRAYER OVER THE OFFERINGS
Cleanse your people, Lord, we pray,
from every taint of wickedness,
that their gifts may be pleasing to you;
and do not let them cling to false joys,
for you promise them the rewards of your truth.
Through Christ our Lord.

COMMUNION ANTIPHON   Psalm 119 (118):4-5
You have laid down your precepts to be carefully kept; /
may my ways be firm in keeping your statutes.

PRAYER AFTER COMMUNION
Graciously raise up, O Lord,
those you renew with this Sacrament,
that we may come to possess your salvation
both in mystery and in the manner of our life.
Through Christ our Lord.

Reflection

"By the Finger of God . . ."

Jesus employs three metaphors in today's Gospel—a divided kingdom, a fallen house, and the finger of God. The first two images connote dissension and anarchy as Jesus responds to the accusation that he is in league with Beelzebul or Satan for calling a demon out of a mute person. Skillfully, Jesus turns his accusers' logic inside out and appeals to a stronger power that has arrived in their midst—the "finger of God," the in-breaking of a new kingdom, a divine kingdom. Beelzebul is viewed as the strong one by the onlookers, but one stronger than he has come to defeat him.

Jesus' use of a figure of speech from the Hebrew Scriptures—"the finger of God" (Exod 8:15)—is a ray of light in an otherwise shadowy controversy story. He relates his own activity to God's work in the world and challenges his onlookers to choose light over darkness, good over evil.

This Gospel story reminds us that we also can fail to see the presence of God all around us. Let us ask ourselves: Are we too weighed down by the darkness near and far to recognize the many ways God continues to bring light into the world? Or are we alert to the signs of new life in one another, in our Church, and in our world?

Our calling as Christians is to allow the Spirit of God to transform us so that we may become tangible signs of the victory of God's love over evil, of God's light in the darkness.

Sr. Ephrem Hollermann

Ephrem Hollermann, OSB, is a former prioress of Saint Benedict's Monastery, St. Joseph, Minnesota, and professor emerita of theology at the College of Saint Benedict and Saint John's University.

Evening

God, come to my assistance.
Lord, make haste to help me.

(opt. hymn, pp. 360–65)

PSALM 33:12-19

Blessed the nation whose God is the LORD,
the people God has chosen as a heritage.
From the heavens the LORD looks forth,
and sees the whole human race.

From the heavenly dwelling God gazes
on all the dwellers on the earth,
God who shapes the hearts of them all,
and considers all their deeds.

A ruler is not saved by a great army,
nor a warrior preserved by great strength.
A vain hope for safety is the horse;
despite its power it cannot save.

Behold, the eyes of the LORD
are on those who fear him,
who hope in God's faithful love,
to rescue their soul from death,
to keep them alive in famine.

Glory to the Father . . .

SCRIPTURE   1 Corinthians 1:21-25

S]ince in the wisdom of God the world did not come to
know God through wisdom, it was the will of God
through the foolishness of the proclamation to save those
who have faith. For Jews demand signs and Greeks look for
wisdom, but we proclaim Christ crucified, a stumbling

block to Jews and foolishness to Gentiles, but to those who are called, Jews and Greeks alike, Christ the power of God and the wisdom of God. For the foolishness of God is wiser than human wisdom, and the weakness of God is stronger than human strength.

READ, PONDER, PRAY on a word or phrase from these readings or another of today's Scriptures (*Lectio Divina*, p. 359)

ANTIPHON
The kingdom of God has come upon you.

CANTICLE OF MARY *(inside back cover)*

INTERCESSIONS
God of fidelity and truth, your gaze is infinite mercy.
In hope we pray: R⁊. God, in your love, hear our prayer.

Lead orphaned children to families that will love and care for them. R⁊.

Help us to make food and resources accessible for everyone. R⁊.

Give solace and peace to those who have lost loved ones to violence. R⁊.

Our Father . . .

May God strengthen us to see Christ in everyone and love our neighbor as ourselves, by the power and gifts of the Holy Spirit. Amen.

Friday, March 17

Morning

O Lord, open my lips.
And my mouth will proclaim your praise.

(opt. hymn, pp. 360–65)

PSALM 12

Save me, O LORD, for the holy ones are no more;
the faithful have vanished from the human race.
They babble vanities, one to another,
with cunning lips, with divided heart.

May the LORD destroy all cunning lips,
the tongue that utters boastful words,
Those who say, "We prevail with our tongue;
our lips are our own, who can command us?"

"For the poor who are oppressed and the needy who sigh,
now will I arise," says the LORD;
"I will grant them the salvation for which they long."
The words of the LORD are words without alloy,
silver from the furnace, seven times refined.

It is you, O LORD, who will keep us safe,
and protect us forever from this generation.
The wicked prowl on every side,
while baseness is exalted by the human race.

Glory to the Father . . .

SCRIPTURE   Isaiah 31:1, 4a-d, 5

Ah! Those who go down to Egypt for help, / who rely on
horses; / Who put their trust in chariots because of
their number, / and in horsemen because of their combined

power, / But look not to the Holy One of Israel / nor seek the LORD! / For thus says the LORD to me: / As a lion or its young / growling over the prey, / With a band of shepherds / assembled against it, / Is neither dismayed by their shouts / nor cowed by their noise, / So shall the LORD of hosts come down. / Like hovering birds, so the LORD of hosts / shall shield Jerusalem, / To shield and deliver, / to spare and rescue.

READ, PONDER, PRAY on a word or phrase from these readings or another of today's Scriptures (*Lectio Divina*, p. 359)

ANTIPHON
Our help is in the name of the Lord.

CANTICLE OF ZECHARIAH *(inside front cover)*

INTERCESSIONS
All-knowing God, you gave us your only Son so that we might have eternal life. In company with St. Patrick we humbly pray: R℣. God, come to our aid.

Pour your Word into our hearts, and let it bring forth a harvest of peace and unity where there is war and division. R℣.

Inspire catechists, parents, pastors, and all who nurture the faith of young people. R℣.

Assist emergency aid workers and all who provide for those who hunger or suffer from famine. R℣.

Our Father . . .

May Christ be ever before us, behind us, within us, and around us, by the power of the Holy Spirit. Amen.

Blessed Among Us

Saints Joseph of Arimathea and Nicodemus
Disciples (First Century)

These two saints, both perhaps members of the Sanhedrin, the supreme Jewish council, make significant appearances in the Gospels. Joseph from the town of Arimathea is described as a "good and just man" who, though apparently wealthy, came to follow Jesus. After the crucifixion he requested permission from Pilate to retrieve Jesus' body. With the help of Nicodemus, he wrapped the body in fine linen and had it placed in his own unused family tomb.

Nicodemus was a Pharisee and "a ruler of the Jews." In the Gospel of John he comes to Jesus secretly by night and engages him in theological discussion. "Rabbi," he addresses Jesus respectfully, "we know that you are a teacher come from God; for no one can do these signs that you do, unless God is with him." This prompts the reply from Jesus, "Truly, truly, I say to you, unless one is born anew he cannot see the kingdom of God." Later, John says that Nicodemus spoke on Jesus' behalf before the council, insisting that he receive a fair hearing. This incites a mocking response: "Are you from Galilee too?"

Scripture provides no more information about these two disciples, though Joseph is the subject of later florid legends involving the Holy Grail and his supposed travels to Glastonbury in England.

"Nicodemus said to him, 'How can a man be born when he is old? Can he enter a second time into his mother's womb and be born?' Jesus answered, 'Truly, truly, I say to you, unless one is born of water and the Spirit, he cannot enter the kingdom of God. That which is born of the flesh is flesh, and that which is born of the Spirit is spirit.'"

—John 3:4-5

Mass

Friday of the Third Week of Lent
[*St. Patrick*, opt. memorial]

ENTRANCE ANTIPHON   Psalm 86 (85):8, 10 ·

Among the gods there is none like you, O Lord, / for you
are great and do marvelous deeds; you alone are God.

COLLECT

Pour your grace into our hearts, we pray, O Lord,
that we may be constantly drawn away from unruly desires
and obey by your own gift the heavenly teaching you give us.
Through our Lord Jesus Christ, your Son,
who lives and reigns with you in the unity of the Holy Spirit,
God, for ever and ever.

A reading from the Book of the Prophet Hosea   14:2-10

We will not say to the work of our hands: our god.

Thus says the LORD: / Return, O Israel, to the LORD, your
God; / you have collapsed through your guilt. / Take
with you words, / and return to the LORD; / Say to him,
"Forgive all iniquity, / and receive what is good, that we may
render / as offerings the bullocks from our stalls. / Assyria
will not save us, / nor shall we have horses to mount; / We
shall say no more, 'Our god,' / to the work of our hands; /
for in you the orphan finds compassion."

I will heal their defection, says the LORD, / I will love them
freely; / for my wrath is turned away from them. / I will be
like the dew for Israel: / he shall blossom like the lily; / He
shall strike root like the Lebanon cedar, / and put forth his
shoots. / His splendor shall be like the olive tree / and his
fragrance like the Lebanon cedar. / Again they shall dwell
in his shade / and raise grain; / They shall blossom like the
vine, / and his fame shall be like the wine of Lebanon.

Ephraim! What more has he to do with idols? / I have

humbled him, but I will prosper him. / "I am like a verdant cypress tree"— / Because of me you bear fruit!

Let him who is wise understand these things; / let him who is prudent know them. / Straight are the paths of the LORD, / in them the just walk, / but sinners stumble in them.

The word of the Lord.

RESPONSORIAL PSALM   81:6c-8a, 8bc-9, 10-11ab, 14 and 17

R̶/. (see 11 and 9a) **I am the Lord your God: hear my voice.**

An unfamiliar speech I hear:
  "I relieved his shoulder of the burden;
  his hands were freed from the basket.
In distress you called, and I rescued you." R̶/.

"Unseen, I answered you in thunder;
  I tested you at the waters of Meribah.
Hear, my people, and I will admonish you;
  O Israel, will you not hear me?" R̶/.

"There shall be no strange god among you
  nor shall you worship any alien god.
I, the LORD, am your God
  who led you forth from the land of Egypt." R̶/.

"If only my people would hear me,
  and Israel walk in my ways,
I would feed them with the best of wheat,
  and with honey from the rock I would fill them." R̶/.

GOSPEL ACCLAMATION   Matthew 4:17
Repent, says the Lord;
the Kingdom of heaven is at hand.

A reading from the holy Gospel according to Mark 12:28-34
The Lord our God is one Lord, and you shall love the Lord your God.

O ne of the scribes came to Jesus and asked him, "Which is the first of all the commandments?" Jesus replied,

"The first is this: *Hear, O Israel! The Lord our God is Lord alone! You shall love the Lord your God with all your heart, with all your soul, with all your mind, and with all your strength.* The second is this: *You shall love your neighbor as yourself.* There is no other commandment greater than these." The scribe said to him, "Well said, teacher. You are right in saying, *He is One and there is no other than he. And to love him with all your heart, with all your understanding, with all your strength, and to love your neighbor as yourself* is worth more than all burnt offerings and sacrifices." And when Jesus saw that he answered with understanding, he said to him, "You are not far from the Kingdom of God." And no one dared to ask him any more questions.

The Gospel of the Lord.

PRAYER OVER THE OFFERINGS
Look with favor, we pray, Lord,
on the offerings we dedicate,
that they may be pleasing in your sight
and always be salutary for us.
Through Christ our Lord.

COMMUNION ANTIPHON   Cf. Mark 12:33
To love God with all your heart, and your neighbor as
yourself, / is worth more than any sacrifice.

PRAYER AFTER COMMUNION
May your strength be at work in us, O Lord,
pervading our minds and bodies,
that what we have received
by participating in this Sacrament
may bring us the fullness of redemption.
Through Christ our Lord.

Reflection

The Measure of Our Work

We are busy people. We don't have time to do the things we say we'd like to do. We're overwhelmed with deadlines, projects, and meetings. We are often tired and stressed. And we wouldn't have it any other way. Our work defines us. Our worth is measured by the value of our portfolios. Our power is centered in who takes our calls.

We *are* our resumes. We take pride in our ability to get things done. Accomplishment is our "god." Activity is our liturgy. Our calendars and planners are our hymnals.

Such emphasis on work and accomplishment has been disastrous for the people of Israel. They have lost their soul, Hosea laments. In their pursuit of economic power and political stature, God's people lost sight of what makes them God's people: compassion for the suffering, justice for the poor, welcome to the stranger. The prophet pleads, "We shall say no more, 'Our god,' to the work of our hands; for in you the orphan finds compassion." What matters more than our work is the good that inspires it and is realized from it.

These days of Lent call us to consider to what extent our work has become "our god." Do we let the pursuit of career, the drive to succeed, the satisfaction of creating take precedence over everything—and everyone—in our lives? Have our ambition and pursuit of wealth made us "orphans" isolated from the people we love most?

As Hosea prophesies, maybe it's time to let ourselves be "replanted" in the compassion of God.

Deacon Jay Cormier

Jay Cormier, a deacon serving in the Diocese of Manchester, New Hampshire, teaches at Saint Anselm College and Pope John XXIII National Seminary.

Evening

God, come to my assistance.
Lord, make haste to help me.

(opt. hymn, pp. 360–65)

PSALM 37:1-6, 16-17
Do not fret because of the wicked;
do not envy those who do evil,
for they wither quickly like grass
and fade like the green of the fields.

Trust in the LORD and do good;
then you will dwell in the land and find safe pasture.
Find your delight in the LORD,
who grants your heart's desire.

Commit your way to the LORD;
if you trust, then God will act,
and make your righteousness shine like the light,
your justice like the noonday sun.

How much better the little of the righteous,
than the overflowing wealth of the wicked;
for the arms of the wicked shall be broken,
and the LORD will support the righteous.

Glory to the Father . . .

SCRIPTURE   2 John 3-6
Grace, mercy, and peace will be with us from God the
Father and from Jesus Christ the Father's Son in truth
and love.
   I rejoiced greatly to find some of your children walking
in the truth just as we were commanded by the Father. But
now, Lady, I ask you, not as though I were writing a new

commandment but the one we have had from the beginning: let us love one another. For this is love, that we walk according to his commandments; this is the commandment, as you heard from the beginning, in which you should walk.

READ, PONDER, PRAY on a word or phrase from these readings or another of today's Scriptures (*Lectio Divina*, p. 359)

ANTIPHON
Love of God and neighbor is the greatest commandment.

CANTICLE OF MARY *(inside back cover)*

INTERCESSIONS
Righteous God, you are the delight of all who know your truth and love. We praise you and pray: R̸. **God of grace and mercy, hear our prayer.**

Help us to welcome immigrants, refugees, newcomers, and the lonely. R̸.

Nurture integrity with knowledge and love of learning in educators, students, and school board personnel. R̸.

Give peace to the dying and those who wait beside them. R̸.

Our Father . . .

May God bless us with peace and give success to the work of our minds, hearts, and hands, through Jesus, the face of God's mercy. Amen.

Saturday, March 18

Morning

O Lord, open my lips.
And my mouth will proclaim your praise.

(opt. hymn, pp. 360–65)

PSALM 103:1-2, 11-14, 17-18

Bless the LORD, O my soul,
and all within me, the holy name of God.
Bless the LORD, O my soul,
and never forget all God's benefits.

For as the heavens are high above the earth,
so strong the mercy for those who fear God.
As far as the east is from the west,
so far from us does God remove our transgressions.

As a father has compassion on his children,
divine compassion is on those who fear the LORD,
who knows of what we are made,
who remembers that we are dust.

But the love of the LORD is everlasting
upon those who revere godly ways,
upon children's children divine righteousness
for those who keep the covenant,
and remember to fulfill its commands.

Glory to the Father . . .

SCRIPTURE   Deuteronomy 4:32-35

A sk now of the days of old, before your time, ever since
God created humankind upon the earth; ask from one
end of the sky to the other: Did anything so great ever hap-

pen before? Was it ever heard of? Did a people ever hear the voice of God speaking from the midst of fire, as you did, and live? Or did any god venture to go and take a nation for himself from the midst of another nation, by testings, by signs and wonders, by war, with strong hand and outstretched arm, and by great terrors, all of which the LORD, your God, did for you in Egypt before your very eyes? All this you were allowed to see that you might know that the LORD is God; there is no other.

READ, PONDER, PRAY on a word or phrase from these readings or another of today's Scriptures (*Lectio Divina*, p. 359)

ANTIPHON
Let us strive to know the Lord.

CANTICLE OF ZECHARIAH *(inside front cover)*

INTERCESSIONS
God of compassion, your mercy spans from east to west. In faith we pray: R̥. **Favor us with your love, O God.**

Uphold and relieve those who suffer persecution for their faith. R̥.

Protect firefighters, law enforcement, and emergency aid workers from harm. R̥.

Nurture patience in coaches, confidence in athletes, and goodness in all who enjoy sports. R̥.

Our Father . . .

May God order our days in peace, guide us by the light of the Holy Spirit, and bring us together to everlasting life, through Jesus, our brother. Amen.

Blessed Among Us

St. Cyril of Jerusalem
Doctor of the Church (ca. 315–386)

St. Cyril, known for his moderate temperament, deplored the intrusion of politics into the body of Christ and the tendency of theological differences to end in bitter factionalism. But his was a time of violent controversy, when compromise was reckoned as treason, and it seemed that one's own orthodoxy could be affirmed only by the condemnation of another's error.

Named bishop of Jerusalem in 350, Cyril found himself embroiled in controversies inherited from his predecessor. Jurisdictional disputes with the bishop of Caesarea resulted in Cyril's formal investigation by a local synod. Among the gravest accusations was that Cyril had sold church property—namely, gifts from the emperor—to give alms to the famine-stricken poor. Cyril was condemned and forced into exile. He returned after some years to find himself caught in battles over the Arian heresy. Cyril was accused by members of each side of being too sympathetic to the other. Of his thirty-five years as a bishop, nearly sixteen were spent in exile.

In 1882 Cyril was named a Doctor of the Church, largely on the basis of his *Catechetical Lectures*. These talks, delivered to adult catechumens, represent one of the first systematic accounts of Christian theology, centered on the articles of the creed. They underline Cyril's determination to present the faith in a positive light and to maintain a balance between correct belief and holy action.

"The way of godliness consists of these two parts, pious doctrines and good works. Neither are the doctrines acceptable to God without good works, nor does God accept works accomplished otherwise than as linked with pious doctrines."

—St. Cyril of Jerusalem

Mass

Saturday of the Third Week of Lent
[*St. Cyril of Jerusalem*, opt. memorial]

ENTRANCE ANTIPHON　　　　　　　　　　　　Psalm 103 (102):2-3
Bless the Lord, O my soul, and never forget all his
benefits; / it is he who forgives all your sins.

COLLECT
Rejoicing in this annual celebration
of our Lenten observance,
we pray, O Lord,
that, with our hearts set on the paschal mysteries,
we may be gladdened by their full effects.
Through our Lord Jesus Christ, your Son,
who lives and reigns with you in the unity of the Holy Spirit,
God, for ever and ever.

A reading from the Book of the Prophet Hosea　　　　6:1-6

What I want is love, not sacrifice.

Come, let us return to the LORD, / it is he who has rent,
but he will heal us; / he has struck us, but he will bind
our wounds. / He will revive us after two days; / on the third
day he will raise us up, / to live in his presence. / Let us
know, let us strive to know the LORD; / as certain as the dawn
is his coming, / and his judgment shines forth like the light
of day! / He will come to us like the rain, / like spring rain
that waters the earth."

　　What can I do with you, Ephraim? / What can I do with
you, Judah? / Your piety is like a morning cloud, / like the
dew that early passes away. / For this reason I smote them
through the prophets, / I slew them by the words of my

mouth; / For it is love that I desire, not sacrifice, / and knowledge of God rather than burnt offerings.

The word of the Lord.

RESPONSORIAL PSALM　　　　　51:3-4, 18-19, 20-21ab

℟. (see Hosea 6:6) **It is mercy I desire, and not sacrifice.**

Have mercy on me, O God, in your goodness;
　in the greatness of your compassion wipe out my
　　offense.
Thoroughly wash me from my guilt
　and of my sin cleanse me. ℟.

For you are not pleased with sacrifices;
　should I offer a burnt offering, you would not accept it.
My sacrifice, O God, is a contrite spirit;
　a heart contrite and humbled, O God, you will not
　　spurn. ℟.

Be bountiful, O LORD, to Zion in your kindness
　by rebuilding the walls of Jerusalem;
Then shall you be pleased with due sacrifices,
　burnt offerings and holocausts. ℟.

GOSPEL ACCLAMATION　　　　　　　　Psalm 95:8

If today you hear his voice,
harden not your hearts.

A reading from the holy Gospel according to Luke　18:9-14

The tax collector went home justified, not the Pharisee.

Jesus addressed this parable to those who were convinced of their own righteousness and despised everyone else. "Two people went up to the temple area to pray; one was a Pharisee and the other was a tax collector. The Pharisee took up his position and spoke this prayer to himself, 'O God, I thank you that I am not like the rest of humanity—greedy, dishonest, adulterous—or even like this tax collector. I fast twice a week, and I pay tithes on my whole income.' But the tax collector stood off at a distance and would not even raise his eyes to heaven but beat his breast and prayed, 'O God, be merciful to me a sinner.' I tell you, the latter went home justified, not the former; for everyone who exalts himself will be humbled, and the one who humbles himself will be exalted."

The Gospel of the Lord.

PRAYER OVER THE OFFERINGS

O God, by whose grace it comes to pass
that we may approach your mysteries
with minds made pure,
grant, we pray,
that, in reverently handing them on,
we may offer you fitting homage.
Through Christ our Lord.

COMMUNION ANTIPHON   Luke 18:13

The tax collector stood at a distance, beating his breast
and saying: / O God, be merciful to me, a sinner.

PRAYER AFTER COMMUNION

May we truly revere, O merciful God,
these holy gifts, by which you ceaselessly nourish us,
and may we always partake of them
with abundant faith in our heart.
Through Christ our Lord.

Reflection

Make Me New!

Like most laments, Psalm 51 begins with a cry directly to God. We call out with four imperatives: have mercy, blot out, wash, cleanse. But in the middle section of the psalm, we admit we are our own worst enemy: "I know my evil well; it stares me in the face" (v. 5). We acknowledge that if God condemns us, God would be in the right! We say this in truth, knowing that God does not owe us mercy; rather, it is always a gift. We also say this in absolute freedom, confident of God's constant inclination to forgive.

After this admission, we begin our petition: teach me, cleanse me (literally, "un-sin me"), wash me. Turn away your face from the sin that stares me in the face. But this petition is only the introduction to the boldest request of all. Right at the center of the psalm we take our courage in hand and beg of God: "Create a pure heart for me, O God; / renew a steadfast spirit within me" (v. 12). We are not asking God to just forgive and forget. We ask, "Make me new and start from the very center of my being." This is total surrender to God. This is our way of dealing with the enemy that is ourselves. We beg, "Make me new!"

It is not easy to trust God this much. It is not easy to let the potter start over with the clay. Looking ahead, this is why I think the resurrection is Jesus' greatest act of obedience— and ours too! It is total surrender to God's gift of life, to God's creating hand.

Sr. Irene Nowell, adapted from *Pleading, Cursing, Praising*

Irene Nowell, OSB, is a member of Mount St. Scholastica Monastery in Atchison, Kansas. She is an editorial advisor to Give Us This Day *and the author of* Wisdom: The Good Life.

Evening

God, come to my assistance.
Lord, make haste to help me.

(opt. hymn, pp. 360–65)

PSALM 1
Blessed indeed are those
who follow not the counsel of the wicked,
nor stand in the path with sinners,
nor abide in the company of scorners,
but whose delight is the law of the LORD,
and who ponder God's law day and night.

Such people are like trees that are planted
beside the flowing waters,
that yield their fruit in due season,
and whose leaves shall never fade;
and all that they do shall prosper.

Not so are the wicked, not so!
For they, like winnowed chaff,
shall be driven away by the wind.

When the wicked are judged they shall not rise,
nor shall sinners in the council of the righteous;
for the LORD knows the way of the righteous,
but the way of the wicked will perish.

Glory to the Father . . .

SCRIPTURE   James 4:6b-10
Scripture] says: / "God resists the proud, / but gives grace
to the humble." / So submit yourselves to God. Resist
the devil, and he will flee from you. Draw near to God, and
he will draw near to you. Cleanse your hands, you sinners,

and purify your hearts, you of two minds. Begin to lament, to mourn, to weep. Let your laughter be turned into mourning and your joy into dejection. Humble yourselves before the Lord and he will exalt you.

READ, PONDER, PRAY on a word or phrase from these readings or another of today's Scriptures (*Lectio Divina*, p. 359)

ANTIPHON
O God, be merciful to me a sinner.

CANTICLE OF MARY *(inside back cover)*

INTERCESSIONS
God Most High, you call us to yourself. In trust we pray:
R̷. Let us find our delight in you, O God.

Strengthen your Church's work of reconciliation
and unity. R̷.

Help us to witness to your hospitality in our welcome to
one another. R̷.

Open our minds to wonder and our hearts to gratitude
for the marvels of nature. R̷.

Our Father . . .

May God bless us, be gracious to us, and fill our hearts
with the peace of Christ, by the power of the Holy Spirit.
Amen.

Sunday, March 19

Morning

O Lord, open my lips.
And my mouth will proclaim your praise.

(opt. hymn, pp. 360–65)

PSALM 148:1b-6, 14

Praise the LORD from the heavens;
praise the Lord in the heights.
Praise the Lord, all his angels;
praise the Lord, all his hosts.

Praise the Lord, sun and moon;
praise the Lord, all shining stars.
Praise the Lord, highest heavens,
and the waters above the heavens.

Let them praise the name of the LORD,
who commanded, and they were created.
God established them forever and ever,
gave a law which shall not pass away.

The Lord exalts the strength of the people,
and is the praise of all the faithful,
the praise of the children of Israel,
of the people to whom our God is close.

Glory to the Father . . .

SCRIPTURE   2 Samuel 23:1b-4

The oracle of David, son of Jesse; / the oracle of the man God raised up, / Anointed of the God of Jacob, / favorite of the Mighty One of Israel. / The spirit of the LORD spoke

Illustration by Martin Erspamer, OSB.

through me; / his word was on my tongue. / The God of Israel spoke; / of me the Rock of Israel said, / "One who rules over humankind with justice, / who rules in the fear of God, / Is like the light at sunrise / on a cloudless morning, / making the land's vegetation glisten after rain."

READ, PONDER, PRAY on a word or phrase from these readings or another of today's Scriptures (*Lectio Divina*, p. 359)

ANTIPHON
The Lord sees the heart.

CANTICLE OF ZECHARIAH *(inside front cover)*

INTERCESSIONS
Shepherding God, you shine your light upon us through Jesus. In hope we pray: R̰. God, in your loving-kindness, hear our prayer.

You rule the earth with justice: prosper efforts to lessen violence to safeguard churches, schools, and all public places. R̰.

You guide us by your Spirit: strengthen the faith of catechumens, sponsors, and all the baptized. R̰.

You breathe life into the world: protect the unborn, and give mothers skilled care and support during and after childbirth. R̰.

Our Father . . .

May the Spirit of God rest upon our hearts and guide us along every good path, now and always. Amen.

Mass

Fourth Sunday of Lent

ENTRANCE ANTIPHON   Cf. Isaiah 66:10-11

Rejoice, Jerusalem, and all who love her. / Be joyful, all who were in mourning; / exult and be satisfied at her consoling breast.

(The Gloria is omitted.)

COLLECT

O God, who through your Word
reconcile the human race to yourself in a wonderful way,
grant, we pray,
that with prompt devotion and eager faith
the Christian people may hasten
toward the solemn celebrations to come.
Through our Lord Jesus Christ, your Son,
who lives and reigns with you in the unity of the Holy Spirit,
God, for ever and ever.

A reading from the first Book of Samuel   16:1b, 6-7, 10-13a

David is anointed as king of Israel.

The LORD said to Samuel: "Fill your horn with oil, and be on your way. I am sending you to Jesse of Bethlehem, for I have chosen my king from among his sons."

As Jesse and his sons came to the sacrifice, Samuel looked at Eliab and thought, "Surely the LORD's anointed is here before him." But the LORD said to Samuel: "Do not judge from his appearance or from his lofty stature, because I have rejected him. Not as man sees does God see, because man sees the appearance but the LORD looks into the heart." In the same way Jesse presented seven sons before Samuel, but

Samuel said to Jesse, "The LORD has not chosen any one of these." Then Samuel asked Jesse, "Are these all the sons you have?" Jesse replied, "There is still the youngest, who is tending the sheep." Samuel said to Jesse, "Send for him; we will not begin the sacrificial banquet until he arrives here." Jesse sent and had the young man brought to them. He was ruddy, a youth handsome to behold and making a splendid appearance. The LORD said, "There—anoint him, for this is the one!" Then Samuel, with the horn of oil in hand, anointed David in the presence of his brothers; and from that day on, the spirit of the LORD rushed upon David.

The word of the Lord.

RESPONSORIAL PSALM   23:1-3a, 3b-4, 5, 6

R̸. (1) **The Lord is my shepherd; there is nothing I shall want.**

The LORD is my shepherd; I shall not want.
  In verdant pastures he gives me repose;
beside restful waters he leads me;
  he refreshes my soul. R̸.

He guides me in right paths
  for his name's sake.
Even though I walk in the dark valley
  I fear no evil; for you are at my side
with your rod and your staff
  that give me courage. R̸.

You spread the table before me
  in the sight of my foes;
you anoint my head with oil;
  my cup overflows. R̸.

Only goodness and kindness follow me
  all the days of my life;

and I shall dwell in the house of the LORD
    for years to come. R℣.

A reading from the Letter of Saint Paul to the Ephesians
                                          5:8-14

Arise from the dead, and Christ will give you light.

Brothers and sisters: You were once darkness, but now
you are light in the Lord. Live as children of light, for
light produces every kind of goodness and righteousness
and truth. Try to learn what is pleasing to the Lord. Take
no part in the fruitless works of darkness; rather expose
them, for it is shameful even to mention the things done by
them in secret; but everything exposed by the light becomes
visible, for everything that becomes visible is light. Therefore, it says: / "Awake, O sleeper, / and arise from the dead,
/ and Christ will give you light."
The word of the Lord.

GOSPEL ACCLAMATION   John 8:12
I am the light of the world, says the Lord;
whoever follows me will have the light of life.

A reading from the holy Gospel according to John
                  9:1-41 (Shorter Form [ ], 9:1, 6-9, 13-17, 34-38)

*The man who was blind went off and
washed himself and came back able to see.*

[As Jesus passed by he saw a man blind from birth.] His
disciples asked him, "Rabbi, who sinned, this man
or his parents, that he was born blind?" Jesus answered,
"Neither he nor his parents sinned; it is so that the works
of God might be made visible through him. We have to do
the works of the one who sent me while it is day. Night is
coming when no one can work. While I am in the world, I
am the light of the world." When he had said this, [he spat

on the ground and made clay with the saliva, and smeared the clay on his eyes, and said to him, "Go wash in the Pool of Siloam"—which means Sent—. So he went and washed, and came back able to see.

His neighbors and those who had seen him earlier as a beggar said, "Isn't this the one who used to sit and beg?" Some said, "It is," but others said, "No, he just looks like him." He said, "I am."] So they said to him, "How were your eyes opened?" He replied, "The man called Jesus made clay and anointed my eyes and told me, 'Go to Siloam and wash.' So I went there and washed and was able to see." And they said to him, "Where is he?" He said, "I don't know."

[They brought the one who was once blind to the Pharisees. Now Jesus had made clay and opened his eyes on a sabbath. So then the Pharisees also asked him how he was able to see. He said to them, "He put clay on my eyes, and I washed, and now I can see." So some of the Pharisees said, "This man is not from God, because he does not keep the sabbath." But others said, "How can a sinful man do such signs?" And there was a division among them. So they said to the blind man again, "What do you have to say about him, since he opened your eyes?" He said, "He is a prophet."]

Now the Jews did not believe that he had been blind and gained his sight until they summoned the parents of the one who had gained his sight. They asked them, "Is this your son, who you say was born blind? How does he now see?" His parents answered and said, "We know that this is our son and that he was born blind. We do not know how he sees now, nor do we know who opened his eyes. Ask him, he is of age; he can speak for himself." His parents said this because they were afraid of the Jews, for the Jews had already agreed that if anyone acknowledged him as the Christ, he would be expelled from the synagogue. For this reason his parents said, "He is of age; question him."

So a second time they called the man who had been blind and said to him, "Give God the praise! We know that this man is a sinner." He replied, "If he is a sinner, I do not know. One thing I do know is that I was blind and now I see." So they said to him, "What did he do to you? How did he open your eyes?" He answered them, "I told you already and you did not listen. Why do you want to hear it again? Do you want to become his disciples, too?" They ridiculed him and said, "You are that man's disciple; we are disciples of Moses! We know that God spoke to Moses, but we do not know where this one is from." The man answered and said to them, "This is what is so amazing, that you do not know where he is from, yet he opened my eyes. We know that God does not listen to sinners, but if one is devout and does his will, he listens to him. It is unheard of that anyone ever opened the eyes of a person born blind. If this man were not from God, he would not be able to do anything." [They answered and said to him, "You were born totally in sin, and are you trying to teach us?" Then they threw him out.

When Jesus heard that they had thrown him out, he found him and said, "Do you believe in the Son of Man?" He answered and said, "Who is he, sir, that I may believe in him?" Jesus said to him, "You have seen him, and the one speaking with you is he." He said, "I do believe, Lord," and he worshiped him.] Then Jesus said, "I came into this world for judgment, so that those who do not see might see, and those who do see might become blind."

Some of the Pharisees who were with him heard this and said to him, "Surely we are not also blind, are we?" Jesus said to them, "If you were blind, you would have no sin; but now you are saying, 'We see,' so your sin remains."

The Gospel of the Lord.

CREED (p. 332)

PRAYER OVER THE OFFERINGS

We place before you with joy these offerings,
which bring eternal remedy, O Lord,
praying that we may both faithfully revere them
and present them to you, as is fitting,
for the salvation of all the world.
Through Christ our Lord.

COMMUNION ANTIPHON   Cf. John 9:11, 38

The Lord anointed my eyes: I went, I washed, / I saw and
I believed in God.

PRAYER AFTER COMMUNION

O God, who enlighten everyone who comes into this
    world,
illuminate our hearts, we pray,
with the splendor of your grace,
that we may always ponder
what is worthy and pleasing to your majesty
and love you in all sincerity.
Through Christ our Lord.

Reflection

Beyond Words and Appearances

We search for ways to speak about what life in Christ means.
But it goes beyond words, so we turn to metaphors and
stories.

That is why the gospel of John spends so much time with
the story of the man born blind. It is, as John often calls Jesus'
miracles, a "sign." It is a sign of what Christ brings to the
world. Jesus opens us up to life in a new way. He brings a new

dimension, a new depth. [For us,] it is as radical a change as what this man experiences, seeing the world for the first time. Now we can see, not just as humans see, but as God sees. We see what is most real. We see beyond appearances. We see with the heart.

The light for this kind of seeing is all around us. And it changes the way we see. We see others differently. We stop judging people by the way they look, or what they have. We begin to see others as they are, in their uniqueness. We begin to respect others and learn from them in new ways, appreciating the mystery they carry within. We see ourselves differently, too. We stop judging ourselves according to what others think of us. We begin to see ourselves as God sees us, as we are, as we are loved. And so we become more loving toward ourselves and more free to change.

We see life differently. It's no longer about choosing sides, or using others, or hoarding things. It's not something we have to fight, or something we must endure. We see life as a gift. We savor it. We begin to use it differently. Life becomes an adventure. It offers one opportunity after another.

This way of seeing changes everything. It doesn't mean that life becomes easy. There may still be hardship, pain, and suffering; but because we are different, they will not defeat us. Even there we'll see the seeds of growth. And we'll know that we're not alone.

Fr. Mark Villano, adapted from *Journey to Jerusalem*

Mark A. Villano is Director of University Outreach at the University Catholic Center at UCLA. Visit his website at mark-a-villano.com.

Evening

God, come to my assistance.
Lord, make haste to help me.

(opt. hymn, pp. 360–65)

PSALM 116:10-19

I trusted, even when I said,
"I am sorely afflicted,"
and when I said in my alarm,
"All people are untruthful."

How can I repay the LORD
for all the goodness shown to me?
The cup of salvation I will raise;
I will call on the name of the LORD.

My vows to the LORD I will fulfill
before all the people.
How precious in the eyes of the LORD
is the death of God's faithful.

Your servant, LORD, your servant am I,
you have loosened my bonds.
I will offer you a thanksgiving sacrifice;
I will call on the name of the LORD.

My vows to the LORD I will fulfill
before all the people,
in the courts of the house of the LORD,
in your midst, O Jerusalem.

Glory to the Father . . .

SCRIPTURE   1 John 1:5-9

Now this is the message that we have heard from him
and proclaim to you: God is light, and in him there is

no darkness at all. If we say, "We have fellowship with him," while we continue to walk in darkness, we lie and do not act in truth. But if we walk in the light as he is in the light, then we have fellowship with one another, and the blood of his Son Jesus cleanses us from all sin. If we say, "We are without sin," we deceive ourselves, and the truth is not in us. If we acknowledge our sins, he is faithful and just and will forgive our sins and cleanse us from every wrongdoing.

READ, PONDER, PRAY on a word or phrase from these readings or another of today's Scriptures (*Lectio Divina*, p. 359)

ANTIPHON
Awake, arise from the dead, and Christ will give you light.

CANTICLE OF MARY *(inside back cover)*

INTERCESSIONS
God of the living, you light our way through our encounter with Jesus. In hope we pray: ℟. **Be with us in our need, O God.**

Heal those who suffer from betrayal, trauma, or wounded relationships. ℟.

Strengthen us in our vocation and commitments, and guide those who are discerning direction in their lives. ℟.

Give holy perseverance to those who face trials or bear heavy responsibility. ℟.

Our Father . . .

May almighty God bless us, forgive our sin, and bring us to everlasting life. Amen.

Within the Word

Has God Abandoned Us?

As we consider the world of which we are a part, we might be overwhelmed by the apparent collapse of so much that once provided stability and meaning—the social norms we relied on for unity and direction, the political structures that promised security and prosperity, and even the religious institutions we turned to for insight and fulfillment. We might ask the same question posed by the people at the time of the prophet Isaiah: has God abandoned us?

The first reading for Wednesday of the Fourth Week of Lent (Isa 49:8-15) calls to mind the time of Israel's return to Jerusalem after a long period of exile. These were not the same people who had been taken to Babylon some seventy years earlier; this was a new generation, a people who never knew the joys of living in their own land, under the protection of their own God. For many of them, restoration seemed to be more a dream than a promise. The announcement they heard must have been mindboggling. They were told this was "a time of favor . . . a day of salvation." They were told that when they returned to the home of their ancestors they would "establish the land . . . apportion the desolate heritages." They would have to work hard at restoration but were given the assurance that "the LORD has comforted his people, and will have compassion on his suffering ones."

Still the people doubted: "The LORD has forsaken me; my Lord has forgotten me." But God would not be deterred. God's bond with this people was stronger and more intimate than that of a woman who had given birth to a child and had then fed it with the nourishment of her own body. One cannot get more intimate than that. With such reassurance, how could Israel possibly doubt God's care?

But then, how could we? This is the same God who loves us, with the same maternal attachment. Like the Israelites, we too have watched so much we formerly relied upon crumble or go up in flames. Many are terrorized when they come to realize what Pope Francis meant when he said: "What we are experiencing is *not simply an epoch of changes, but an epochal change.*" In the face of such consternation, where can we turn? Whom can we trust?

What are we thinking when we hear Wednesday's poignant passage from Isaiah? Can we honestly respond, "Thanks be to God"? Do we realize the implications of the words we speak? Like the Israelites, we too will have to work at restoration. Perhaps an "epochal change" calls for something new, a genuine transformation. Is it possible this might be our time of favor? Our day of salvation? Is this just a dream? Or is it a promise?

Lent is a time of transformation—not merely of Jesus in his passion, death, and resurrection, but of all of us as we die to one way of living in order to rise into another. It can be a time when we move away from exclusionary lines of conflict and separation into authentic dialogue and synodality, away from selfish isolation and hoarding into expressions of our interconnectedness and interdependency. It can be done. God has promised: "I will not forget you."

—Sr. Dianne Bergant

Dianne Bergant, CSA, is Carroll Stuhlmueller, CP, Distinguished Professor Emerita of Old Testament Studies at Catholic Theological Union in Chicago. She is author of numerous books, including the Psalms *volumes in the* New Collegeville Bible Commentary.

Monday, March 20

Morning

O Lord, open my lips.
And my mouth will proclaim your praise.

(opt. hymn, pp. 360–65)

PSALM 112:1b-9

Blessed are those who fear the LORD,
who take great delight in God's commands.
Their descendants shall be powerful on earth;
the generation of the upright will be blest.

Riches and wealth are in their houses;
their righteousness stands firm forever.
A light rises in the darkness for the upright;
they are generous, loving and righteous.

It goes well for those who deal generously and lend,
who conduct their affairs with justice.
They will never be moved;
forever shall the righteous be remembered.

They have no fear of evil news;
with a firm heart, they trust in the LORD.
With steadfast hearts they will not fear;
they will see the downfall of their foes.

Openhanded, they give to the poor;
their righteousness stands firm forever.
Their might shall be exalted in glory.

Glory to the Father . . .

SCRIPTURE   Sirach 14:20; 15:1-4, 6

Happy those who meditate on Wisdom, / and fix their
gaze on knowledge.

Whoever fears the LORD will do this; / whoever is practiced in the Law will come to Wisdom. / She will meet him like a mother; / like a young bride she will receive him, / She will feed him with the bread of learning, / and give him the water of understanding to drink. / He will lean upon her and not fall; / he will trust in her and not be put to shame. / Joy and gladness he will find, / and an everlasting name he will inherit.

READ, PONDER, PRAY on a word or phrase from these readings or another of today's Scriptures (*Lectio Divina*, p. 359)

ANTIPHON

His faith was credited to him as righteousness.

CANTICLE OF ZECHARIAH *(inside front cover)*

INTERCESSIONS

Holy God, in company with your humble and faith-filled servant Joseph, we pray: R̸. **God of the covenant, hear our prayer.**

Help us to welcome spring with attention to your life-giving Word and its presence in all creation. R̸.

Give wisdom, guidance, and peace to parents who are challenged by difficult decisions. R̸.

Deepen your Church's love for the poor and hospitality to refugees. R̸.

Our Father . . .

May God bless us and strengthen us in our vocation to love, through Jesus, Mary, and Joseph. Amen.

Blessed Among Us

St. Cuthbert
Bishop (ca. 634–687)

St. Cuthbert grew up as a shepherd in Northumbria. There, at the age of fifteen, he entered the first of a series of monasteries in which he spent his life, eventually becoming prior of the Abbey of Lindisfarne. Monks at that time were also missionaries and evangelists, and Cuthbert spent much of his time traveling throughout the region, visiting remote villages to preach the Gospel and spread the faith. Known for his ardent prayer and asceticism, he liked to pray while standing in the frigid sea with arms outstretched, as birds and otters gathered round to witness the spectacle.

After many years at Lindisfarne, Cuthbert received permission from his abbot to retire to a hermitage on a desolate island where he lived entirely on the barley he grew in his garden. Eventually, his election as bishop of Lindisfarne compelled him to leave this happy seclusion. For two years he attended faithfully to his duties as bishop, "protecting the people committed to his charge by constant prayer, and exciting them, by most wholesome admonitions, to heavenly practices." But after Christmas of 686, sensing that his race was nearly complete, he announced that he would be returning to his island hermitage. "Tell us, my lord bishop," one of his monks asked, "when may we hope for your return?" "When you shall bring back my body," he replied. Three months later he died peacefully in an attitude of prayer.

"He saved the needy man from the hand of the stronger, and the poor and destitute from those who would oppress them. He comforted the weak and sorrowful; but he took care to recall those who were sinfully rejoicing to that sorrow which is according to godliness."
                                        —The Life of St. Cuthbert

Mass

St. Joseph, Spouse of the Blessed Virgin Mary, Solemnity

ENTRANCE ANTIPHON   Cf. Luke 12:42
Behold, a faithful and prudent steward, / whom the Lord
set over his household.

GLORIA (p. 331)

COLLECT
Grant, we pray, almighty God,
that by Saint Joseph's intercession
your Church may constantly watch over
the unfolding of the mysteries of human salvation,
whose beginnings you entrusted to his faithful care.
Through our Lord Jesus Christ, your Son,
who lives and reigns with you in the unity of the Holy Spirit,
God, for ever and ever.

A reading from the second Book of Samuel
7:4-5a, 12-14a, 16

*The Lord God will give him the throne of David,
his father (Luke 1:32).*

The LORD spoke to Nathan and said: "Go, tell my servant
David, 'When your time comes and you rest with your
ancestors, I will raise up your heir after you, sprung from
your loins, and I will make his kingdom firm. It is he who
shall build a house for my name. And I will make his royal
throne firm forever. I will be a father to him, and he shall
be a son to me. Your house and your kingdom shall endure
forever before me; your throne shall stand firm forever.'"
The word of the Lord.

RESPONSORIAL PSALM   89:2-3, 4-5, 27 and 29

R̷. (37) **The son of David will live for ever.**

The promises of the LORD I will sing forever;
   through all generations my mouth shall proclaim your
      faithfulness,
For you have said, "My kindness is established forever";
   in heaven you have confirmed your faithfulness. R̷.

"I have made a covenant with my chosen one,
   I have sworn to David my servant:
Forever will I confirm your posterity
   and establish your throne for all generations." R̷.

"He shall say of me, 'You are my father,
   my God, the Rock, my savior.'
Forever I will maintain my kindness toward him,
   and my covenant with him stands firm." R̷.

A reading from the Letter of Saint Paul to the Romans
                                          4:13, 16-18, 22

Abraham believed, hoping against hope.

Brothers and sisters: It was not through the law that the
promise was made to Abraham and his descendants
that he would inherit the world, but through the righteousness that comes from faith. For this reason, it depends on
faith, so that it may be a gift, and the promise may be guar-
anteed to all his descendants, not to those who only adhere
to the law but to those who follow the faith of Abraham, who
is the father of all of us, as it is written, *I have made you
father of many nations*. He is our father in the sight of God,
in whom he believed, who gives life to the dead and calls
into being what does not exist. He believed, hoping against
hope, that he would become *the father of many nations*,

according to what was said, *Thus shall your descendants be.* That is why *it was credited to him as righteousness.*

The word of the Lord.

GOSPEL ACCLAMATION   Psalm 84:5
Blessed are those who dwell in your house, O Lord; they never cease to praise you.

A reading from the holy Gospel according to Matthew
1:16, 18-21, 24a (alt. Luke 2:41-51a)

Joseph did as the angel of the Lord had commanded him.

Jacob was the father of Joseph, the husband of Mary. Of her was born Jesus who is called the Christ.

Now this is how the birth of Jesus Christ came about. When his mother Mary was betrothed to Joseph, but before they lived together, she was found with child through the Holy Spirit. Joseph her husband, since he was a righteous man, yet unwilling to expose her to shame, decided to divorce her quietly. Such was his intention when, behold, the angel of the Lord appeared to him in a dream and said, "Joseph, son of David, do not be afraid to take Mary your wife into your home. For it is through the Holy Spirit that this child has been conceived in her. She will bear a son and you are to name him Jesus, because he will save his people from their sins." When Joseph awoke, he did as the angel of the Lord had commanded him and took his wife into his home.

The Gospel of the Lord.

CREED (p. 332)

PRAYER OVER THE OFFERINGS
We pray, O Lord,
that, just as Saint Joseph served with loving care
your Only Begotten Son, born of the Virgin Mary,
so we may be worthy to minister
with a pure heart at your altar.
Through Christ our Lord.

COMMUNION ANTIPHON   Matthew 25:21
Well done, good and faithful servant. / Come, share your
master's joy.

PRAYER AFTER COMMUNION
Defend with unfailing protection,
O Lord, we pray,
the family you have nourished
with food from this altar,
as they rejoice at the Solemnity of Saint Joseph,
and graciously keep safe your gifts among them.
Through Christ our Lord.

Reflection

Just Like That?

Joseph must have been devastated when he learned Mary was
pregnant. But the law and his culture gave him a clear next
step. He would "divorce her quietly" and not expose Mary
to shame.

Then the angel visited him, and suddenly his next step was
not so clear. Matthew makes it sound simple. Joseph woke
up and did as the Lord commanded—just like that. But was
it really that easy? For me—maybe for most of us—God's call

comes as a whisper, a feeling, a series of "coincidences." And when God calls us to do something risky, we often doubt and question if this is *really* what God is asking of us.

Joseph may have doubted and questioned. He probably did. But like his ancestor Abraham, he "believed, hoping against hope" that God's word was true. Joseph's righteousness comes not from following the law but from believing in God's promise. He took the risk of trusting God and simply embracing the next step God set out for him.

That's why Matthew makes it sound so simple. I don't think he meant to say Joseph had no doubts. But the simple truth is that Joseph was willing to act on faith and do what God asked.

When we're faced with our own next step and we wonder if this is *really* what God is asking us to do, the answer is simple. Be like Joseph.

Nick Wagner

Nick Wagner, a writer in San Jose, California, is the cofounder and codirector of TeamRCIA.com—a free resource to help parish teams form Christians for life. He is the author of Field Hospital Catechesis: The Core Content for RCIA Formation.

Evening

God, come to my assistance.
Lord, make haste to help me.

(opt. hymn, pp. 360–65)

PSALM 111:1b-2, 5-10
I will thank the LORD with all my heart,
in the meeting of the just and the assembly.
Great are the works of the LORD,
to be pondered by all who delight in them.

You give food to those who revere you;
you are mindful of your covenant forever.
You have shown mighty works to your people
by giving them the heritage of nations.

Your handiwork is justice and truth,
your precepts are all of them sure,
standing firm forever and ever,
wrought in uprightness and truth.

You have sent redemption to your people,
and established your covenant forever.
Holy your name, to be feared.

Fear of the LORD is the beginning of wisdom;
understanding marks all who live by it.
Your praise endures forever!

Glory to the Father . . .

SCRIPTURE   Romans 8:28-30
We know that all things work for good for those who
love God, who are called according to his purpose.
For those he foreknew he also predestined to be conformed
to the image of his Son, so that he might be the firstborn

among many brothers. And those he predestined he also called; and those he called he also justified; and those he justified he also glorified.

READ, PONDER, PRAY on a word or phrase from these readings or another of today's Scriptures (*Lectio Divina*, p. 359)

ANTIPHON

Great are the works of the Lord, to be pondered by all who delight in them.

CANTICLE OF MARY *(inside back cover)*

INTERCESSIONS

Redeeming God, you entrusted Jesus to the care of Joseph and Mary. In faith we pray: ℟. **Help us to be faithful, O God.**

Inspire the craft and artistry of carpenters, architects, and builders. ℟.

Deepen the bonds of love and friendship between spouses. ℟.

Strengthen us to begin every good work with prayer. ℟.

Our Father . . .

May God fill us with peace and grant us a happy death, through Jesus, the Son of Joseph and Mary. Amen.

Tuesday, March 21

Morning

O Lord, open my lips.
And my mouth will proclaim your praise.

(opt. hymn, pp. 360–65)

PSALM 33:8-13, 20-22

Let all the earth fear the LORD,
all who live in the world show reverence.
God spoke, and it came to be;
commanded and it stood in place.

The LORD frustrates the designs of the nations,
and defeats the plans of the peoples.
The designs of the LORD stand forever,
the plans of God's heart from age to age.

Blessed the nation whose God is the LORD,
the people God has chosen as a heritage.
From the heavens the LORD looks forth,
and sees the whole human race.

Our soul is waiting for the LORD,
our God, our help and our shield.
In you do our hearts find joy;
we trust in your holy name.
May your faithful love be upon us,
as we hope in you, O LORD.

Glory to the Father . . .

SCRIPTURE   Zechariah 14:6-9

On that day there will no longer be cold or frost. There
will be one continuous day—it is known to the LORD—

not day and night, for in the evening there will be light.
On that day, fresh water will flow from Jerusalem, half to
the eastern sea, and half to the western sea. This will be so
in summer and in winter. The LORD will be king over the
whole earth; on that day the LORD will be the only one, and
the LORD's name the only one.

READ, PONDER, PRAY on a word or phrase from these readings or
another of today's Scriptures (*Lectio Divina*, p. 359)

ANTIPHON
**Where these waters flow they refresh; everything lives
where the river goes.**

CANTICLE OF ZECHARIAH *(inside front cover)*

INTERCESSIONS
**God of our joy, the basis of wisdom is fear of the Lord.
In company with St. Benedict and all the saints we pray:
R̷. Teach us your ways, O God.**

**Encourage those who experience a call to the religious or
monastic life. R̷.**

**Enlighten all people to reverence the fragility and beauty
of the natural world. R̷.**

**Embolden elected officials to engage in fruitful dialogue
and discernment for the common good. R̷.**

Our Father . . .

**May God bless us with peace and guide us with wisdom's
clear light, through Jesus, our brother. Amen.**

Blessed Among Us

St. Maria Josefa de Guerra
Founder, Institute of the Servants of Jesus (1842–1912)

Maria Josefa de Guerra was born in Vitoria, Spain, the daughter of a chair maker who died when she was seven. As she later liked to say, she was "born with a religious vocation." But she struggled for some time to find her way, trying one congregation and then another. Before taking vows with the Handmaids of Mary Serving the Sick, she experienced doubts. After months of consultation with her archbishop and other spiritual advisors, she decided to found her own institute, the Servants of Jesus.

The mission of the institute was to offer care for the sick and dying, whether in hospitals or in their homes. The Servant of Jesus was instructed to "provide for the sick, whom she accompanies unto the door of eternity, a blessing better than that of a missionary, who, with his preaching, calls those who are lost to the right path of life." The institute made its first foundation in Bilbao in 1871. Maria remained the superior for the next forty years, during which time she founded forty-three houses and welcomed over one thousand sisters.

She died on March 20, 1912. She was canonized in 2000, becoming the first Basque woman saint.

"Don't believe, sisters, that assistance consists only in giving medicines and food to the sick. There is another type of assistance . . . the assistance of the heart that enters in sympathy with the person who suffers and goes to meet his necessities."

—St. Maria Josefa de Guerra

Mass

Tuesday of the Fourth Week of Lent*

* The following readings may be used on any Lenten day this week,
  especially in Years B and C when the Gospel of the Man Born Blind is
  not read on the Fourth Sunday of Lent: Micah 7:7-9; John 9:1-41.

ENTRANCE ANTIPHON   Cf. Isaiah 55:1

**All who are thirsty, come to the waters, says the Lord. /
Though you have no money, come and drink with joy.**

COLLECT

May the venerable exercises of holy devotion
shape the hearts of your faithful, O Lord,
to welcome worthily the Paschal Mystery
and proclaim the praises of your salvation.
Through our Lord Jesus Christ, your Son,
who lives and reigns with you in the unity of the Holy Spirit,
God, for ever and ever.

A reading from the Book of the Prophet Ezekiel   47:1-9, 12

*I saw water flowing from the temple, and all who were
touched by it were saved (see Roman Missal).*

The angel brought me, Ezekiel, back to the entrance of
the temple of the LORD, and I saw water flowing out
from beneath the threshold of the temple toward the east,
for the façade of the temple was toward the east; the water
flowed down from the right side of the temple, south of the
altar. He led me outside by the north gate, and around to
the outer gate facing the east, where I saw water trickling
from the right side. Then when he had walked off to the east
with a measuring cord in his hand, he measured off a thousand cubits and had me wade through the water, which was
ankle-deep. He measured off another thousand and once

more had me wade through the water, which was now knee-deep. Again he measured off a thousand and had me wade; the water was up to my waist. Once more he measured off a thousand, but there was now a river through which I could not wade; for the water had risen so high it had become a river that could not be crossed except by swimming. He asked me, "Have you seen this, son of man?" Then he brought me to the bank of the river, where he had me sit. Along the bank of the river I saw very many trees on both sides. He said to me, "This water flows into the eastern district down upon the Arabah, and empties into the sea, the salt waters, which it makes fresh. Wherever the river flows, every sort of living creature that can multiply shall live, and there shall be abundant fish, for wherever this water comes the sea shall be made fresh. Along both banks of the river, fruit trees of every kind shall grow; their leaves shall not fade, nor their fruit fail. Every month they shall bear fresh fruit, for they shall be watered by the flow from the sanctuary. Their fruit shall serve for food, and their leaves for medicine."

The word of the Lord.

RESPONSORIAL PSALM   46:2-3, 5-6, 8-9
R℟. (8) **The Lord of hosts is with us; our stronghold is the God of Jacob.**

God is our refuge and our strength,
    an ever-present help in distress.
Therefore we fear not, though the earth be shaken
    and mountains plunge into the depths of the sea. R℟.

There is a stream whose runlets gladden the city of God,
    the holy dwelling of the Most High.
God is in its midst; it shall not be disturbed;
    God will help it at the break of dawn. R℟.

The LORD of hosts is with us;
　our stronghold is the God of Jacob.
Come! behold the deeds of the LORD,
　the astounding things he has wrought on earth. R̡.

GOSPEL ACCLAMATION　　　　　　　　　Psalm 51:12a, 14a
A clean heart create for me, O God;
give me back the joy of your salvation.

A reading from the holy Gospel according to John　5:1-16

Immediately the man became well.

There was a feast of the Jews, and Jesus went up to Jerusalem. Now there is in Jerusalem at the Sheep Gate a pool called in Hebrew Bethesda, with five porticoes. In these lay a large number of ill, blind, lame, and crippled. One man was there who had been ill for thirty-eight years. When Jesus saw him lying there and knew that he had been ill for a long time, he said to him, "Do you want to be well?" The sick man answered him, "Sir, I have no one to put me into the pool when the water is stirred up; while I am on my way, someone else gets down there before me." Jesus said to him, "Rise, take up your mat, and walk." Immediately the man became well, took up his mat, and walked.

Now that day was a sabbath. So the Jews said to the man who was cured, "It is the sabbath, and it is not lawful for you to carry your mat." He answered them, "The man who made me well told me, 'Take up your mat and walk.'" They asked him, "Who is the man who told you, 'Take it up and walk'?" The man who was healed did not know who it was, for Jesus had slipped away, since there was a crowd there. After this Jesus found him in the temple area and said to him, "Look, you are well; do not sin any more, so that nothing worse may happen to you." The man went and told the Jews that Jesus was the one who had made him well.

Therefore, the Jews began to persecute Jesus because he did this on a sabbath.

The Gospel of the Lord.

PRAYER OVER THE OFFERINGS
We offer to you, O Lord,
these gifts which you yourself have bestowed;
may they attest to your care as Creator
for this our mortal life,
and effect in us the healing
that brings us immortality.
Through Christ our Lord.

COMMUNION ANTIPHON   Cf. Psalm 23 (22):1-2
The Lord is my shepherd; there is nothing I shall want. /
Fresh and green are the pastures where he gives me
repose, / near restful waters he leads me.

PRAYER AFTER COMMUNION
Purify our minds, O Lord, we pray,
and renew them with this heavenly Sacrament,
that we may find help for our bodies
now and likewise in times to come.
Through Christ our Lord.

Reflection

An Overflowing Gift

No place on earth is lower than the Dead Sea. And few places
are drier and more desolate than the land surrounding it. No
creatures live in the sea's salty waters, and little can survive

its extreme temperatures. Against the backdrop of this dry and desolate landscape, we hear today's first reading.

About fifteen miles to the east, and three thousand feet above in the hills of Jerusalem, an angel shows Ezekiel a vision of water flowing from the Temple. It starts with a trickle and then becomes a river that is ankle deep, knee deep, waist deep, until it flows over his head. From the riverbanks, the angel shows Ezekiel how this Temple—which is a symbol of God's presence—gives life to all creation, calling to mind the river flowing through the Garden of Eden (Gen 2:10). But now, in the context of Israel's own desolation, God sends a river to make the desert lands fertile and the Dead Sea a life-giving water.

Though given thousands of years ago, this message has much to say to our own times, our personal and collective desolations. It reminds us that God's grace is an overflowing gift offered to all who are open to receive it. And no matter how chaotic and desolate our lives become, God is always at work, pouring out his healing, cleansing, and life-giving power.

From the very place of Ezekiel's vision, Jesus speaks of this river, this promise, this Spirit: "Let anyone who thirsts come to me and drink. . . . Rivers of living water will flow from within [them]" (John 7:37-38).

What dry and desolate part of my own life needs the refreshment of the Holy Spirit?

Fr. Daniel Groody

Fr. Daniel Groody, CSC, is Vice President and Associate Provost of Undergraduate Affairs at the University of Notre Dame.
He is author of the recently released A Theology of Migration: The Bodies of Refugees and the Body of Christ.

Evening

God, come to my assistance.
Lord, make haste to help me.

(opt. hymn, pp. 360–65)

PSALM 11

In the LORD I have taken refuge.
How can you say to my soul,
"Fly like a bird to the mountain!

"Look, the wicked are bending their bow!
They are fixing their arrow on the string,
to shoot the upright of heart in the dark.
Foundations once destroyed,
what can the righteous do?"

The LORD is in his holy temple;
in heaven is the throne of the LORD,
whose eyes behold the world,
whose gaze inspects the human race.

The LORD inspects the righteous and the wicked,
and hates the lover of violence,
sending fire and brimstone on the wicked,
a scorching wind to fill their cup.
For the LORD is righteous and loves righteous deeds;
the upright shall behold the face of God.

Glory to the Father . . .

SCRIPTURE   Acts 3:1-8

Now Peter and John were going up to the temple area
for the three o'clock hour of prayer. And a man crippled from birth was carried and placed at the gate of the
temple called "the Beautiful Gate" every day to beg for alms
from the people who entered the temple. When he saw Peter

and John about to go into the temple, he asked for alms. But Peter looked intently at him, as did John, and said, "Look at us." He paid attention to them, expecting to receive something from them. Peter said, "I have neither silver nor gold, but what I do have I give you: in the name of Jesus Christ the Nazorean, [rise and] walk." Then Peter took him by the right hand and raised him up, and immediately his feet and ankles grew strong. He leaped up, stood, and walked around, and went into the temple with them, walking and jumping and praising God.

READ, PONDER, PRAY on a word or phrase from these readings or another of today's Scriptures (*Lectio Divina*, p. 359)

ANTIPHON
Rise, take up your mat, and walk.

CANTICLE OF MARY *(inside back cover)*

INTERCESSIONS
Triune God, you show us how to love one another.
We praise you and pray: ℟. **Lead us along the everlasting way, O God.**

Help us to find joy in our work. ℟.

Renew your Church through preparations for the Synod. ℟.

Bless hospitality professionals and those who operate shelters, pantries, and services to the poor. ℟.

Our Father . . .

May God strengthen our faith, fulfill our hope, and lead us to know the fullness of God's love, through Jesus, our everlasting joy. Amen.

Wednesday, March 22

Morning

O Lord, open my lips.
And my mouth will proclaim your praise.

(opt. hymn, pp. 360–65)

PSALM 104:24-31

How many are your works, O LORD!
In wisdom you have made them all.
The earth is full of your creatures.

Vast and wide is the span of the sea,
with its creeping things past counting,
living things great and small.
The ships are moving there,
and Leviathan you made to play with.

All of these look to you
to give them their food in due season.
You give it, they gather it up;
you open wide your hand, they are well filled.

You hide your face, they are dismayed;
you take away their breath, they die,
returning to the dust from which they came.
When you send forth your breath, they are created,
and you renew the face of the earth.

May the glory of the LORD last forever!
May the LORD rejoice in these works!

Glory to the Father . . .

SCRIPTURE   Deuteronomy 32:36-37, 38b-39

Surely, the LORD will do justice for his people; / on his
servants he will have pity. / When he sees their strength

is gone, / and neither bond nor free is left, / He will say, Where are their gods, / the rock in whom they took refuge? / Let them rise up now and help you! / Let them be your protection! / See now that I, I alone, am he, / and there is no god besides me. / It is I who bring both death and life, / I who inflict wounds and heal them, / and from my hand no one can deliver.

READ, PONDER, PRAY on a word or phrase from these readings or another of today's Scriptures (*Lectio Divina*, p. 359)

ANTIPHON
It is I who form you and set you as a covenant for the people.

CANTICLE OF ZECHARIAH *(inside front cover)*

INTERCESSIONS
Wondrous God, in wisdom you have created all things. Trusting in you we pray: R̸. **Renew the face of the earth, O God.**

Advance dialogue and unity among Christians. R̸.

Show pity on the people in Ukraine, and strengthen them in their zeal for justice. R̸.

Help us to address climate change, and increase our awareness of those who are most adversely affected by environmental crises. R̸.

Our Father . . .

May God balance our past sorrows with present joys, and lead us to see the splendor of God's creative work all around us, through Jesus our Savior. Amen.

Blessed Among Us

Blessed Clemens August von Galen
Bishop (1878–1946)

Born in Westphalia to an aristocratic family, Clemens von Galen was ordained a priest in 1904. In September 1933, in the early months of the Third Reich, he was consecrated as bishop of Munster. From early on, Bishop von Galen regarded the Nazis as an idolatrous cult, and he used his pulpit to issue a series of defiant sermons: "Not one of us is certain that he will not any day be dragged from his house and carried off to the cells of some concentration camp. I know full well that this may happen to me, perhaps now or on some future day."

As details emerged of the Nazi euthanasia program—which ultimately claimed 100,000 lives—Bishop von Galen spoke out courageously: "Once [we] admit the right to kill unproductive persons, then none of us can be sure of his life. A curse on men and on the German people if we break the holy commandment 'Thou shalt not kill.' . . . Woe to us German people if we not only license this heinous offence but allow it to be committed with impunity."

Having thus incurred the Fuhrer's wrath, the bishop was subjected to constant harassment, though his international reputation spared his life. He survived the destruction of his cathedral by Allied bombing, and then the war. In 1946 he was named a cardinal, but he died only a few days later. He was beatified in 2005.

"I call aloud as a German man, as an honorable citizen, as representative of the Christian religion, as a Catholic bishop: We demand Justice!"

—Blessed Clemens August von Galen

Mass

Wednesday of the Fourth Week of Lent

ENTRANCE ANTIPHON   Psalm 69 (68):14

I pray to you, O Lord, for a time of your favor. / In your great mercy, answer me, O God, / with your salvation that never fails.

COLLECT

O God, who reward the merits of the just
and offer pardon to sinners who do penance,
have mercy, we pray, on those who call upon you,
that the admission of our guilt
may serve to obtain your pardon for our sins.
Through our Lord Jesus Christ, your Son,
who lives and reigns with you in the unity of the Holy Spirit,
God, for ever and ever.

A reading from the Book of the Prophet Isaiah   49:8-15

I have given you as a covenant to the people, to restore the land.

Thus says the LORD: / In a time of favor I answer you, / on the day of salvation I help you; / and I have kept you and given you as a covenant to the people, / To restore the land / and allot the desolate heritages, / Saying to the prisoners: Come out! / To those in darkness: Show yourselves! / Along the ways they shall find pasture, / on every bare height shall their pastures be. / They shall not hunger or thirst, / nor shall the scorching wind or the sun strike them; / For he who pities them leads them / and guides them beside springs of water. / I will cut a road through all my mountains, / and make my highways level. / See, some shall come from afar, / others from the north and the west, / and some from the land of Syene. / Sing out, O heavens, and rejoice, O earth,

/ break forth into song, you mountains. / For the LORD comforts his people / and shows mercy to his afflicted.

But Zion said, "The LORD has forsaken me; / my Lord has forgotten me." / Can a mother forget her infant, / be without tenderness for the child of her womb? / Even should she forget, / I will never forget you.

The word of the Lord.

RESPONSORIAL PSALM   145:8-9, 13cd-14, 17-18

R℣. (8a) **The Lord is gracious and merciful.**

The LORD is gracious and merciful,
    slow to anger and of great kindness.
The LORD is good to all
    and compassionate toward all his works. R℣.

The LORD is faithful in all his words
    and holy in all his works.
The LORD lifts up all who are falling
    and raises up all who are bowed down. R℣.

The LORD is just in all his ways
    and holy in all his works.
The LORD is near to all who call upon him,
    to all who call upon him in truth. R℣.

GOSPEL ACCLAMATION   John 11:25a, 26
I am the resurrection and the life, says the Lord;
whoever believes in me will never die.

A reading from the holy Gospel according to John   5:17-30

*As the Father raises the dead and gives them life,
so also does the Son give life to those whom he chooses.*

esus answered the Jews: "My Father is at work until now, so I am at work." For this reason they tried all the more to kill him, because he not only broke the sabbath but he also called God his own father, making himself equal to God.

Jesus answered and said to them, "Amen, amen, I say to you, the Son cannot do anything on his own, but only what he sees the Father doing; for what he does, the Son will do also. For the Father loves the Son and shows him everything that he himself does, and he will show him greater works than these, so that you may be amazed. For just as the Father raises the dead and gives life, so also does the Son give life to whomever he wishes. Nor does the Father judge anyone, but he has given all judgment to the Son, so that all may honor the Son just as they honor the Father. Whoever does not honor the Son does not honor the Father who sent him. Amen, amen, I say to you, whoever hears my word and believes in the one who sent me has eternal life and will not come to condemnation, but has passed from death to life. Amen, amen, I say to you, the hour is coming and is now here when the dead will hear the voice of the Son of God, and those who hear will live. For just as the Father has life in himself, so also he gave to the Son the possession of life in himself. And he gave him power to exercise judgment, because he is the Son of Man. Do not be amazed at this, because the hour is coming in which all who are in the tombs will hear his voice and will come out, those who have done good deeds to the resurrection of life, but those who have done wicked deeds to the resurrection of condemnation.

"I cannot do anything on my own; I judge as I hear, and my judgment is just, because I do not seek my own will but the will of the one who sent me."

The Gospel of the Lord.

PRAYER OVER THE OFFERINGS
May the power of this sacrifice, O Lord, we pray,
mercifully wipe away what is old in us,
and increase in us grace of salvation and newness of life.
Through Christ our Lord.

COMMUNION ANTIPHON   John 3:17
God did not send his Son into the world / to judge the
world, / but that the world might be saved through him.

PRAYER AFTER COMMUNION
May your heavenly gifts, O Lord, we pray,
which you bestow as a heavenly remedy on your people,
not bring judgment to those who receive them.
Through Christ our Lord.

Reflection

"Come Out!"

After ten years in the balmy Gulf South, moving back to
central Minnesota was a big transition for our family. Our
first winter back lasted from October well into April, with
snow flurries rather than lilies decorating the Easter Sunday
landscape white. More than just the cold, it was the long
winter of being indoors, not seeing as many people out and
about, a long stretch of hunkering down that was a tough
adjustment. In early May, with warmer temperatures came
an amazing sight: people! It was a joy to return to the park,
to the outdoor market, even just to being outdoors and seeing
neighbors passing. The joy of life in community returns
palpably with the spring in the Upper Midwest.

Today's readings bring to mind this coming to life, this sense of freedom and flourishing, especially after a period of darkness and confinement: *Come out! . . . Show yourselves!* God has promised to restore our landscape—whether the natural world that year after year comes to life in the spring, or our inner landscape of the spirit that may be dormant, parched, or afflicted in the wake of a disaster.

God's Word and Spirit restore and give life, as they have done since the beginning of creation. And the beauty of this restoration is that it calls us out of ourselves, into community. When God calls us tenderly to come out, we will find ourselves with others, and there is much joy in that.

Daniella Zsupan-Jerome

Daniella Zsupan-Jerome, PhD, is director of ministerial formation and field education at Saint John's University School of Theology and Seminary in Collegeville, Minnesota. She is author of Connected Toward Communion: The Church and Social Communication in the Digital Age.

Evening

God, come to my assistance.
Lord, make haste to help me.

(opt. hymn, pp. 360–65)

PSALM 105:1-9
Give thanks and proclaim the name of the LORD;
make known God's deeds among the peoples.

O sing to God, sing praise;
tell all the wonderful works of the Lord!
Glory in the holy name of God;
let hearts that seek the LORD rejoice.

Turn to the LORD who is strong;
constantly seek God's face.
Remember the wonders the Lord has done,
great marvels and words of judgment.

O children of Abraham, God's servant,
O descendants of Jacob the chosen one,
it is the LORD who is our God,
whose judgments are in all the earth.

The Lord remembers the covenant forever:
the promise ordained for a thousand generations,
the covenant made with Abraham,
the oath that was sworn to Isaac.

Glory to the Father . . .

SCRIPTURE   2 Corinthians 5:6-10
So we are always courageous, although we know that
while we are at home in the body we are away from the
Lord, for we walk by faith, not by sight. Yet we are courageous, and we would rather leave the body and go home to

the Lord. Therefore, we aspire to please him, whether we are at home or away. For we must all appear before the judgment seat of Christ, so that each one may receive recompense, according to what he did in the body, whether good or evil.

READ, PONDER, PRAY on a word or phrase from these readings or another of today's Scriptures (*Lectio Divina*, p. 359)

ANTIPHON
Whoever hears my word and believes in the one who sent me has eternal life.

CANTICLE OF MARY *(inside back cover)*

INTERCESSIONS
Gracious and merciful God, you are slow to anger and full of kindness. With humble hearts we pray: R℔. Help us, O God.

Gather in your warm embrace children who are orphaned, abandoned, or neglected. R℔.

Energize us to expand support services, employment opportunities, and aid for those who have been released from prison. R℔.

Give courage and hope to those who are terminally ill. R℔.

Our Father . . .

May God lead us to deep and sincere prayer, and bless us with an increase of faith, hope, and love, through Jesus, the resurrection and the life. Amen.

Thursday, March 23

Morning

O Lord, open my lips.
And my mouth will proclaim your praise.

(opt. hymn, pp. 360–65)

PSALM 86:11-17

Teach me, O LORD, your way,
so that I may walk in your truth,
single-heartedly revering your name.

I will praise you, Lord my God, with all my heart,
and glorify your name forever.
Your faithful love to me has been great;
you have saved me from the depths of Sheol.

The proud have risen against me, O God;
a band of the ruthless seeks my life.
To you they pay no heed.

But you, O God, are compassionate and gracious,
slow to anger, O Lord,
abundant in love and fidelity;
turn and take pity on me.

O give your strength to your servant,
and save the child of your handmaid.
Show me the sign of your favor,
that my foes may see to their shame
that you, O LORD, give me comfort and help.

Glory to the Father . . .

SCRIPTURE   Numbers 14:13-14a, 15-16, 19

Moses said to the LORD: "The Egyptians will hear of this,
for by your power you brought out this people from

among them. They will tell the inhabitants of this land, who have heard that you, LORD, are in the midst of this people! If now you slay this people all at once, the nations who have heard such reports of you will say, 'The LORD was not able to bring this people into the land he swore to give them; that is why he slaughtered them in the wilderness.' Pardon, then, the iniquity of this people in keeping with your great kindness, even as you have forgiven them from Egypt until now."

READ, PONDER, PRAY on a word or phrase from these readings or another of today's Scriptures (*Lectio Divina*, p. 359)

ANTIPHON
The Lord is slow to anger and abounding in kindness.

CANTICLE OF ZECHARIAH *(inside front cover)*

INTERCESSIONS
God of infinite love, you gave your only Son so that we may have eternal life. In hope we pray: ℟. God, come to our aid.

Teach us your way so that we may walk in your truth and praise you wholeheartedly. ℟.

Save those who experience depression or despair. ℟.

Strengthen those who care for elders or loved ones with special needs. ℟.

Our Father . . .

May God show us kindness and give us peace, through Jesus, our companion and friend. Amen.

Blessed Among Us

St. Rebecca Ar-Rayès
Nun (1832–1914)

Rebecca Ar-Rayès (Rafqa Butrusia) was born in 1832 to a Maronite Christian family in Lebanon. In 1855 she entered a convent in Ghazir—the same year as a terrible outbreak of violence by Druze militia against the Christian population. While thousands of Christians were massacred, Rebecca and the other sisters were hidden by friendly Arabs. When her congregation dissolved, she entered a new convent of the Baladiya Order. She cheerfully took to contemplative life, eagerly performing any assignment and even volunteering to share the punishment for the infractions of other sisters.

So privileged did Rebecca feel in her new life that she feared she would become spoiled. She prayed to God that she might experience some of Christ's suffering and so relieve the suffering of others. Soon after, she lost her vision; this was followed by increasing paralysis that allowed her only to knit and pray the rosary. She accepted these ordeals without a murmur. Her sufferings, she said, were nothing compared to Christ's agony. "I have sins to expiate, but he, in his love for us, has borne an infinite degree of opprobrium and so much suffering, and we think so little of it."

She died on March 23, 1914, at eighty-one. She was canonized in 2001.

"May the sick, the afflicted, the war refugees, and all victims of hatred, yesterday and today, find in St. Rafqa a companion on the road, so that, through her intercession, they will continue to search in the night for reasons to hope again and build peace."

—Pope John Paul II

Mass

Thursday of the Fourth Week of Lent

[*St. Turibius of Mogrovejo*, opt. memorial]

ENTRANCE ANTIPHON   Cf. Psalm 105 (104):3-4

Let the hearts that seek the Lord rejoice; / turn to the
Lord and his strength; / constantly seek his face.

COLLECT

We invoke your mercy in humble prayer, O Lord,
that you may cause us, your servants,
corrected by penance and schooled by good works,
to persevere sincerely in your commands
and come safely to the paschal festivities.
Through our Lord Jesus Christ, your Son,
who lives and reigns with you in the unity of the Holy Spirit,
God, for ever and ever.

A reading from the Book of Exodus   32:7-14

Relent in punishing your people.

The LORD said to Moses, "Go down at once to your
people whom you brought out of the land of Egypt,
for they have become depraved. They have soon turned
aside from the way I pointed out to them, making for themselves a molten calf and worshiping it, sacrificing to it and
crying out, 'This is your God, O Israel, who brought you
out of the land of Egypt!'" The LORD said to Moses, "I see
how stiff-necked this people is. Let me alone, then, that my
wrath may blaze up against them to consume them. Then
I will make of you a great nation."

But Moses implored the LORD, his God, saying, "Why,
O LORD, should your wrath blaze up against your own
people, whom you brought out of the land of Egypt with

such great power and with so strong a hand? Why should the Egyptians say, 'With evil intent he brought them out, that he might kill them in the mountains and exterminate them from the face of the earth'? Let your blazing wrath die down; relent in punishing your people. Remember your servants Abraham, Isaac and Israel, and how you swore to them by your own self, saying, 'I will make your descendants as numerous as the stars in the sky; and all this land that I promised, I will give your descendants as their perpetual heritage.'" So the LORD relented in the punishment he had threatened to inflict on his people.

The word of the Lord.

RESPONSORIAL PSALM   106:19-20, 21-22, 23
R̸. (4a) **Remember us, O Lord, as you favor your people.**

Our fathers made a calf in Horeb
  and adored a molten image;
They exchanged their glory
  for the image of a grass-eating bullock. R̸.

They forgot the God who had saved them,
  who had done great deeds in Egypt,
Wondrous deeds in the land of Ham,
  terrible things at the Red Sea. R̸.

Then he spoke of exterminating them,
  but Moses, his chosen one,
Withstood him in the breach
  to turn back his destructive wrath. R̸.

GOSPEL ACCLAMATION   John 3:16
God so loved the world that he gave his only-begotten
    Son,
so that everyone who believes in him might have eternal
    life.

A reading from the holy Gospel according to John 5:31-47

The one who will accuse you is Moses,
in whom you have placed your hope.

Jesus said to the Jews: "If I testify on my own behalf, my testimony is not true. But there is another who testifies on my behalf, and I know that the testimony he gives on my behalf is true. You sent emissaries to John, and he testified to the truth. I do not accept human testimony, but I say this so that you may be saved. He was a burning and shining lamp, and for a while you were content to rejoice in his light. But I have testimony greater than John's. The works that the Father gave me to accomplish, these works that I perform testify on my behalf that the Father has sent me. Moreover, the Father who sent me has testified on my behalf. But you have never heard his voice nor seen his form, and you do not have his word remaining in you, because you do not believe in the one whom he has sent. You search the Scriptures, because you think you have eternal life through them; even they testify on my behalf. But you do not want to come to me to have life.

"I do not accept human praise; moreover, I know that you do not have the love of God in you. I came in the name of my Father, but you do not accept me; yet if another comes in his own name, you will accept him. How can you believe, when you accept praise from one another and do not seek the praise that comes from the only God? Do not think that I will accuse you before the Father: the one who will accuse you is Moses, in whom you have placed your hope. For if you had believed Moses, you would have believed me, because he wrote about me. But if you do not believe his writings, how will you believe my words?"

The Gospel of the Lord.

PRAYER OVER THE OFFERINGS
Grant, we pray, almighty God,
that what we offer in sacrifice
may cleanse us in our frailty from every evil
and always grant us your protection.
Through Christ our Lord.

COMMUNION ANTIPHON   Jeremiah 31:33
I will place my law within them, and I will write it upon
their hearts; / and I will be their God, and they shall be
my people, says the Lord.

PRAYER AFTER COMMUNION
May this Sacrament we have received purify us, we pray,
O Lord,
and grant your servants freedom from all blame,
that those bound by a guilty conscience
may glory in the fullness of heavenly remedy.
Through Christ our Lord.

Reflection

No Beating Around the Bush

This funny kid I sat near on my middle school bus, more of
a star hockey player with a mischievous streak than a devoted
student, shocked me one morning when he carried a thick
paperback book onboard. The book, *How to Argue and Win
Every Time* by celebrity lawyer Gerry Spence, was not home-
work for a class. My friend wasn't unaccustomed to getting in
trouble, and he probably wanted to prepare for the next time
his teacher or mother tried to bust him for something.

I don't know anything about the book, but it sounds like something Moses might have appreciated. So often he found himself caught between the Lord and the perpetually disappointing Hebrew people. In today's passage, he comes to the people's defense yet again to stave off the Lord's wrath. It's a masterclass of argumentation that reveals his extensive experience in the genre. Moses flatters the Lord (great power, strong hand). He says freeing the Israelites just to kill them in the desert could lead others to rightly question the Lord's goodness and wisdom. And Moses uses the Lord's own promises to Abraham, Isaac, and Jacob in his appeal for compassion.

I love this scene. There is no stuffy formality between God and Moses, no beating around the bush. We see a strong disagreement that reflects intimacy in the relationship, and only after the conflict can reconciliation come. It reads like just the type of loving family squabble that many of us might relate to even today. This is the type of relationship the Lord desires to have with us: open, honest, and, in the end, always full of mercy.

Mike Jordan Laskey

Michael Jordan Laskey is the communications director for the Jesuit Conference of Canada and the United States and the author of The Ministry of Peace and Justice.

Evening

God, come to my assistance.
Lord, make haste to help me.

(opt. hymn, pp. 360–65)

PSALM 89:20-28

Then you spoke in a vision.
To your faithful ones you said,
"I have bestowed my help on a warrior,
I have exalted one chosen from the people.

"I have found my servant David,
and with my holy oil anointed him.
My hand shall always be with him,
and my arm shall make him strong.

"The enemy shall never outwit him,
nor shall the son of iniquity humble him.
I will beat down his foes before him,
and those who hate him I will strike.

"My love and my faithfulness shall be with him;
by my name his might shall be exalted.
I will stretch out his hand to the Sea,
and his right hand upon the Rivers.

"He will call out to me, 'You are my father,
my God, the rock of my salvation.'
I for my part will make him my firstborn,
the highest of the kings of the earth."

Glory to the Father . . .

SCRIPTURE   1 Corinthians 15:13-17

f there is no resurrection of the dead, then neither has
Christ been raised. And if Christ has not been raised,

then empty [too] is our preaching; empty, too, your faith.
Then we are also false witnesses to God, because we testified
against God that he raised Christ, whom he did not raise if
in fact the dead are not raised. For if the dead are not raised,
neither has Christ been raised, and if Christ has not been
raised, your faith is vain; you are still in your sins.

READ, PONDER, PRAY on a word or phrase from these readings or
another of today's Scriptures (*Lectio Divina*, p. 359)

ANTIPHON
The Father who sent me has testified on my behalf.

CANTICLE OF MARY *(inside back cover)*

INTERCESSIONS
God of the covenant, you are forever faithful and true in
your love. With trust we pray: ℞. **God, in your wisdom,
hear our prayer.**

Pour your grace and blessing upon Muslims as they
begin Ramadan. ℞.

Advance dialogue, understanding, and respect among
Christians, Muslims, and Jews. ℞.

Comfort and heal those who suffer relationship
wounds. ℞.

Our Father . . .

May the God of peace sanctify us completely, and may we
be kept blameless at the coming of our Lord Jesus Christ,
by the power of the Holy Spirit. Amen.

Friday, March 24

Morning

O Lord, open my lips.
And my mouth will proclaim your praise.

(opt. hymn, pp. 360–65)

PSALM 88:10b-19
I call to you, LORD, all day long;
to you I stretch out my hands.

Will you work your wonders for the dead?
Will the shades rise up to praise you?
From the grave, who can tell of your love?
From the place of perdition your faithfulness?
Will your wonders be known in the dark,
in the land of oblivion your righteousness?

But I, O LORD, cry out to you;
in the morning my prayer comes before you.
Why do you reject me, O LORD?
Why do you hide your face from me?

I am wretched, close to death from my youth.
I have borne your trials; I am numb.
Your fury has swept down upon me;
your terrors have utterly destroyed me.

They surround me all the day like a flood;
together they close in against me.
Friend and neighbor you have taken away:
my one companion is darkness.

Glory to the Father . . .

SCRIPTURE   Genesis 37:17b-20, 23-24a

Joseph went after his brothers and found them in Dothan. They saw him from a distance, and before he reached them, they plotted to kill him. They said to one another: "Here comes that dreamer! Come now, let us kill him and throw him into one of the cisterns here; we could say that a wild beast devoured him. We will see then what comes of his dreams."

So when Joseph came up to his brothers, they stripped him of his tunic, the long ornamented tunic he had on; then they took him and threw him into the cistern.

READ, PONDER, PRAY on a word or phrase from these readings or another of today's Scriptures (*Lectio Divina*, p. 359)

ANTIPHON

If the righteous one is the son of God, God will help him.

CANTICLE OF ZECHARIAH *(inside front cover)*

INTERCESSIONS

Merciful God, you are near the brokenhearted and you rescue those in distress. In hope we pray: ℟. **O God, hear our cries for help.**

Lead victims of abuse to find help and support for healing. ℟.

Prosper the work of environmentalists and biologists, and lead us to prevent further environmental disasters. ℟.

Ease the burdens of those who experience mental illness, and encircle them with your healing presence. ℟.

Our Father . . .

May God strengthen us in faithfulness and love, and bring all things to perfection in Christ, by the power of the Holy Spirit. Amen.

Blessed Among Us

St. Oscar Romero
Archbishop and Martyr (1917–1980)

In 2015, the Vatican decreed that Archbishop Oscar Romero of San Salvador had died as a martyr "in hatred of the faith," opening the way for his beatification, and ultimately his canonization in 2018. For an archbishop slain at the altar while saying Mass, this decree might have seemed unremarkable. But for many years Romero's cause was blocked by powerful prelates who claimed he had not died for his faith but for mixing himself up in politics. This charge was answered by the postulator of Romero's cause who said his assassination "was not caused by motives that were simply political, but by hatred for a faith that, imbued with charity, would not be silent in the face of the injustices that relentlessly and cruelly slaughtered the poor and their defenders."

Romero's canonization did not simply enlarge the Church's understanding of martyrdom; he offered a powerful example of what it means to be a disciple of Jesus Christ in a world marked by violence and injustice. While many saints have exemplified a model of holiness in the form of escape from a sinful world, Romero's holiness was expressed in solidarity with a wounded world. Many saints practiced charity, but Romero combined charity with a passion for justice. He answered the call for holy witnesses who are faithful to the end, who challenge both the Church and the world, and who are willing to speak the truth and pay up personally.

"One who is committed to the poor must risk the same fate as the poor. And in El Salvador we know what the fate of the poor signifies: to disappear, to be tortured, to be captive, and to be found dead."

—St. Oscar Romero

Mass

Friday of the Fourth Week of Lent

ENTRANCE ANTIPHON   Cf. Psalm 54 (53):3-4

O God, save me by your name; / by your power, defend
my cause. / O God, hear my prayer; / give ear to the
words of my mouth.

COLLECT

O God, who have prepared
fitting helps for us in our weakness,
grant, we pray, that we may receive
their healing effects with joy
and reflect them in a holy way of life.
Through our Lord Jesus Christ, your Son,
who lives and reigns with you in the unity of the Holy Spirit,
God, for ever and ever.

A reading from the Book of Wisdom   2:1a, 12-22

Let us condemn him to a shameful death.

The wicked said among themselves, / thinking not
aright: / "Let us beset the just one, because he is
obnoxious to us; / he sets himself against our doings, /
Reproaches us for transgressions of the law / and charges
us with violations of our training. / He professes to have
knowledge of God / and styles himself a child of the LORD.
/ To us he is the censure of our thoughts; / merely to see him
is a hardship for us, / Because his life is not like that of
others, / and different are his ways. / He judges us debased;
/ he holds aloof from our paths as from things impure. / He
calls blest the destiny of the just / and boasts that God is his
Father. / Let us see whether his words be true; / let us find
out what will happen to him. / For if the just one be the son

of God, he will defend him / and deliver him from the hand of his foes. / With revilement and torture let us put him to the test / that we may have proof of his gentleness / and try his patience. / Let us condemn him to a shameful death; / for according to his own words, God will take care of him." / These were their thoughts, but they erred; / for their wickedness blinded them, / and they knew not the hidden counsels of God; / neither did they count on a recompense of holiness / nor discern the innocent souls' reward.

The word of the Lord.

RESPONSORIAL PSALM   34:17-18, 19-20, 21 and 23

R̶̸. (19a) **The Lord is close to the brokenhearted.**

The LORD confronts the evildoers,
    to destroy remembrance of them from the earth.
When the just cry out, the LORD hears them,
    and from all their distress he rescues them. R̶̸.

The LORD is close to the brokenhearted;
    and those who are crushed in spirit he saves.
Many are the troubles of the just man,
    but out of them all the LORD delivers him. R̶̸.

He watches over all his bones;
    not one of them shall be broken.
The LORD redeems the lives of his servants;
    no one incurs guilt who takes refuge in him. R̶̸.

GOSPEL ACCLAMATION   Matthew 4:4b

One does not live on bread alone,
but on every word that comes forth from the mouth of
    God.

A reading from the holy Gospel according to John

7:1-2, 10, 25-30

They tried to arrest him, but his hour had not yet come.

Jesus moved about within Galilee; he did not wish to travel in Judea, because the Jews were trying to kill him. But the Jewish feast of Tabernacles was near.

But when his brothers had gone up to the feast, he himself also went up, not openly but as it were in secret.

Some of the inhabitants of Jerusalem said, "Is he not the one they are trying to kill? And look, he is speaking openly and they say nothing to him. Could the authorities have realized that he is the Christ? But we know where he is from. When the Christ comes, no one will know where he is from." So Jesus cried out in the temple area as he was teaching and said, "You know me and also know where I am from. Yet I did not come on my own, but the one who sent me, whom you do not know, is true. I know him, because I am from him, and he sent me." So they tried to arrest him, but no one laid a hand upon him, because his hour had not yet come.

The Gospel of the Lord.

PRAYER OVER THE OFFERINGS
May this sacrifice, almighty God,
cleanse us by its mighty power
and lead us to approach its source
with ever greater purity.
Through Christ our Lord.

COMMUNION ANTIPHON   Ephesians 1:7
In Christ, we have redemption by his Blood, / and forgiveness of our sins, / in accord with the riches of his grace.

PRAYER AFTER COMMUNION
Grant, we pray, O Lord,
that, as we pass from old to new,
so, with former ways left behind,
we may be renewed in holiness of mind.
Through Christ our Lord.

Reflection

The Refuge We Seek

The Lord is close to the brokenhearted.

Recent years have been hard. Our screens and minds are overwhelmed with the images of police shootings, school shootings, and mass shootings; fires, floods, and hurricanes; crying children and distraught mothers; chain link fences and razor wires. So much pain.

In grief, we cry out to God. Like a tidal wave, the emotion begins in the belly and then swells, filling the chest and then the throat, the mouth, the air. In trouble and despair, confusion or frustration, when God seems far away, we cry out.

Although the temples, chapels, and cathedrals of the world have provided sanctuary for the people of God throughout time, the place of refuge or safety we seek is not a space created below ceilings or between walls. It does not require stained glass or pews, big screens, projectors, or coffee bars. No, we find sanctuary any time when, in the Spirit, we enter the presence of the living God. Sanctuary is the place where we empty our hearts before the Lord, pouring out our pain, anger, and sorrow like water. But it is also a place of remembrance and restoration where we can find and enter that space through worship.

Worship is not a form of entertainment for a crowd of religious spectators. It is the way we remind our souls of who God is and what he has done.

Donna Barber, *Bread for the Resistance*

Donna Barber is cofounder and executive director of The Voices Project, *an organization that influences culture through training and promoting leaders of color.*

Evening

God, come to my assistance.
Lord, make haste to help me.

(opt. hymn, pp. 360–65)

PSALM 85:9-14

I will hear what the LORD God speaks,
who speaks of peace to his faithful people,
and those who turn to God in their hearts.
For those who fear God, salvation is near,
and the Lord's glory will dwell in our land.

Merciful love and faithfulness have met;
righteousness and peace have kissed.
Faithfulness shall spring from the earth,
and righteousness look down from heaven.

Also the LORD will bestow a great bounty,
and our earth shall yield its increase.
Righteousness will march as a vanguard,
and guide God's steps on the way.

Glory to the Father . . .

SCRIPTURE   Ephesians 1:15-18

I, too, hearing of your faith in the Lord Jesus and of your love for all the holy ones, do not cease giving thanks for you, remembering you in my prayers, that the God of our Lord Jesus Christ, the Father of glory, may give you a spirit of wisdom and revelation resulting in knowledge of him. May the eyes of [your] hearts be enlightened, that you may know what is the hope that belongs to his call, what are the riches of glory in his inheritance among the holy ones.

READ, PONDER, PRAY on a word or phrase from these readings or another of today's Scriptures (*Lectio Divina*, p. 359)

ANTIPHON
Jesus came that we might know the Father.

CANTICLE OF MARY *(inside back cover)*

INTERCESSIONS
Supporting God, you strengthen and uphold us in our weakness. In faith we pray: R̈. Gracious God, fill us with your Spirit.

Favor farmers and all who cultivate the earth with clement weather, just wages, and appreciation for the food they provide. R̈.

Come to the aid of those who seek healing of addiction, and help us to provide plentiful services for them and their families. R̈.

Animate countries at war to negotiate peace and to address conflict in nonviolent ways. R̈.

Our Father . . .

May God open our eyes to the beauty that surrounds us, strengthen us in our Lenten practices, and bring us to Easter with joy and peace, through Jesus our Redeemer. Amen.

Saturday, March 25

Morning

O Lord, open my lips.
And my mouth will proclaim your praise.

(opt. hymn, pp. 360–65)

PSALM 138:1-3, 6-8
I thank you, LORD, with all my heart;
you have heard the words of my mouth.
In the presence of the angels I praise you.
I bow down toward your holy temple.

I give thanks to your name
for you have exalted over all
your name and your promise.
On the day I called, you answered me;
you increased the strength of my soul.

The LORD is high, yet looks on the lowly,
and the haughty God knows from afar.
You give me life though I walk amid affliction;
you stretch out your hand against the anger of my foes.

With your right hand you save me;
the LORD will accomplish this for me.
O LORD, your merciful love is eternal;
discard not the work of your hands.

Glory to the Father . . .

SCRIPTURE   Zephaniah 3:14, 15b-18a
Shout for joy, daughter Zion! / sing joyfully, Israel! / Be glad and exult with all your heart, / daughter Jerusalem! / The King of Israel, the LORD, is in your midst, / you

have no further misfortune to fear. / On that day, it shall be said to Jerusalem: / Do not fear, Zion, / do not be discouraged! / The LORD, your God, is in your midst, / a mighty savior, / Who will rejoice over you with gladness, / and renew you in his love, / Who will sing joyfully because of you, / as on festival days.

READ, PONDER, PRAY on a word or phrase from these readings or another of today's Scriptures (*Lectio Divina*, p. 359)

ANTIPHON
You will conceive and bear a son, and you shall name him Jesus.

CANTICLE OF ZECHARIAH *(inside front cover)*

INTERCESSIONS
God of our joy, Mary's "yes" is our source of redemption. In faith we pray: R̝. **Lead us along your everlasting way, O God.**

Give us peace and good zeal to live as disciples in the state of life we embrace. R̝.

Help us to be mindful of ways in which we may support and assist pregnant women and mothers of young children. R̝.

Fill your Church with gratitude and exaltation for the greatness of your love. R̝.

Our Father . . .

May God bless us with songs of praise and thanksgiving for all the good God has done for us, through Jesus our Savior. Amen.

Blessed Among Us

Ida B. Wells
Champion of Justice (1862–1931)

Born into slavery in Mississippi, Ida B. Wells's struggle against racial injustice began in 1884 when a train conductor tried to evict her from her first-class seat to make room for a white man. Her successful suit against the train company won her a national reputation, and she became editor of a Black newspaper in Memphis, *The Free Speech and Headlight*.

When, in 1892, three Black men were lynched in Memphis, Wells was galvanized to action. In the years since Emancipation, lynching had become the ultimate form of white terrorism in the South. Though the pretext was often some alleged "outrage" against (white) womanhood, Wells conducted exhaustive research documenting the actual causes: failure to show proper deference to whites, registering to vote, "talking back," complaining about work, or sheer bad luck. Whatever the reasons, it was a reminder that the underlying code of slavery lived on. Christian ministers, meanwhile, were generally oblivious to the parallels between this public violence and the death of Jesus on a cross.

Following her editorials, an outraged mob destroyed her press and would have lynched her too if she had been present. Settling in Chicago, she became a "journalist in exile," tirelessly carrying on the fight against lynching, until her death on March 31, 1931. She did not live to see success (there were 28 recorded lynchings in 1931), but her courageous witness lit a torch that others carried across the generations. In 2022, Congress passed the Emmet Till Anti-Lynching Act.

"We submit all to the sober judgment of the Nation, confident that, in this cause, as well as all others, 'Truth is mighty and will prevail.'"

—Ida B. Wells

Mass

The Annunciation of the Lord, Solemnity

ENTRANCE ANTIPHON   Hebrews 10:5, 7
The Lord said, as he entered the world: / Behold, I come to do your will, O God.

GLORIA (p. 331)

COLLECT
O God, who willed that your Word
should take on the reality of human flesh
in the womb of the Virgin Mary,
grant, we pray,
that we, who confess our Redeemer to be God and man,
may merit to become partakers even in his divine nature.
Who lives and reigns with you in the unity of the
    Holy Spirit,
God, for ever and ever.

A reading from the Book of the Prophet Isaiah

7:10-14; 8:10

Behold, the virgin shall conceive.

The LORD spoke to Ahaz, saying: Ask for a sign from the LORD, your God; let it be deep as the nether world, or high as the sky! But Ahaz answered, "I will not ask! I will not tempt the LORD!" Then Isaiah said: Listen, O house of David! Is it not enough for you to weary people, must you also weary my God? Therefore the Lord himself will give you this sign: the virgin shall be with child, and bear a son, and shall name him Emmanuel, which means "God is with us!"

The word of the Lord.

RESPONSORIAL PSALM   40:7-8a, 8b-9, 10, 11

R℣. (8a and 9a) **Here I am, Lord; I come to do your will.**

Sacrifice or oblation you wished not,
   but ears open to obedience you gave me.
Holocausts or sin-offerings you sought not;
   then said I, "Behold I come." R℣.

"In the written scroll it is prescribed for me,
To do your will, O my God, is my delight,
   and your law is within my heart!" R℣.

I announced your justice in the vast assembly;
   I did not restrain my lips, as you, O LORD, know. R℣.

Your justice I kept not hid within my heart;
   your faithfulness and your salvation I have spoken of;
I have made no secret of your kindness and your truth
   in the vast assembly. R℣.

A reading from the Letter to the Hebrews   10:4-10

*As is written of me in the scroll, behold,
   I come to do your will, O God.*

Brothers and sisters: It is impossible that the blood of
bulls and goats take away sins. For this reason, when
Christ came into the world, he said: / "Sacrifice and offering
you did not desire, / but a body you prepared for me; / in
holocausts and sin offerings you took no delight. / Then I
said, 'As is written of me in the scroll, / behold, I come to
do your will, O God.' " / First he says, "Sacrifices and offerings, holocausts and sin offerings, you neither desired nor
delighted in." These are offered according to the law. Then
he says, "Behold, I come to do your will." He takes away the
first to establish the second. By this "will," we have been
consecrated through the offering of the Body of Jesus Christ
once for all.

The word of the Lord.

GOSPEL ACCLAMATION   John 1:14ab

The Word of God became flesh and made his dwelling
    among us;
and we saw his glory.

A reading from the holy Gospel according to Luke 1:26-38

Behold, you will conceive in your womb and bear a son.

The angel Gabriel was sent from God to a town of Galilee
called Nazareth, to a virgin betrothed to a man named
Joseph, of the house of David, and the virgin's name was
Mary. And coming to her, he said, "Hail, full of grace! The
Lord is with you." But she was greatly troubled at what was
said and pondered what sort of greeting this might be. Then
the angel said to her, "Do not be afraid, Mary, for you have
found favor with God. Behold, you will conceive in your
womb and bear a son, and you shall name him Jesus. He
will be great and will be called Son of the Most High, and
the Lord God will give him the throne of David his father,
and he will rule over the house of Jacob forever, and of his
Kingdom there will be no end." But Mary said to the angel,
"How can this be, since I have no relations with a man?"
And the angel said to her in reply, "The Holy Spirit will
come upon you, and the power of the Most High will over-
shadow you. Therefore the child to be born will be called
holy, the Son of God. And behold, Elizabeth, your relative,
has also conceived a son in her old age, and this is the sixth
month for her who was called barren; for nothing will be
impossible for God." Mary said, "Behold, I am the handmaid of the Lord. May it be done to me according to your
word." Then the angel departed from her.

The Gospel of the Lord.

CREED (p. 332)

PRAYER OVER THE OFFERINGS
Be pleased, almighty God,
to accept your Church's offering,
so that she, who is aware that her beginnings
lie in the Incarnation of your Only Begotten Son,
may rejoice to celebrate his mysteries on this Solemnity.
Who lives and reigns for ever and ever.

COMMUNION ANTIPHON   Isaiah 7:14
Behold, a Virgin shall conceive and bear a son; / and his
name will be called Emmanuel.

PRAYER AFTER COMMUNION
Confirm in our minds the mysteries of the true faith,
we pray, O Lord,
so that, confessing that he who was conceived of the
     Virgin Mary
is true God and true man,
we may, through the saving power of his Resurrection,
merit to attain eternal joy.
Through Christ our Lord.

Reflection

The Weight of Light

Fiat. It brought a universe into being. *Fiat lux*—let there be
light. With a breath, an unbearable radiance poured into the
darkness at creation.

   Fiat, said Mary to Gabriel. And with a breath, that infinite,
unbearable Light poured into a young woman in a small
town, until she swayed with the weight of it. *Fiat*, cried Jesus
in the Garden of Gethsemane. Once again the universe was

borne on a breath, carried across the shoulders of God incarnate.

We hear these assents as "let it be done to me." Yet the Greek word Luke uses—*genoito*—means more than passive assent. It whispers of birth and growth, of what we might become. None of the events set in motion by these *fiats* are complete. They were each a "yes" to becoming. The light that tore through the darkness all those billions of years ago is still flaring out, igniting suns whose light will not reach us for a hundred billion years.

Mary said "yes" to becoming the Christ-bearer. Even now she bears our prayers aloft, swaying under the weight of our needs. And with a word ripped from the depths, Jesus became the redeemer of our sins past and present and even of the future. Light still careening through our darkness, moving heaven and earth.

Light has no weight, the physicists tell us. Except when it is in motion. Then it has power that can sweep the dust of dead stars together with enough force to bring the very earth we stand on into being. Dare I take on the weight of light? Dare I say "yes" to moving toward what God hopes for me?

Fiat. Fiat lux. Let me be aflame with the Gospel, heavy with the light of Christ.

Michelle Francl-Donnay

Michelle Francl-Donnay is a wife and mother, a professor of chemistry, and an adjunct scholar at the Vatican Observatory. She is author of Prayer: Biblical Wisdom for Seeking God *in the Little Rock Scripture Study* Alive in the Word *series. Her website is* michellefrancldonnay.com.

Evening

God, come to my assistance.
Lord, make haste to help me.

(opt. hymn, pp. 360–65)

PSALM 87

Founded by God on the holy mountain,
the LORD loves the gates of Zion,
more than all the dwellings of Jacob.
Of you are told glorious things,
you, O city of God!

"Rahab and Babylon I will count
among those who know me;
Of Tyre, Philistia, Ethiopia, it is told,
'There was this one born.'
But of Zion it shall be said,
'Each one was born in her.'"

God, the Most High, will establish her.
In the register of peoples the LORD writes,
"Here was this one born."
The singers cry out in chorus,
"All my wellsprings are in you."

Glory to the Father . . .

SCRIPTURE   Ephesians 1:11-14

I n [Christ] we were also chosen, destined in accord with
the purpose of the One who accomplishes all things according to the intention of his will, so that we might exist
for the praise of his glory, we who first hoped in Christ. In
him you also, who have heard the word of truth, the gospel
of your salvation, and have believed in him, were sealed
with the promised holy Spirit, which is the first installment

of our inheritance toward redemption as God's possession, to the praise of his glory.

READ, PONDER, PRAY on a word or phrase from these readings or another of today's Scriptures (*Lectio Divina*, p. 359)

ANTIPHON
May the eyes of our hearts be enlightened to know the hope to which we are called.

CANTICLE OF MARY *(inside back cover)*

INTERCESSIONS
Most High God, we echo Mary's words of praise and pray in faith: R℣. Your will be done, O God.

Help us to embrace mystery and to ponder your Word in our hearts. R℣.

Keep vigil with those who wait for an organ transplant. R℣.

Bring to light all that needs to be healed and transformed in your Church. R℣.

Our Father . . .

May God make of our hearts wellsprings of joy and renew us in love, through Jesus, our saving hope. Amen.

HL. LAZARUS VON BETHANIEN

Sunday, March 26

Morning

O Lord, open my lips.
And my mouth will proclaim your praise.

(opt. hymn, pp. 360–65)

PSALM 96:1-9

O sing a new song to the LORD;
sing to the LORD, all the earth.
O sing to the LORD; bless God's name.
Proclaim divine salvation day by day.
Tell among the nations God's glory,
divine wonders among all the peoples.

For the LORD is great and highly to be praised,
to be feared above all gods.
For the idols of the nations are naught.
It was the LORD who made the heavens.
Greatness and splendor abound in God's presence,
strength and honor in the holy place.

Ascribe to the LORD, you families of peoples,
Ascribe to the LORD glory and power;
Ascribe to the LORD the glory of God's name.

Bring an offering and enter God's courts;
worship the LORD in holy splendor.
O tremble before God, all the earth.

Glory to the Father . . .

SCRIPTURE   2 Kings 4:32b-37

[E]lisha] found the boy dead, lying on the bed. He went
in, closed the door on them both, and prayed to the

St. Lazarus of Bethany by Nikola Sarić.

LORD. Then he lay upon the child on the bed, placing his mouth upon the child's mouth, his eyes upon the eyes, and his hands upon the hands. As Elisha stretched himself over the child, the boy's flesh became warm. He arose, paced up and down the room, and then once more stretched himself over him, and the boy sneezed seven times and opened his eyes. Elisha summoned Gehazi and said, "Call the Shunammite." He called her, and she came to him, and Elisha said to her, "Take your son." She came in and fell at his feet in homage; then she took her son and left.

READ, PONDER, PRAY on a word or phrase from these readings or another of today's Scriptures (*Lectio Divina*, p. 359)

ANTIPHON
I know that whatever you ask of God, God will give you.

CANTICLE OF ZECHARIAH *(inside front cover)*

INTERCESSIONS
Saving God, splendor abounds in your presence. With joy we pray: R⁊. **Let us acclaim your goodness, O God.**

You raise the dead to life: animate your Church to proclaim the Good News in word, deed, worship, and prayer. R⁊.

You rule the world with justice: help us to address deceitful practices, structural racism, and exploitation of those who are vulnerable. R⁊.

You answer the pleas of the faithful: heed the prayers of those who care for a sick child or parent. R⁊.

Our Father . . .

May God heal us of every sin and illness, bless us with peace, and bring us together to everlasting life, through Jesus, the resurrection and the life. Amen.

Mass

Fifth Sunday of Lent

ENTRANCE ANTIPHON   Cf. Psalm 43 (42):1-2

Give me justice, O God, / and plead my cause against a
nation that is faithless. / From the deceitful and cunning
rescue me, / for you, O God, are my strength.

(The Gloria is omitted.)

COLLECT

By your help, we beseech you, Lord our God,
may we walk eagerly in that same charity
with which, out of love for the world,
your Son handed himself over to death.
Through our Lord Jesus Christ, your Son,
who lives and reigns with you in the unity of the Holy Spirit,
God, for ever and ever.

A reading from the Book of the Prophet Ezekiel 37:12-14

I will put my spirit in you that you may live.

Thus says the Lord GOD: O my people, I will open your
graves and have you rise from them, and bring you
back to the land of Israel. Then you shall know that I am
the LORD, when I open your graves and have you rise from
them, O my people! I will put my spirit in you that you may
live, and I will settle you upon your land; thus you shall
know that I am the LORD. I have promised, and I will do it,
says the LORD.

The word of the Lord.

RESPONSORIAL PSALM   130:1-2, 3-4, 5-6, 7-8

℞. (7) **With the Lord there is mercy and fullness of redemption.**

Out of the depths I cry to you, O LORD;
  LORD, hear my voice!
Let your ears be attentive
  to my voice in supplication. ℞.

If you, O LORD, mark iniquities,
  LORD, who can stand?
But with you is forgiveness,
  that you may be revered. ℞.

I trust in the LORD;
  my soul trusts in his word.
More than sentinels wait for the dawn,
  let Israel wait for the LORD. ℞.

For with the LORD is kindness
  and with him is plenteous redemption;
and he will redeem Israel
  from all their iniquities. ℞.

A reading from the Letter of Saint Paul to the Romans
                                            8:8-11

*The Spirit of the One who raised
Jesus from the dead dwells in you.*

Brothers and sisters: Those who are in the flesh cannot please God. But you are not in the flesh; on the contrary, you are in the spirit, if only the Spirit of God dwells in you. Whoever does not have the Spirit of Christ does not belong to him. But if Christ is in you, although the body is dead because of sin, the spirit is alive because of righteousness. If the Spirit of the One who raised Jesus from the dead dwells in you, the One who raised Christ from the dead will give life to your mortal bodies also, through his Spirit dwelling in you.

The word of the Lord.

GOSPEL ACCLAMATION   John 11:25a, 26

I am the resurrection and the life, says the Lord;
whoever believes in me, even if he dies, will never die.

A reading from the holy Gospel according to John

11:1-45 (Shorter Form [ ], 11:3-7, 17, 20-27, 33b-45)

I am the resurrection and the life.

Now a man was ill, Lazarus from Bethany, the village of Mary and her sister Martha. Mary was the one who had anointed the Lord with perfumed oil and dried his feet with her hair; it was her brother Lazarus who was ill. So [the sisters (of Lazarus) sent word to Jesus saying, "Master, the one you love is ill." When Jesus heard this he said, "This illness is not to end in death, but is for the glory of God, that the Son of God may be glorified through it." Now Jesus loved Martha and her sister and Lazarus. So when he heard that he was ill, he remained for two days in the place where he was. Then after this he said to his disciples, "Let us go back to Judea."] The disciples said to him, "Rabbi, the Jews were just trying to stone you, and you want to go back there?" Jesus answered, "Are there not twelve hours in a day? If one walks during the day, he does not stumble, because he sees the light of this world. But if one walks at night, he stumbles, because the light is not in him." He said this, and then told them, "Our friend Lazarus is asleep, but I am going to awaken him." So the disciples said to him, "Master, if he is asleep, he will be saved." But Jesus was talking about his death, while they thought that he meant ordinary sleep. So then Jesus said to them clearly, "Lazarus has died. And I am glad for you that I was not there, that you may believe.

Let us go to him." So Thomas, called Didymus, said to his fellow disciples, "Let us also go to die with him."

[When Jesus arrived, he found that Lazarus had already been in the tomb for four days.] Now Bethany was near Jerusalem, only about two miles away. And many of the Jews had come to Martha and Mary to comfort them about their brother. [When Martha heard that Jesus was coming, she went to meet him; but Mary sat at home. Martha said to Jesus, "Lord, if you had been here, my brother would not have died. But even now I know that whatever you ask of God, God will give you." Jesus said to her, "Your brother will rise." Martha said to him, "I know he will rise, in the resurrection on the last day." Jesus told her, "I am the resurrection and the life; whoever believes in me, even if he dies, will live, and everyone who lives and believes in me will never die. Do you believe this?" She said to him, "Yes, Lord. I have come to believe that you are the Christ, the Son of God, the one who is coming into the world."]

When she had said this, she went and called her sister Mary secretly, saying, "The teacher is here and is asking for you." As soon as she heard this, she rose quickly and went to him. For Jesus had not yet come into the village, but was still where Martha had met him. So when the Jews who were with her in the house comforting her saw Mary get up quickly and go out, they followed her, presuming that she was going to the tomb to weep there. When Mary came to where Jesus was and saw him, she fell at his feet and said to him, "Lord, if you had been here, my brother would not have died." When Jesus saw her weeping and the Jews who had come with her weeping, [he became perturbed and deeply troubled, and said, "Where have you laid him?" They said to him, "Sir, come and see." And Jesus wept. So the Jews said, "See how he loved him." But some of them said, "Could not the one who opened the eyes of the blind man have done something so that this man would not have died?"

So Jesus, perturbed again, came to the tomb. It was a cave, and a stone lay across it. Jesus said, "Take away the stone." Martha, the dead man's sister, said to him, "Lord, by now there will be a stench; he has been dead for four days." Jesus said to her, "Did I not tell you that if you believe you will see the glory of God?" So they took away the stone. And Jesus raised his eyes and said, "Father, I thank you for hearing me. I know that you always hear me; but because of the crowd here I have said this, that they may believe that you sent me." And when he had said this, he cried out in a loud voice, "Lazarus, come out!" The dead man came out, tied hand and foot with burial bands, and his face was wrapped in a cloth. So Jesus said to them, "Untie him and let him go."

Now many of the Jews who had come to Mary and seen what he had done began to believe in him.]

The Gospel of the Lord.

CREED (p. 332)

PRAYER OVER THE OFFERINGS
Hear us, almighty God,
and, having instilled in your servants
the teachings of the Christian faith,
graciously purify them
by the working of this sacrifice.
Through Christ our Lord.

COMMUNION ANTIPHON   Cf. John 11:26
Everyone who lives and believes in me / will not die for ever, says the Lord.

PRAYER AFTER COMMUNION
We pray, almighty God,
that we may always be counted among the members of
Christ,
in whose Body and Blood we have communion.
Who lives and reigns for ever and ever.

Reflection

Full of Hope and Promise

It's the Fifth Sunday of Lent, and many of us are probably groaning inwardly, "How long, O Lord? Will Easter ever get here?" If this is the case for you, then take heart—and take a long, deep look at each of today's readings. They are shot full of hope and promise.

It is so easy to downgrade resurrection to a vague notion or merely embrace it as just another theological construct among many. In fact, and shockingly, a large percentage of Christians doubt the reality of resurrection.

What I find so hopeful on this Lenten Lord's Day is that God does not pitch resurrection to us as a possibility or even a probability *but as a fact*—and, not only as a fact, but *a promise.* "I will open your graves and have you rise from them . . ." Twice this fact is declared, and then God makes it a promise.

Paul, writing to the Romans, takes up the theme of resurrection, linking the resurrection of Jesus with the resurrection that awaits you and me. How? Why? Because we have been imbued with the same Spirit with which Jesus and Ezekiel's people were filled. It is the same Spirit promised by the risen Jesus, sent upon the disciples and all the Church on Pentecost.

The Lazarus narrative takes the general notion of resurrection and gives it specificity. Lazarus's being raised by Jesus prefigures and anticipates Jesus' own rising up. It is an icon, a promise to us.

So, if you are struggling and feeling overwhelmed by the Lenten journey, take heart. The best is yet to come—the promise of him who said, "I am the resurrection and the life."

Fr. John Meoska

John Meoska, OSB, is a monk of Saint John's Abbey and an avid woodworker.

Evening

God, come to my assistance.
Lord, make haste to help me.

(opt. hymn, pp. 360–65)

PSALM 24:1-6

The LORD's is the earth and its fullness,
the world, and those who dwell in it.
It is the Lord who set it on the seas,
and made it firm on the rivers.

Who shall climb the mountain of the LORD?
Who shall stand in God's holy place?
The clean of hands and pure of heart,
whose souls are not set on vain things,
who have not sworn deceitful words.

Blessings from the LORD shall they receive,
and right reward from the God who saves them.
Such are the people who seek the Lord,
who seek the face of the God of Jacob.

Glory to the Father . . .

SCRIPTURE   1 John 5:9-12

If we accept human testimony, the testimony of God is surely greater. Now the testimony of God is this, that he has testified on behalf of his Son. Whoever believes in the Son of God has this testimony within himself. Whoever does not believe God has made him a liar by not believing the testimony God has given about his Son. And this is the testimony: God gave us eternal life, and this life is in his Son. Whoever possesses the Son has life; whoever does not possess the Son of God does not have life.

READ, PONDER, PRAY on a word or phrase from these readings or another of today's Scriptures (*Lectio Divina*, p. 359)

ANTIPHON

I am the resurrection and the life; whoever believes in me will live.

CANTICLE OF MARY *(inside back cover)*

INTERCESSIONS

Living God, through our encounter with Jesus you transform our hearts. In hope we pray: R̦. Lead us to your light, O God.

Unite people of good will to end wars, violence, and poverty. R̦.

Teach us to contemplate your presence in creation, and prosper efforts to reverse climate change. R̦.

Give everlasting peace and joy to the faithful departed. R̦.

Our Father . . .

May God bless us with compassion and strengthen us for life in the Spirit, through Jesus, our power and promise. Amen.

Within the Word

Lazarus, a Pivotal Figure

What would it be like to be raised from the dead only to have to suffer death again? Some people who have undergone near-death experiences claim that it transformed their entire attitude. They no longer feared death. The story of Lazarus that we hear on the fifth Sunday of Lent is a biblical case in point. What must Lazarus have thought when Jesus called him out of the tomb in a shocking display of power over death? Was he grateful? Afraid? Upset? His resuscitation, after all, was only temporary. He would have to submit to death once more in order to gain "eternal life" (John 10:28).

The story of Lazarus, whose name means "God helps," is found only in John's Gospel (11:1–12:11). It is, in fact, a pivotal narrative. It is the sixth and last great "sign" (the Johannine expression for *miracle*) that concludes the "Book of Signs" (1:19–12:50). The Lazarus narrative leads to the "Book of Glory" (chaps. 13–20), which climaxes in the greatest sign of all, Jesus' own resurrection (not resuscitation) from the dead. The text of the Lazarus story is fraught with Johannine drama and irony. Lazarus's being raised from the dead ironically leads to the plot to kill Jesus, who has the audacity to speak and act in the name of his heavenly Father—and Lazarus is targeted at the same time (12:10)!

What are we to make of this marvelous account as Lent proceeds towards the climax of Easter, the feast of the resurrection? Although the lengthy narrative is rich in detail, three features stand out. First, the text emphasizes that Jesus *loved*

Lazarus. Jesus was indeed a close friend of this family—Lazarus and his sisters Martha and Mary—who lived in Bethany, near Jerusalem. When Lazarus fell gravely ill, Martha pleaded with Jesus to come and heal him. For seemingly mysterious reasons, Jesus dallies and arrives too late. Lazarus is already in the tomb four days, an indication in the Jewish culture of the day that he was truly dead.

Enter the second feature—the profound emotional dimensions of the text. A series of Greek verbs (vv. 33-35, 38) emphasize the deep emotions this death evokes. Jesus himself "became perturbed and deeply troubled," and he "wept," so that even his Jewish opponents remark, "See how he loved him" (v. 36). Paradoxically, in the gospel that most emphasizes Jesus' divinity, this text displays his true participation in our humanity. Jesus is touched by human suffering and shows the depth of his own humanness.

Finally, we see the true purpose of the story. It is not so much about *death* but *life*. When Lazarus emerges from the tomb, Jesus commands, "Untie him and let him go" (v. 44). In Jesus, death cannot bind humanity. Lazarus's death is an opportunity for Jesus to manifest without a doubt that he, and he alone, is "the resurrection and the life" (v. 25). It is a validation of what the gospel has been claiming all along: Jesus is the Messiah, the Son of God, who holds the power to give "eternal life" to all who would embrace his call (v. 27).

Yes, Lazarus had to experience death again, as we all must. But our Easter faith tells us it is not the final word.

—Fr. Ronald D. Witherup

Ronald D. Witherup, PSS, is former Superior General of the Sulpicians. He is author of numerous books, including Paul: Proclaiming Christ Crucified *in the* Alive in the Word *series and* Galatians: Life in the New Creation.

Monday, March 27

Morning

O Lord, open my lips.
And my mouth will proclaim your praise.

(opt. hymn, pp. 360–65)

PSALM 103:1-5, 11-14
Bless the LORD, O my soul,
and all within me, the holy name of God.
Bless the LORD, O my soul,
and never forget all God's benefits.

It is the Lord who forgives all your sins,
who heals every one of your ills,
who redeems your life from the grave,
who crowns you with love and compassion,
who fills your life with good things,
renewing your youth like an eagle's.

For as the heavens are high above the earth,
so strong the mercy for those who fear God.
As far as the east is from the west,
so far from us does God remove our transgressions.

As a father has compassion on his children,
divine compassion is on those who fear the LORD,
who knows of what we are made,
who remembers that we are dust.

Glory to the Father . . .

SCRIPTURE   Deuteronomy 19:15-19

One witness alone shall not stand against someone in
regard to any crime or any offense that may have been

committed; a charge shall stand only on the testimony of two or three witnesses.

If a hostile witness rises against someone to accuse that person of wrongdoing, the two parties in the dispute shall appear in the presence of the LORD, in the presence of the priests and judges in office at that time, and the judges must investigate it thoroughly. If the witness is a false witness and has falsely accused the other, you shall do to the false witness just as that false witness planned to do to the other. Thus shall you purge the evil from your midst.

READ, PONDER, PRAY on a word or phrase from these readings or another of today's Scriptures (*Lectio Divina*, p. 359)

ANTIPHON
Susanna was saved from the lies of false witnesses.

CANTICLE OF ZECHARIAH *(inside front cover)*

INTERCESSIONS
Loving God, you fill our life with good things. With grateful hearts we pray: ℟. **Show us mercy, O God.**

Give justice to those who are falsely accused. ℟.

Inspire efforts to cultivate cures and immunizations for contagious diseases. ℟.

Sensitize us to the rhythm and patterns of the natural world, and kindle in us a deep connection with all of creation. ℟.

Our Father . . .

May God lead us from death to life, from falsehood to truth, from hate to love, through Jesus, our peace. Amen.

Blessed Among Us

St. John of Egypt
Hermit (ca. 304–394)

St. John was one of the most famous of the early desert fathers, and his ascetic exploits were honored by many saints, including Augustine, Jerome, and John Cassian. He spent his early life as a carpenter before receiving a call to a life of prayer and solitude. He then apprenticed himself to an elderly monk who trained his capacity for obedience by forcing him to perform seemingly ridiculous exercises, like faithfully watering a dead twig or moving heavy rocks from one place to another.

Upon his master's death, John set out for the desert wilderness. From a cave he constructed a cell in which he walled himself in, except for a window through which he received donations of food. He received visitors only on Saturdays and Sundays. The other days he spent in prayer. Pilgrims flocked to see him, drawn by his renowned gifts of prophecy, healing, and the ability to read people's souls. Even the emperor sent messengers to receive his wisdom.

John spent over forty years in this life. At the age of ninety, when he sensed that his end was near, he closed his window and instructed that no one disturb him for three days. At the conclusion of that period, he was found to have expired while kneeling in prayer.

"Am I a saint, or a prophet like God's true servants? I am a sinful and weak man. . . . Live always in the fear of God, and never forget his benefits."

—St. John of Egypt

Mass

Monday of the Fifth Week of Lent *

* The following readings may be used on any day this week, especially in
Years B and C when the Gospel of Lazarus is not read on the Fifth
Sunday of Lent: 2 Kgs 4:18b-21, 32-37; John 11:1-45.

Entrance Antiphon   Cf. Psalm 56 (55):2

Have mercy on me, O God, for people assail me; / they
fight me all day long and oppress me.

Collect

O God, by whose wondrous grace
we are enriched with every blessing,
grant us so to pass from former ways to newness of life,
that we may be made ready for the glory of the heavenly
    Kingdom.
Through our Lord Jesus Christ, your Son,
who lives and reigns with you in the unity of the Holy Spirit,
God, for ever and ever.

A reading from the Book of the Prophet Daniel

13:41c-62 (Longer Form, 13:1-9, 15-17, 19-30, 33-62)

*Here I am about to die, though I have
done none of the things charged against me.*

The assembly condemned Susanna to death.

But Susanna cried aloud: "O eternal God, you know
what is hidden and are aware of all things before they come
to be: you know that they have testified falsely against me.
Here I am about to die, though I have done none of the
things with which these wicked men have charged me."

The Lord heard her prayer. As she was being led to exe-
cution, God stirred up the holy spirit of a young boy named
Daniel, and he cried aloud: "I will have no part in the death

of this woman." All the people turned and asked him, "What is this you are saying?" He stood in their midst and continued, "Are you such fools, O children of Israel! To condemn a woman of Israel without examination and without clear evidence? Return to court, for they have testified falsely against her."

Then all the people returned in haste. To Daniel the elders said, "Come, sit with us and inform us, since God has given you the prestige of old age." But he replied, "Separate these two far from each other that I may examine them."

After they were separated one from the other, he called one of them and said: "How you have grown evil with age! Now have your past sins come to term: passing unjust sentences, condemning the innocent, and freeing the guilty, although the Lord says, 'The innocent and the just you shall not put to death.' Now, then, if you were a witness, tell me under what tree you saw them together." "Under a mastic tree," he answered. Daniel replied, "Your fine lie has cost you your head, for the angel of God shall receive the sentence from him and split you in two." Putting him to one side, he ordered the other one to be brought. Daniel said to him, "Offspring of Canaan, not of Judah, beauty has seduced you, lust has subverted your conscience. This is how you acted with the daughters of Israel, and in their fear they yielded to you; but a daughter of Judah did not tolerate your wickedness. Now, then, tell me under what tree you surprised them together." "Under an oak," he said. Daniel replied, "Your fine lie has cost you also your head, for the angel of God waits with a sword to cut you in two so as to make an end of you both."

The whole assembly cried aloud, blessing God who saves those who hope in him. They rose up against the two elders, for by their own words Daniel had convicted them of perjury. According to the law of Moses, they inflicted on them the penalty they had plotted to impose on their neighbor: they put them to death. Thus was innocent blood spared that day.

The word of the Lord.

RESPONSORIAL PSALM   23:1-3a, 3b-4, 5, 6

R̸. (4ab) **Even though I walk in the dark valley I fear no evil; for you are at my side.**

The LORD is my shepherd; I shall not want.
  In verdant pastures he gives me repose;
Beside restful waters he leads me;
  he refreshes my soul. R̸.

He guides me in right paths
  for his name's sake.
Even though I walk in the dark valley
  I fear no evil; for you are at my side
With your rod and your staff
  that give me courage. R̸.

You spread the table before me
  in the sight of my foes;
You anoint my head with oil;
  my cup overflows. R̸.

Only goodness and kindness follow me
  all the days of my life;
And I shall dwell in the house of the LORD
  for years to come. R̸.

GOSPEL ACCLAMATION   Ezekiel 33:11

I take no pleasure in the death of the wicked man, says
    the Lord,
but rather in his conversion, that he may live.

A reading from the holy Gospel according to John   8:1-11

Let the person without sin be the first to throw a stone.

Jesus went to the Mount of Olives. But early in the morning he arrived again in the temple area, and all the people started coming to him, and he sat down and taught them. Then the scribes and the Pharisees brought a woman who had been caught in adultery and made her stand in the middle. They said to him, "Teacher, this woman was caught in the very act of committing adultery. Now in the law, Moses commanded us to stone such women. So what do you say?" They said this to test him, so that they could have some charge to bring against him. Jesus bent down and began to write on the ground with his finger. But when they continued asking him, he straightened up and said to them, "Let the one among you who is without sin be the first to throw a stone at her." Again he bent down and wrote on the ground. And in response, they went away one by one, beginning with the elders. So he was left alone with the woman before him. Then Jesus straightened up and said to her, "Woman, where are they? Has no one condemned you?" She replied, "No one, sir." Then Jesus said, "Neither do I condemn you. Go, and from now on do not sin any more."
The Gospel of the Lord.

Prayer over the Offerings
Grant, we pray, O Lord,
that, preparing to celebrate the holy mysteries,
we may bring before you as the fruit of bodily penance
a joyful purity of heart.
Through Christ our Lord.

Communion Antiphon

When the Gospel of the Adulterous Woman is read: John 8:10-11

**Has no one condemned you, woman? No one, Lord. /
Neither shall I condemn you. From now on, sin no more.**

When another Gospel is read: John 8:12

**I am the light of the world, says the Lord; / whoever
follows me will not walk in the darkness,. / but will have
the light of life.**

Prayer after Communion

**Strengthened by the blessing of your Sacraments, we pray,
    O Lord,
that through them we may constantly be cleansed of
    our faults
and, by following Christ,
hasten our steps upward toward you.
Through Christ our Lord.**

Reflection

Resisting the Mob

In the swirl of their shouting crowds, today's readings exemplify the need for integrity to resist the mob. And the mob is calling for blood.

One way to view these stories is to see in them an exemplar of integrity: an image of a single person standing resolute in opposition to the braying populace, unbowed, a spine of steel. But in these two narratives about a lone woman faced with a mob, a more complex narrative emerges. Justice is rendered not by *fiat* but by insightful social leveraging. These stories are the product of a complex cultural lineage, certainly told many times before. The authors could have chosen to sharpen things up, to make a point more clearly, to clean up the edges.

Yet they didn't. Daniel steps forward, and engages skillfully with the judges. Jesus imposes a moment of reflection, and turns the issue back to the crowd. Each account charts the rushing river of a complex social movement—its headlong stampede fueled by righteous indignation—as it suddenly changes course. One new element shifts the whole frame.

The call of integrity can reasonably lead us to ignore the crowd, delete the app, and turn toward who we really are, the core of our being. There is value to this. But the layers of Scripture push back at any sense that virtue emerges only from isolation, as if our "true self" is an individual untouched by commerce with others.

"Reading the room" is not customarily cited as an element of virtue. In these stories, however, it is decisive, suggesting a wider horizon for the divine judgment than we may have imagined, as God tenderly "reads the room" of our hearts.

Nancy Dallavalle

Nancy Dallavalle is associate professor of religious studies at Fairfield University in Fairfield, Connecticut.

Evening

God, come to my assistance.
Lord, make haste to help me.

(opt. hymn, pp. 360–65)

PSALM 34:12-19
Come, children, and hear me,
that I may teach you the fear of the LORD.
Who is eager for life
and longs to see prosperous days?

Guard your tongue from evil,
and your lips from speaking deceit.
Turn aside from evil and do good.
Seek after peace, and pursue it.

The eyes of the LORD are on the righteous;
God's ears are open to their cry.
The LORD's face is turned against the wicked
to cut off their remembrance from the earth.

When the righteous cry out, the LORD hears,
and rescues them in all their distress.
The LORD is close to the brokenhearted,
and saves those whose spirit is crushed.

Glory to the Father . . .

SCRIPTURE   James 4:11-12
Do not speak evil of one another. . . . Whoever speaks evil of a brother or judges his brother speaks evil of the law and judges the law. If you judge the law, you are not a doer of the law but a judge. There is one lawgiver and judge who is able to save or to destroy. Who then are you to judge your neighbor?

READ, PONDER, PRAY on a word or phrase from these readings or another of today's Scriptures (*Lectio Divina*, p. 359)

ANTIPHON

Those who condemned the woman went away one by one.

CANTICLE OF MARY *(inside back cover)*

INTERCESSIONS

Compassionate God, you are wisdom and truth. In hope we pray: R̸. Gracious God, hear our prayer.

Broaden and prosper our efforts to stop human trafficking. R̸.

Heal those who continue to suffer from COVID-19 and the pandemic. R̸.

Safeguard public transportation personnel and all travelers. R̸.

Our Father . . .

May God bless us with every gift of the Spirit so we may seek peace and pursue it, now and always. Amen.

Tuesday, March 28

Morning

O Lord, open my lips.
And my mouth will proclaim your praise.

(opt. hymn, pp. 360–65)

PSALM 5:2-6, 12-13
To my words give ear, O LORD;
give heed to my sighs.
Attend to the sound of my cry,
my Sovereign and my God.

To you do I pray, O LORD.
In the morning you hear my voice;
in the morning I plead and watch before you.

You are no God who delights in evil;
no sinner is your guest.
The boastful shall not stand before your eyes.

All who take refuge in you shall be glad,
and ever cry out their joy.
You shelter them; in you they rejoice,
those who love your name.
It is you who bless the righteous, O LORD,
you surround them with your favor like a shield.

Glory to the Father . . .

SCRIPTURE   Ecclesiastes 7:8-10, 13-14
Better is the end of a thing than its beginning; / better
is a patient spirit than a lofty one. / Do not let anger
upset your spirit, / for anger lodges in the bosom of a fool.
   Do not say: How is it that former times were better than
these? For it is not out of wisdom that you ask about this.

Consider the work of God. Who can make straight what God has made crooked? On a good day enjoy good things, and on an evil day consider: Both the one and the other God has made, so that no one may find the least fault with him.

READ, PONDER, PRAY on a word or phrase from these readings or another of today's Scriptures (*Lectio Divina*, p. 359)

ANTIPHON
The people complained against God and against Moses.

CANTICLE OF ZECHARIAH *(inside front cover)*

INTERCESSIONS
Sovereign God, you surround us with favor like a shield. In trust we pray: R̂. God, hear our prayer.

Help us to share our support and joy with those who are preparing to receive the sacraments of initiation. R̂.

Give journalists, reporters, and social media personnel perseverance, honesty, and good zeal for communicating the truth. R̂.

Lead juries, judges, and lawmakers to rule with impartiality and right judgment. R̂.

Our Father . . .

May God lead us along the everlasting way by the light of Christ and the aid of the Holy Spirit. Amen.

Blessed Among Us

Moses
Liberator and Mystic

At the heart of the Exodus, the foundational story of Israel, lies the figure of Moses, one of the great and mysterious characters in the Bible. In his *Life of Moses*, St. Gregory of Nyssa reads this story as a symbolic treatise on mystical prayer. More recently, liberation theologians have fastened on the social and political dimensions of the Exodus. Moses is the paradigmatic liberator, the human agent of God's desire to bring people out of bondage. Perhaps he was both—mystic and liberator.

What is certain is that Moses' role in the Exodus is rooted in his unique relationship with God. In their first encounter, God speaks to him from the midst of a burning bush and reveals himself as one who hears the cry of the oppressed. Moses' mission is inseparable from his intimate communion with the Lord, with whom he would speak "face to face, as a man speaks to his friend." Later mystics were fascinated by the information that Moses entered into a cloud to speak with God—an image familiar in the annals of mystical literature. But in the end, the significant issue is not that God spoke to Moses; it matters what was said. The topic was not simply God's glory but the liberation of the oppressed. Thus, Moses reflects the essential fusion of the mystical and the political.

After forty years in the wilderness, Moses lived only to look over the Promised Land from the heights of Mt. Nebo. There he died alone, and there the Lord performed the last rites of friendship by burying Moses in a secret place.

"Thus says the Lord, the God of Israel, 'Let my people go.'"

—Moses, speaking to Pharaoh (Exodus 5:1)

Mass
Tuesday of the Fifth Week of Lent

ENTRANCE ANTIPHON　　　　　　　　　　　　Psalm 27 (26):14

Wait for the Lord; be strong; / be stouthearted, and wait for the Lord!

COLLECT

Grant us, we pray, O Lord,
perseverance in obeying your will,
that in our days the people dedicated to your service
may grow in both merit and number.
Through our Lord Jesus Christ, your Son,
who lives and reigns with you in the unity of the Holy Spirit,
God, for ever and ever.

A reading from the Book of Numbers　　　　　21:4-9

Whoever looks at the bronze serpent, shall live.

From Mount Hor the children of Israel set out on the Red Sea road, to bypass the land of Edom. But with their patience worn out by the journey, the people complained against God and Moses, "Why have you brought us up from Egypt to die in this desert, where there is no food or water? We are disgusted with this wretched food!"

In punishment the LORD sent among the people saraph serpents, which bit the people so that many of them died. Then the people came to Moses and said, "We have sinned in complaining against the LORD and you. Pray the LORD to take the serpents away from us." So Moses prayed for the people, and the LORD said to Moses, "Make a saraph and mount it on a pole, and whoever looks at it after being bitten will live." Moses accordingly made a bronze serpent and mounted it on a pole, and whenever anyone who had been bitten by a serpent looked at the bronze serpent, he lived. The word of the Lord.

RESPONSORIAL PSALM 102:2-3, 16-18, 19-21

R℣. (2) O Lord, hear my prayer, and let my cry come to you.

O LORD, hear my prayer,
  and let my cry come to you.
Hide not your face from me
  in the day of my distress.
Incline your ear to me;
  in the day when I call, answer me speedily. R℣.

The nations shall revere your name, O LORD,
  and all the kings of the earth your glory,
When the LORD has rebuilt Zion
  and appeared in his glory;
When he has regarded the prayer of the destitute,
  and not despised their prayer. R℣.

Let this be written for the generation to come,
  and let his future creatures praise the LORD:
"The LORD looked down from his holy height,
  from heaven he beheld the earth,
To hear the groaning of the prisoners,
  to release those doomed to die." R℣.

GOSPEL ACCLAMATION
The seed is the word of God, Christ is the sower;
all who come to him will live for ever.

A reading from the holy Gospel according to John 8:21-30

When you have lifted up the Son of Man,
then you will know that I am he.

Jesus said to the Pharisees: "I am going away and you
will look for me, but you will die in your sin. Where I
am going you cannot come." So the Jews said, "He is not
going to kill himself, is he, because he said, 'Where I am
going you cannot come'?" He said to them, "You belong to

what is below, I belong to what is above. You belong to this world, but I do not belong to this world. That is why I told you that you will die in your sins. For if you do not believe that I AM, you will die in your sins." So they said to him, "Who are you?" Jesus said to them, "What I told you from the beginning. I have much to say about you in condemnation. But the one who sent me is true, and what I heard from him I tell the world." They did not realize that he was speaking to them of the Father. So Jesus said to them, "When you lift up the Son of Man, then you will realize that I AM, and that I do nothing on my own, but I say only what the Father taught me. The one who sent me is with me. He has not left me alone, because I always do what is pleasing to him." Because he spoke this way, many came to believe in him.

The Gospel of the Lord.

PRAYER OVER THE OFFERINGS

We offer you, O Lord, the sacrifice of conciliation,
that, being moved to compassion,
you may both pardon our offenses
and direct our wavering hearts.
Through Christ our Lord.

COMMUNION ANTIPHON   John 12:32

When I am lifted up from the earth, / I will draw all to myself, says the Lord.

PRAYER AFTER COMMUNION

Grant, we pray, almighty God,
that, ever seeking what is divine,
we may always be worthy
to approach these heavenly gifts.
Through Christ our Lord.

Reflection

The One Who Sends Us Is With Us

What is God's I Am? On one occasion a teacher asked a class of high-school students, "If you had the power to make God cease to be God, what would you remove?" One of the students responded, "I would remove God's longing to be with others." Did the young man realize that what he would remove from God is the name Isaiah gave to God, "Emmanuel," which means "God is with us"?

God's "with-ness" is God's I Am-ness. Notice what God said to Moses: "I AM sent me to you" (Exod 3:14). Examine the implications! In the act of creation, God endowed human nature with that same I Am-ness which is God's I AM. We are created in the image and likeness of God, and we bear God's propensity to be sent and to be with. This is how we are the image and likeness of God. This solidarity with God and others demands that we serve God by being with others in their needs, to be "I AM" for others.

. . . Our salvation is to follow this way of God that was marked out for us by Jesus, who "though he was in the form of God . . . did not deem equality with God something to be grasped at" (Phil 2:6).

The mind is boggled! The Son of God externally surrenders his triune with-ness that he might be God's I AM with all men and women. Service to others, then, is the way we empty ourselves—and it is this service that becomes our salvation because it is our freedom to share the I AM of God with others.

Msgr. John J. McIlhon, adapted from *Forty Days Plus Three*

John J. McIlhon (1922–2006) was a priest of the Diocese of Des Moines and served as a retreat director, teacher, hospital chaplain, and pastor.

Evening

God, come to my assistance.
Lord, make haste to help me.

(opt. hymn, pp. 360–65)

PSALM 99:1-2, 5-9

The LORD is king; the peoples tremble.
God is enthroned on the cherubim; earth quakes.
The LORD is great in Zion,
exalted over all the peoples.

Exalt the LORD our God;
bow down before God's footstool,
for the Lord our God is holy!

Among God's priests were Aaron and Moses;
among those who invoked God's name was Samuel.
They cried out to the LORD, who answered.

To them the Lord spoke in the pillar of cloud.
They obeyed the decrees and the statutes
which the Lord had given them.

O LORD our God, you answered them.
For them you were a God who forgives,
and yet you punished their offenses.

Exalt the LORD our God;
bow down before the holy mountain,
for the LORD our God is holy.

Glory to the Father . . .

SCRIPTURE   2 Corinthians 4:13-16

Since, then, we have the same spirit of faith, according
to what is written, "I believed, therefore I spoke," we
too believe and therefore speak, knowing that the one who

raised the Lord Jesus will raise us also with Jesus and place us with you in his presence. Everything indeed is for you, so that the grace bestowed in abundance on more and more people may cause the thanksgiving to overflow for the glory of God.

Therefore, we are not discouraged; rather, although our outer self is wasting away, our inner self is being renewed day by day.

READ, PONDER, PRAY on a word or phrase from these readings or another of today's Scriptures (*Lectio Divina*, p. 359)

ANTIPHON
The one who sent me is true, and what I heard from him I tell the world.

CANTICLE OF MARY *(inside back cover)*

INTERCESSIONS
God of mystery, heaven and earth tremble in your presence. In awe we pray: R̷. **God, incline your ear to us.**

Sow in the hearts of all people a deep respect for life at all its stages, from conception to death. R̷.

Safeguard all who are without safe shelter and all who work through the night. R̷.

Uphold those who experience difficulty in their transition toward less independence. R̷.

Our Father . . .

May God guide us by the light of the Word, and fill our hearts with the peace of Christ, now and forever. Amen.

Wednesday, March 29

Morning

O Lord, open my lips.
And my mouth will proclaim your praise.

(opt. hymn, pp. 360–65)

PSALM 147:1, 5-11
How good to sing psalms to our God;
how pleasant to chant fitting praise!

Our Lord is great and almighty;
God's wisdom can never be measured.
The LORD lifts up the lowly,
and casts down the wicked to the ground.
O sing to the LORD, giving thanks;
sing psalms to our God with the lyre.

The Lord covers the heavens with clouds;
and prepares the rain for the earth,
making mountains sprout with grass,
and plants to serve human needs.

God provides the cattle with their food,
and what young ravens call for.
The Lord's delight is not in the strength of horses,
nor God's pleasure in a warrior's stride.
The LORD delights in those who revere him,
those who wait for God's faithful love.

Glory to the Father . . .

SCRIPTURE   2 Maccabees 7:20, 22-23

Most admirable and worthy of everlasting remembrance
was the mother who, seeing her seven sons perish in
a single day, bore it courageously because of her hope in

the Lord. "I do not know how you came to be in my womb; it was not I who gave you breath and life, nor was it I who arranged the elements you are made of. Therefore, since it is the Creator of the universe who shaped the beginning of humankind and brought about the origin of everything, he, in his mercy, will give you back both breath and life, because you now disregard yourselves for the sake of his law."

READ, PONDER, PRAY on a word or phrase from these readings or another of today's Scriptures (*Lectio Divina*, p. 359)

ANTIPHON

Blessed be those who yielded their bodies to martyrdom rather than serve any false god.

CANTICLE OF ZECHARIAH *(inside front cover)*

INTERCESSIONS

Tenderhearted God, you lift up the lowly and heal the brokenhearted. In trust we pray: R͡. Renew us by your Spirit, O God.

You bring back exiles: watch over refugees, migrants, and those exiled from their home. R͡.

You delight in those who revere you: inspire us to practice greater charity and deeper prayer. R͡.

You satisfy those who wait for your merciful love: fulfill the hopes of those who seek healing or a new beginning. R͡.

Our Father . . .

May God give us the grace to know Jesus more intimately and to call upon the name of the Lord, by the power of the Holy Spirit. Amen.

Blessed Among Us

Marc Chagall
Artist (1887–1985)

Marc Chagall was born to a Hasidic Jewish family in a town in Belarus, part of the Russian Empire. Determined to become an artist, he moved to Paris, where his distinctive style drew on various modernist influences. His work was marked by recurring dreamlike images of his homeland—rural villages filled with floating cows, fiddlers, roosters, and weddings. After travels in Palestine, biblical images also entered his work. In 1938, following the Kristallnacht pogrom in Germany, Chagall painted his "White Crucifixion," depicting Jesus on the cross, clothed with a Jewish prayer shawl as a loincloth, and surrounded by scenes of Jewish persecution. This painting, which is apparently a favorite of Pope Francis, not only emphasizes the Jewishness of Jesus but relates the crucifixion to the contemporary passion of the Jews and the ongoing suffering of humanity. Christ, for Chagall, symbolized "the true type of the Jewish martyr." And as the Holocaust unfolded, the number of martyrs swelled beyond imagination.

Chagall and his wife managed to escape to New York in 1941. His wife died two years later. After the war he returned to France, where he became one of the most celebrated and beloved artists of his time. The visual symbols of his lost village in Belarus—of suffering, love, work, and hope—became the common treasury of humanity. He died on March 28, 1985.

"For me Christ is a great poet, the master whose poetry is already forgotten by the modern world."

—Marc Chagall

Mass
Wednesday of the Fifth Week of Lent

ENTRANCE ANTIPHON   Cf. Psalm 18 (17):48-49

My deliverer from angry nations, you set me above my
assailants; / you saved me from the violent man, O Lord.

COLLECT

Enlighten, O God of compassion,
the hearts of your children, sanctified by penance,
and in your kindness
grant those you stir to a sense of devotion
a gracious hearing when they cry out to you.
Through our Lord Jesus Christ, your Son,
who lives and reigns with you in the unity of the Holy Spirit,
God, for ever and ever.

A reading from the Book of the Prophet Daniel

3:14-20, 91-92, 95

The Lord has sent his angel to deliver his servants.

King Nebuchadnezzar said: "Is it true, Shadrach,
Meshach, and Abednego, that you will not serve my
god, or worship the golden statue that I set up? Be ready
now to fall down and worship the statue I had made, whenever you hear the sound of the trumpet, flute, lyre, harp,
psaltery, bagpipe, and all the other musical instruments;
otherwise, you shall be instantly cast into the white-hot
furnace; and who is the God who can deliver you out of my
hands?" Shadrach, Meshach, and Abednego answered King
Nebuchadnezzar, "There is no need for us to defend ourselves before you in this matter. If our God, whom we serve,
can save us from the white-hot furnace and from your
hands, O king, may he save us! But even if he will not, know,
O king, that we will not serve your god or worship the
golden statue that you set up."

King Nebuchadnezzar's face became livid with utter rage against Shadrach, Meshach, and Abednego. He ordered the furnace to be heated seven times more than usual and had some of the strongest men in his army bind Shadrach, Meshach, and Abednego and cast them into the white-hot furnace.

Nebuchadnezzar rose in haste and asked his nobles, "Did we not cast three men bound into the fire?" "Assuredly, O king," they answered. "But," he replied, "I see four men unfettered and unhurt, walking in the fire, and the fourth looks like a son of God." Nebuchadnezzar exclaimed, "Blessed be the God of Shadrach, Meshach, and Abednego, who sent his angel to deliver the servants who trusted in him; they disobeyed the royal command and yielded their bodies rather than serve or worship any god except their own God."

The word of the Lord.

RESPONSORIAL PSALM   Daniel 3:52, 53, 54, 55, 56

R℣. (52b) **Glory and praise for ever!**

"Blessed are you, O Lord, the God of our fathers,
    praiseworthy and exalted above all forever;
And blessed is your holy and glorious name,
    praiseworthy and exalted above all for all ages." R℣.

"Blessed are you in the temple of your holy glory,
    praiseworthy and exalted above all forever." R℣.

"Blessed are you on the throne of your Kingdom,
    praiseworthy and exalted above all forever." R℣.

"Blessed are you who look into the depths
    from your throne upon the cherubim;
    praiseworthy and exalted above all forever." R℣.

"Blessed are you in the firmament of heaven,
   praiseworthy and glorious forever." ℟.

GOSPEL ACCLAMATION   See Luke 8:15
Blessed are they who have kept the word with a generous
   heart
and yield a harvest through perseverance.

A reading from the holy Gospel according to John   8:31-42

If the Son makes you free, you will be free indeed.

Jesus said to those Jews who believed in him, "If you
remain in my word, you will truly be my disciples, and
you will know the truth, and the truth will set you free."
They answered him, "We are descendants of Abraham and
have never been enslaved to anyone. How can you say, 'You
will become free'?" Jesus answered them, "Amen, amen,
I say to you, everyone who commits sin is a slave of sin.
A slave does not remain in a household forever, but a son
always remains. So if the Son frees you, then you will truly
be free. I know that you are descendants of Abraham. But
you are trying to kill me, because my word has no room
among you. I tell you what I have seen in the Father's presence; then do what you have heard from the Father."

They answered and said to him, "Our father is Abraham."
Jesus said to them, "If you were Abraham's children, you
would be doing the works of Abraham. But now you are
trying to kill me, a man who has told you the truth that I
heard from God; Abraham did not do this. You are doing
the works of your father!" So they said to him, "We were
not born of fornication. We have one Father, God." Jesus
said to them, "If God were your Father, you would love me,
for I came from God and am here; I did not come on my
own, but he sent me."

The Gospel of the Lord.

PRAYER OVER THE OFFERINGS

**Receive back, O Lord, these sacrificial offerings,
which you have given to be offered
to the honor of your name,
and grant that they may become remedies for our
　　healing.
Through Christ our Lord.**

COMMUNION ANTIPHON　　　　　　　　　Colossians 1:13-14

**God has brought us to the kingdom of his beloved Son, /
in whom we have redemption through his Blood, / the
forgiveness of sins.**

PRAYER AFTER COMMUNION

**May the mysteries we have received, O Lord,
bring us heavenly medicine,
that they may purge all evil from our heart
and strengthen us with eternal protection.
Through Christ our Lord.**

Reflection

Enriched by Communion

If you remain in my word, you will truly be my disciples.

In the very moment when God experiences human mortality,
his human nature reaches the divine. . . . Living the word
and imitating Mary are two other key points of the spirituality
of unity.

Those who live the word give witness to the fact that the
authentic person is simple and because simple, he or she is
also free. All forms of attachment, whether to self or to things,

destroy the self, fragment it, both because attachments nurture pride and self-satisfaction and because they fabricate that "false self" which psychologists call the ego.

The problem people face today is the need to rebuild an integrated self, freeing it from the propensities of the ego, that is to say, freeing it from all forms of greed and possessiveness. For the one who has an integrated self knows how to empty the self, to strip self of everything in order to be enriched by communion with others.

And this is precisely what the gospel teaches.

Mary is the icon of this self-emptying, above all in her desolation at the feet of her crucified son whom she loses. But into that immense emptiness enter all the children of God.

And at the end, unity.

Chiara Lubich, *Essential Writings*

Chiara Lubich (1920–2008), an internationally known religious leader and writer, was the founder of the Focolare, a movement that includes people of all ages, races, and vocations who promote unity, reconciliation, and the spirit of love.

Evening

God, come to my assistance.
Lord, make haste to help me.

(opt. hymn, pp. 360–65)

PSALM 113

Praise, O servants of the LORD,
praise the name of the LORD!
May the name of the LORD be blest
both now and forevermore!
From the rising of the sun to its setting,
praised be the name of the LORD!

High above all nations is the LORD,
above the heavens God's glory.
Who is like the LORD, our God,
who dwells on high,
who stoops from the heights to look down
upon heaven and earth?

From the dust the Lord lifts up the lowly,
from the ash heap raises the poor,
to set them in the company of leaders,
yes, with the leaders of the people.
To the childless wife God gives a home
as a joyful mother of children.

Glory to the Father . . .

SCRIPTURE   Hebrews 1:2-5

In these last days, [God] spoke to us through a son, whom
he made heir of all things and through whom he created
the universe, / who is the refulgence of his glory, / the very
imprint of his being, / and who sustains all things by his
mighty word. / When he had accomplished purification

from sins, / he took his seat at the right hand of the Majesty on high, / as far superior to the angels / as the name he has inherited is more excellent than theirs.

For to which of the angels did God ever say: / "You are my son; this day I have begotten you"? / Or again: / "I will be a father to him, and he shall be a son to me"?

READ, PONDER, PRAY on a word or phrase from these readings or another of today's Scriptures (*Lectio Divina*, p. 359)

ANTIPHON

I came from God and am here; I did not come on my own, but he sent me.

CANTICLE OF MARY *(inside back cover)*

INTERCESSIONS

Ever-present God, you are praised from the rising of the sun to its setting. In faith we pray: R̟. **Holy God, hear our prayer.**

For engaged and newly married couples: strengthen them to grow daily in respect, reverence, and love for one another, we pray: R̟.

For those who are in need of a companion, friend, or mentor: lead them to experience your unconditional love and find welcome in the Church, we pray: R̟.

For those who are anxious or fear death: give them the peace of Christ that casts out all fear, we pray: R̟.

Our Father . . .

May the Lord bless us, fill us with peace, and lead us to the knowledge of God's glory in the face of Jesus Christ. Amen.

Thursday, March 30

Morning

O Lord, open my lips.
And my mouth will proclaim your praise.

(opt. hymn, pp. 360–65)

PSALM 25:12-18, 21-22

Who are they that fear the LORD?
God will show them the path to choose.
Their souls shall live in happiness,
and their descendants shall possess the land.
The friendship of the LORD is for those who fear God;
to them is revealed the covenant.

My eyes are always on the LORD,
who rescues my feet from the snare.
Turn to me and have mercy on me,
for I am alone and poor.

Relieve the anguish of my heart,
and set me free from my distress.
See my lowliness and suffering,
and take away all my sins.

May integrity and virtue protect me,
for I have hoped in you, O LORD.
Grant redemption to Israel, O God,
from all its distress.

Glory to the Father . . .

SCRIPTURE   Amos 8:11-12

See, days are coming—oracle of the Lord GOD— / when
I will send a famine upon the land: / Not a hunger for

bread, or a thirst for water, / but for hearing the word of the
LORD. / They shall stagger from sea to sea / and wander from
north to east / In search of the word of the LORD, / but they
shall not find it.

READ, PONDER, PRAY on a word or phrase from these readings or
another of today's Scriptures (*Lectio Divina*, p. 359)

ANTIPHON
Whoever keeps my word shall never see death.

CANTICLE OF ZECHARIAH *(inside front cover)*

INTERCESSIONS
**God of wondrous deeds, through Jesus you have given
us all things. In faith we pray: R̂. God, in your kindness,
hear our prayer.**

**You rescue our feet from the snare: free the people of
Ukraine and all places where oppression, war, and
injustice rage. R̂.**

**You relieve the anguish of our hearts: help us to heal
divisions in families, communities, and within the
human race. R̂.**

**You free us from our distress: give solace and peace to
those who grieve or are long-suffering. R̂.**

Our Father . . .

**May integrity and virtue protect us, by the power and
mercy of God, in the name of the Father, the Son, and the
Holy Spirit. Amen.**

Blessed Among Us

Servant of God Thea Bowman
African American Franciscan (1937–1990)

Thea Bowman was one of the great treasures of the American Catholic Church. Ablaze with the spirit of love, the memory of struggle, and a faith in God's promises, she impressed her audiences not just with her message but with the nobility of her spirit.

Born in rural Mississippi, she converted to Catholicism while attending parochial school. Later, as a Franciscan nun, she found herself the only African American in a White religious order. But she had no desire to "blend in." She believed her identity as a Black woman entailed a special vocation. She believed the Church must make room for the spiritual traditions of African Americans, including the memory of slavery, but also the spirit of hope and resistance reflected in the spirituals, the importance of family, community, celebration, and remembrance.

She was a spellbinding speaker who preached the Gospel to audiences across the land, including the U.S. bishops. After being diagnosed with incurable cancer, she bore a different kind of witness. She continued to travel and speak, even from her wheelchair. To her other gifts to the Church she added the witness of her courage and trust in God. "I don't make sense of suffering. I try to make sense of life," she said. "I try each day to see God's will." She died on March 30, 1990, at the age of fifty-two. Her cause for canonization is in process.

"What does it mean to be Black and Catholic? It means that I come to my church fully functioning. I bring myself, my Black self, all that I am, all that I have, all that I hope to become."

—Servant of God Thea Bowman

Mass

Thursday of the Fifth Week of Lent

Entrance Antiphon   Hebrews 9:15

Christ is mediator of a New Covenant, / so that by means of his death, those who are called / may receive the promise of an eternal inheritance.

Collect

Be near, O Lord, to those who plead before you,
and look kindly on those who place their hope in your
    mercy,
that, cleansed from the stain of their sins,
they may persevere in holy living
and be made full heirs of your promise.
Through our Lord Jesus Christ, your Son,
who lives and reigns with you in the unity of the Holy Spirit,
God, for ever and ever.

A reading from the Book of Genesis   17:3-9

You will be the father of a multitude of nations.

When Abram prostrated himself, God spoke to him: "My covenant with you is this: you are to become the father of a host of nations. No longer shall you be called Abram; your name shall be Abraham, for I am making you the father of a host of nations. I will render you exceedingly fertile; I will make nations of you; kings shall stem from you. I will maintain my covenant with you and your descendants after you throughout the ages as an everlasting pact, to be your God and the God of your descendants after you. I will give to you and to your descendants after you the land in which you are now staying, the whole land of Canaan, as a permanent possession; and I will be their God."

God also said to Abraham: "On your part, you and your descendants after you must keep my covenant throughout the ages."

The word of the Lord.

RESPONSORIAL PSALM   105:4-5, 6-7, 8-9

R7. (8a) **The Lord remembers his covenant for ever.**

Look to the LORD in his strength;
    seek to serve him constantly.
Recall the wondrous deeds that he has wrought,
    his portents, and the judgments he has uttered. R7.

You descendants of Abraham, his servants,
    sons of Jacob, his chosen ones!
He, the LORD, is our God;
    throughout the earth his judgments prevail. R7.

He remembers forever his covenant
    which he made binding for a thousand generations—
Which he entered into with Abraham
    and by his oath to Isaac. R7.

GOSPEL ACCLAMATION   Psalm 95:8

If today you hear his voice,
harden not your hearts.

A reading from the holy Gospel according to John   8:51-59

Your father, Abraham, rejoiced because he saw my day.

Jesus said to the Jews: "Amen, amen, I say to you, whoever keeps my word will never see death." So the Jews said to him, "Now we are sure that you are possessed. Abraham died, as did the prophets, yet you say, 'Whoever keeps my word will never taste death.' Are you greater than our father Abraham, who died? Or the prophets, who died?

Who do you make yourself out to be?" Jesus answered, "If I glorify myself, my glory is worth nothing; but it is my Father who glorifies me, of whom you say, 'He is our God.' You do not know him, but I know him. And if I should say that I do not know him, I would be like you a liar. But I do know him and I keep his word. Abraham your father rejoiced to see my day; he saw it and was glad." So the Jews said to him, "You are not yet fifty years old and you have seen Abraham?" Jesus said to them, "Amen, amen, I say to you, before Abraham came to be, I AM." So they picked up stones to throw at him; but Jesus hid and went out of the temple area.

The Gospel of the Lord.

PRAYER OVER THE OFFERINGS
Look with favor, Lord, we pray,
on these sacrificial offerings,
that they may profit our conversion
and the salvation of all the world.
Through Christ our Lord.

COMMUNION ANTIPHON   Romans 8:32
God did not spare his own Son, but handed him over for us all; / with him, he has given us all things.

PRAYER AFTER COMMUNION
Nourished by your saving gifts,
we beseech your mercy, Lord,
that by this same Sacrament,
with which you feed us in the present age,
you may make us partakers of life eternal.
Through Christ our Lord.

Reflection

Forever Is Forever

I recently read a clarifying distinction between a contract and a covenant. If one party does something in violation of a *contract*, then the whole contract is considered null and void. The signers of a contract agree to hold up their end only if the other party does. With a *covenant*, however, both parties pledge to hold up their end of the agreement regardless of whether the other party does. A violation of a covenant by one party does not change the agreement by the other party.

When God enters a covenant with Abraham and his descendants, it is forever. This changes the course of human history, but we often forget the significance of it. We default to thinking in terms of a contract, believing God will abandon his side of the covenant if Abraham or his descendants fall short.

The Lord remembers his covenant forever. When we forget this, we argue like the religious leaders in today's Gospel, and we have plenty of leaders who still do that today. But when we remember that God's covenant is forever, we are compelled and inspired by God's unbroken commitment, and we resolve to respond in kind.

A contemporary example of this is a loving parent. Parents who have been loved unconditionally as children instinctively love their own children, no matter how hurtful or broken they become. No matter what children say or do, parents cannot help but continue to love them.

May we remember God's love for us by loving others without distinction.

Fr. Brendan McGuire

Brendan McGuire is pastor of St. Simon Parish, Los Altos, California, and author of a book of Sunday homilies, Weaving the Divine Thread.

Evening

God, come to my assistance.
Lord, make haste to help me.

(opt. hymn, pp. 360–65)

PSALM 136:1-9

O give thanks to the LORD, who is good,
for God's faithful love endures forever.
Give thanks to the God of gods,
for God's faithful love endures forever.
Give thanks to the Lord of lords,
for God's faithful love endures forever.

Who alone has wrought marvelous works,
for God's faithful love endures forever.
who in wisdom made the heavens,
for God's faithful love endures forever;
who spread the earth on the waters,
for God's faithful love endures forever.

It was the Lord who made the great lights,
for God's faithful love endures forever;
the sun to rule in the day,
for God's faithful love endures forever;
the moon and the stars in the night,
for God's faithful love endures forever.

Glory to the Father . . .

SCRIPTURE   Romans 4:1-5

What then can we say that Abraham found, our ancestor according to the flesh? Indeed, if Abraham was
justified on the basis of his works, he has reason to boast;
but this was not so in the sight of God. For what does the
scripture say? "Abraham believed God, and it was credited

to him as righteousness." A worker's wage is credited not as a gift, but as something due. But when one does not work, yet believes in the one who justifies the ungodly, his faith is credited as righteousness.

READ, PONDER, PRAY on a word or phrase from these readings or another of today's Scriptures (*Lectio Divina*, p. 359)

ANTIPHON
Abraham's descendants are those who follow the example of his faith.

CANTICLE OF MARY *(inside back cover)*

INTERCESSIONS
Loving God, your mercy endures forever. In hope we pray: ℟. **Open our hearts to receive your living Word, O God.**

For spiritual directors and companions, confessors, and catechists, we pray: ℟.

For Scripture scholars, translators, and editors, we pray: ℟.

For Church architects, sculptors, and all who create beauty in our worship spaces, we pray: ℟.

Our Father . . .

May the peace of Christ reign in our hearts, and may the love of Christ be the foundation of our lives, by the power of the Holy Spirit. Amen.

Friday, March 31

Morning

O Lord, open my lips.
And my mouth will proclaim your praise.

(opt. hymn, pp. 360–65)

PSALM 69:2-4, 6-7

Save me, O God, for the waters
have risen to my neck.
I have sunk into the mud of the deep,
where there is no foothold.
I have entered the waters of the deep,
where the flood overwhelms me.

I am wearied with crying aloud;
my throat is parched.
My eyes are wasted away
with waiting for my God.

O God, you know my folly;
from you my sins are not hidden.
May those who hope in you not be shamed
because of me, O Lord of hosts;
may those who seek you not be disgraced
because of me, O God of Israel.

Glory to the Father . . .

SCRIPTURE   Job 30:12-16

On my right the young rabble rise up; / they trip my
feet, / they build their approaches for my ruin. / They
tear up my path, / they promote my ruin, / no helper is there
against them. / As through a wide breach they advance; /
amid the uproar they come on in waves; / terrors roll over

me. / My dignity is driven off like the wind, / and my well-being vanishes like a cloud. / And now my life ebbs away from me, / days of affliction have taken hold of me.

READ, PONDER, PRAY on a word or phrase from these readings or another of today's Scriptures (*Lectio Divina*, p. 359)

ANTIPHON
Lord, to you I have entrusted my cause.

CANTICLE OF ZECHARIAH *(inside front cover)*

INTERCESSIONS
Righteous God, your words are Spirit and life. Desiring everlasting life we pray: R̥. **Bring us into eternity, O God.**

For all who are discerning their path of discipleship and love, we pray: R̥.

For all believers and for those who persevere in faith in the midst of struggles and doubts, we pray: R̥.

For those whose earthly life is nearing the end, we pray: R̥.

Our Father . . .

May God strengthen us to be joyful in hope, patient in affliction, and faithful in prayer, through Jesus, our brother. Amen.

Blessed Among Us

St. Maria Skobtsova
Orthodox Nun and Martyr (1891–1945)

Lisa Pilenko was born into an aristocratic family in Russia. A political activist in her youth, twice married and the mother of three, she joined the throng of refugees uprooted by the revolution in 1923 and made her way to Paris. There, after the death of her youngest daughter, she experienced a profound conversion. She emerged with a determination "to be a mother for all, for all who need care, assistance, or protection."

In Paris she immersed herself in social work among the destitute Russian refugees. Increasingly she emphasized the religious dimension of this work, the insight that "each person is the very icon of God incarnate in the world." Her bishop encouraged her to become a nun. Yet, she was determined to pioneer a new form of monasticism, engaged in the world, avoiding "even the subtlest barrier which might separate the heart from the world and its wounds." In 1932 she made her monastic profession and became Mother Maria. In a house in Paris she established a soup kitchen, with her "cell" consisting of a cot in the basement beside the boiler.

After the German occupation of Paris, she worked with her chaplain to hide and rescue Jews, leading eventually to her arrest along with her son. She survived two years in Ravensbruck concentration camp before dying on the eve of Easter, March 31, 1945.

In 2004 she was canonized by the Russian Orthodox Church.

"I am your message, Lord. Throw me like a blazing torch into the night that all may see and understand what it means to be a disciple."

—Mother Maria Skobtsova

Mass
Friday of the Fifth Week of Lent

ENTRANCE ANTIPHON   Cf. Psalm 31 (30):10, 16, 18

Have mercy on me, O Lord, for I am in distress. / Deliver
me from the hands of my enemies and those who pursue
me. / O Lord, let me never be put to shame, for I call
on you.

COLLECT

Pardon the offenses of your peoples, we pray, O Lord,
and in your goodness set us free
from the bonds of the sins
we have committed in our weakness.
Through our Lord Jesus Christ, your Son,
who lives and reigns with you in the unity of the Holy Spirit,
God, for ever and ever.

Or:

O God, who in this season
give your Church the grace
to imitate devoutly the Blessed Virgin Mary
in contemplating the Passion of Christ,
grant, we pray, through her intercession,
that we may cling more firmly each day
to your Only Begotten Son
and come at last to the fullness of his grace.
Who lives and reigns with you in the unity of the
     Holy Spirit,
God, for ever and ever.

A reading from the Book of the Prophet Jeremiah   20:10-13

The LORD God is with me, a mighty hero.

hear the whisperings of many: / "Terror on every side! /
Denounce! let us denounce him!" / All those who were

my friends / are on the watch for any misstep of mine. / "Perhaps he will be trapped; then we can prevail, / and take our vengeance on him." / But the LORD is with me, like a mighty champion: / my persecutors will stumble, they will not triumph. / In their failure they will be put to utter shame, / to lasting, unforgettable confusion. / O LORD of hosts, you who test the just, / who probe mind and heart, / Let me witness the vengeance you take on them, / for to you I have entrusted my cause. / Sing to the LORD, / praise the LORD, / For he has rescued the life of the poor / from the power of the wicked!

The word of the Lord.

RESPONSORIAL PSALM   18:2-3a, 3bc-4, 5-6, 7

℟. (see 7) **In my distress I called upon the Lord, and he
heard my voice.**

I love you, O LORD, my strength,
    O LORD, my rock, my fortress, my deliverer. ℟.

My God, my rock of refuge,
    my shield, the horn of my salvation, my stronghold!
Praised be the LORD, I exclaim,
    and I am safe from my enemies. ℟.

The breakers of death surged round about me,
    the destroying floods overwhelmed me;
The cords of the nether world enmeshed me,
    the snares of death overtook me. ℟.

In my distress I called upon the LORD
    and cried out to my God;
From his temple he heard my voice,
    and my cry to him reached his ears. ℟.

GOSPEL ACCLAMATION   See John 6:63c, 68c
**Your words, Lord, are Spirit and life;
you have the words of everlasting life.**

A reading from the holy Gospel according to John 10:31-42

They wanted to arrest Jesus, but he eluded them.

The Jews picked up rocks to stone Jesus. Jesus answered
them, "I have shown you many good works from my
Father. For which of these are you trying to stone me?" The
Jews answered him, "We are not stoning you for a good
work but for blasphemy. You, a man, are making yourself
God." Jesus answered them, "Is it not written in your law,
'I said, "You are gods"'? If it calls them gods to whom the
word of God came, and Scripture cannot be set aside, can
you say that the one whom the Father has consecrated and
sent into the world blasphemes because I said, 'I am the Son
of God'? If I do not perform my Father's works, do not
believe me; but if I perform them, even if you do not believe
me, believe the works, so that you may realize and understand that the Father is in me and I am in the Father."
Then they tried again to arrest him; but he escaped from
their power.

He went back across the Jordan to the place where John
first baptized, and there he remained. Many came to him
and said, "John performed no sign, but everything John
said about this man was true." And many there began to
believe in him.

The Gospel of the Lord.

PRAYER OVER THE OFFERINGS
**Grant, O merciful God, that we may be worthy
to serve ever fittingly at your altars,
and there to be saved by constant participation.
Through Christ our Lord.**

COMMUNION ANTIPHON   1 Peter 2:24

**Jesus bore our sins in his own body on the cross, / so that
dead to sin, we might live for righteousness. / By his
wounds we have been healed.**

PRAYER AFTER COMMUNION

**May the unfailing protection
of the sacrifice we have received
never leave us, O Lord,
and may it always drive far from us
all that would do us harm.
Through Christ our Lord.**

Reflection

Snares of the Enemy

Vengeance takes center stage in today's readings, just as it
often does in our own lives. We might read Jeremiah's words
and feel uncomfortable hearing his in-your-face prayer asking for justice to be brought down on those who mistreat
him. But the truth is, we've all been Jeremiah at some point.
Someone does something to threaten us, and we imagine
how sweet it would be not only to be free from the threats
but to watch as our enemies get their comeuppance.

Unfortunately, what was once a rarity is becoming the
norm. People on all sides seem to have a thirst for vengeance
and a willingness to take matters into their own hands. Much
like the mob in today's Gospel, modern-day crowds gather
around those considered outsiders and pick up their version
of stones. Where are we in this scene? Do we have a rock in
hand? Are we in the crowd waiting to watch justice play out?
Are we the one who feels threatened? Every one of us has a

choice in how we respond. We can choose fear, or we can choose trust.

Do we believe, truly and without hedging, that God is our "rock of refuge," and we need nothing more? It is only through such deep and abiding trust that we begin to realize we can release ourselves from the snares of the enemy, snares that have no power once we stop giving them oxygen and put everything in God's hands.

Trust in God, and watch the traps and threats fall away.

Mary DeTurris Poust

Mary DeTurris Poust is a writer, retreat leader, and yoga teacher. She writes about the spiritual journey and learning to discover the divine in the everyday. Visit her website, Not Strictly Spiritual, *to see more of her work.*

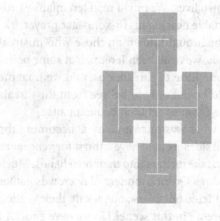

Evening

God, come to my assistance.
Lord, make haste to help me.

(opt. hymn, pp. 360–65)

PSALM 13

How long, O LORD? Will you forget me forever?
How long will you hide your face from me?
How long must I bear grief in my soul,
have sorrow in my heart all day long?
How long shall my enemy prevail over me?

Look, answer me, O LORD my God!
Give light to my eyes lest I fall asleep in death;
lest my enemy say, "I have prevailed over you;"
lest my foes rejoice when they see me fall.

As for me, I trust in your faithful love.
Let my heart rejoice in your salvation.
I will sing to the LORD who has been bountiful with me.

Glory to the Father . . .

SCRIPTURE   1 John 4:13-16

This is how we know that we remain in [God] and he in us, that he has given us of his Spirit. Moreover, we have seen and testify that the Father sent his Son as savior of the world. Whoever acknowledges that Jesus is the Son of God, God remains in him and he in God. We have come to know and to believe in the love God has for us.

God is love, and whoever remains in love remains in God and God in him.

READ, PONDER, PRAY on a word or phrase from these readings or another of today's Scriptures (*Lectio Divina*, p. 359)

ANTIPHON

God remains in everyone who acknowledges that Jesus is the Son of God.

CANTICLE OF MARY *(inside back cover)*

INTERCESSIONS

Ever-living God, you see our grief and, at the right time, take things in hand. In faith we pray: R̊. **God, come to our aid.**

Attune our eyes, minds, and hearts to ways in which we can encourage one another in faith, hope, and love. R̊.

Help us to embrace the beauty of creation and to preserve it for future generations. R̊.

Assist efforts to help communities recover from tragedy, prevent further violence, and thrive. R̊.

Our Father . . .

May God strengthen us to seek and pursue peace, through Jesus, the justice of God. Amen.

The Order of Mass

▐▌ In the name of the Father, and of the Son, and of the
Holy Spirit.

▐▌ **Amen.**

GREETING

A The grace of our Lord Jesus Christ,
and the love of God,
and the communion of the Holy Spirit
be with you all.
And with your spirit.

B Grace to you and peace from God our Father
and the Lord Jesus Christ.
And with your spirit.

C The Lord be with you.
And with your spirit.

PENITENTIAL ACT

Brethren (brothers and sisters), let us acknowledge our sins,
and so prepare ourselves to celebrate the sacred mysteries.
(Pause)

A **I confess to almighty God**
and to you, my brothers and sisters,
that I have greatly sinned,
in my thoughts and in my words,
in what I have done and in what I have failed to do,

And, striking their breast, they say:

through my fault, through my fault,
through my most grievous fault;

Then they continue:

329

therefore I ask blessed Mary ever-Virgin,
all the Angels and Saints,
and you, my brothers and sisters,
to pray for me to the Lord our God.

B Have mercy on us, O Lord.
For we have sinned against you.

Show us, O Lord, your mercy.
And grant us your salvation.

These or other invocations may be used.

C You were sent to heal the contrite of heart:
Lord, have mercy. Or: Kyrie, eleison.
Lord, have mercy. Or: **Kyrie, eleison.**

You came to call sinners:
Christ, have mercy. Or: Christe, eleison.
Christ, have mercy. Or: **Christe, eleison.**

You are seated at the right hand of the Father to
intercede for us:
Lord, have mercy. Or: Kyrie, eleison.
Lord, have mercy. Or: **Kyrie, eleison.**

▮▮ May almighty God have mercy on us,
forgive us our sins,
and bring us to everlasting life.
▮▮ Amen.

KYRIE

The Kyrie, eleison (Lord, have mercy) invocations follow, unless they
have just occurred in a formula of the Penitential Act.

▮▮ Lord, have mercy.	**▮▮** Kyrie, eleison.
▮▮ Lord, have mercy.	**▮▮ Kyrie, eleison.**
▮▮ Christ, have mercy.	**▮▮** Christe, eleison.
▮▮ Christ, have mercy.	**▮▮ Christe, eleison.**
▮▮ Lord, have mercy.	**▮▮** Kyrie, eleison.
▮▮ Lord, have mercy.	**▮▮ Kyrie, eleison.**

GLORIA

**Glory to God in the highest,
and on earth peace to people of good will.**

**We praise you,
we bless you,
we adore you,
we glorify you,
we give you thanks for your great glory,
Lord God, heavenly King,
O God, almighty Father.**

**Lord Jesus Christ, Only Begotten Son,
Lord God, Lamb of God, Son of the Father,
you take away the sins of the world,
    have mercy on us;
you take away the sins of the world,
    receive our prayer;
you are seated at the right hand of the Father,
    have mercy on us.**

**For you alone are the Holy One,
you alone are the Lord,
you alone are the Most High,
Jesus Christ,
with the Holy Spirit,
in the glory of God the Father.
Amen.**

COLLECT (OPENING PRAYER)

LITURGY OF THE WORD

FIRST READING

RESPONSORIAL PSALM

SECOND READING

Gospel Acclamation

Gospel

Cleanse my heart and my lips, almighty God,
that I may worthily proclaim your holy Gospel.

❚❚ The Lord be with you.
❚❚ **And with your spirit.**

❚❚ A reading from the holy Gospel according to N.
❚❚ **Glory to you, O Lord.**

At the end:

❚❚ The Gospel of the Lord.
❚❚ **Praise to you, Lord Jesus Christ.**

Through the words of the Gospel
may our sins be wiped away.

Homily

Profession of Faith
[The Apostles' Creed can be found on p. 357]

Nicene Creed
I believe in one God,
the Father almighty,
maker of heaven and earth,
of all things visible and invisible.

I believe in one Lord Jesus Christ,
the Only Begotten Son of God,
born of the Father before all ages.
God from God, Light from Light,
true God from true God,
begotten, not made, consubstantial with the Father;
through him all things were made.
For us men and for our salvation
he came down from heaven,

At the words that follow, up to and including *and became man,*
all bow.

**and by the Holy Spirit was incarnate of the Virgin Mary,
and became man.**

**For our sake he was crucified under Pontius Pilate,
he suffered death and was buried,
and rose again on the third day
in accordance with the Scriptures.
He ascended into heaven
and is seated at the right hand of the Father.
He will come again in glory
to judge the living and the dead
and his kingdom will have no end.**

**I believe in the Holy Spirit, the Lord, the giver of life,
who proceeds from the Father and the Son,
who with the Father and the Son is adored and glorified,
who has spoken through the prophets.**

**I believe in one, holy, catholic and apostolic Church.
I confess one Baptism for the forgiveness of sins
and I look forward to the resurrection of the dead
and the life of the world to come. Amen.**

PRAYER OF THE FAITHFUL (BIDDING PRAYERS)

LITURGY OF THE EUCHARIST

PRESENTATION AND PREPARATION OF THE GIFTS
Blessed are you, Lord God of all creation,
for through your goodness we have received
the bread we offer you:
fruit of the earth and work of human hands,
it will become for us the bread of life.

Blessed be God for ever.

By the mystery of this water and wine
may we come to share in the divinity of Christ
who humbled himself to share in our humanity.

**Blessed are you, Lord God of all creation,
for through your goodness we have received
the wine we offer you:
fruit of the vine and work of human hands,
it will become our spiritual drink.**

Blessed be God for ever.

With humble spirit and contrite heart
may we be accepted by you, O Lord,
and may our sacrifice in your sight this day
be pleasing to you, Lord God.

Wash me, O Lord, from my iniquity
and cleanse me from my sin.

INVITATION TO PRAYER
Pray, brethren (brothers and sisters),
that my sacrifice and yours
may be acceptable to God,
the almighty Father.

**May the Lord accept the sacrifice at your hands
for the praise and glory of his name,
for our good
and the good of all his holy Church.**

PRAYER OVER THE OFFERINGS

EUCHARISTIC PRAYER
▐▌ The Lord be with you.   ▐▌ **And with your spirit.**
▐▌ Lift up your hearts.   ▐▌ **We lift them up to the Lord.**
▐▌ Let us give thanks to the Lord our God.
▐▌ **It is right and just.**

PREFACE III OF LENT
The fruits of abstinence
(The following Preface is said in Masses of the weekdays of Lent and on days of fasting.)
It is truly right and just, our duty and our salvation,
always and everywhere to give you thanks,
Lord, holy Father, almighty and eternal God.

For you will that our self-denial should give you thanks,
humble our sinful pride,
contribute to the feeding of the poor,
and so help us imitate you in your kindness.

And so we glorify you with countless Angels,
as with one voice of praise we acclaim:

Holy, Holy, Holy Lord God of hosts . . .

PREFACE OF THE SECOND SUNDAY OF LENT
The Transfiguration of the Lord
It is truly right and just, our duty and our salvation,
always and everywhere to give you thanks,
Lord, holy Father, almighty and eternal God,
through Christ our Lord.

For after he had told the disciples of his coming Death,
on the holy mountain he manifested to them his glory,
to show, even by the testimony of the law and the prophets,
that the Passion leads to the glory of the Resurrection.

And so, with the Powers of heaven,
we worship you constantly on earth,
and before your majesty
without end we acclaim:

Holy, Holy, Holy Lord God of hosts . . .

PREFACE OF THE THIRD SUNDAY OF LENT, YEAR A
The Samaritan Woman
It is truly right and just, our duty and our salvation,
always and everywhere to give you thanks,

Lord, holy Father, almighty and eternal God,
through Christ our Lord.

For when he asked the Samaritan woman for water to drink,
he had already created the gift of faith within her
and so ardently did he thirst for her faith,
that he kindled in her the fire of divine love.

And so we, too, give you thanks
and with the Angels
praise your mighty deeds, as we acclaim:

Holy, Holy, Holy Lord God of hosts . . .

PREFACE OF THE FOURTH SUNDAY OF LENT, YEAR A
The Man Born Blind

It is truly right and just, our duty and our salvation,
always and everywhere to give you thanks,
Lord, holy Father, almighty and eternal God,
through Christ our Lord.

By the mystery of the Incarnation,
he has led the human race that walked in darkness
into the radiance of the faith
and has brought those born in slavery to ancient sin
through the waters of regeneration
to make them your adopted children.

Therefore, all creatures of heaven and earth
sing a new song in adoration,
and we, with all the host of Angels,
cry out, and without end acclaim:

Holy, Holy, Holy Lord God of hosts . . .

PREFACE OF THE FIFTH SUNDAY OF LENT, YEAR A
Lazarus

It is truly right and just, our duty and our salvation,
always and everywhere to give you thanks,

Lord, holy Father, almighty and eternal God,
through Christ our Lord.

For as true man he wept for Lazarus his friend
and as eternal God raised him from the tomb,
just as, taking pity on the human race,
he leads us by sacred mysteries to new life.

Through him the host of Angels adores your majesty
and rejoices in your presence for ever.
May our voices, we pray, join with theirs
in one chorus of exultant praise, as we acclaim:

Holy, Holy, Holy Lord God of hosts . . .

PREFACE OF THE SOLEMNITY OF SAINT JOSEPH
The mission of Saint Joseph
It is truly right and just, our duty and our salvation,
always and everywhere to give you thanks,
Lord, holy Father, almighty and eternal God,
and on the Solemnity of Saint Joseph
to give you fitting praise,
to glorify you and bless you.

For this just man was given by you
as spouse to the Virgin Mother of God
and set as a wise and faithful servant
in charge of your household,
to watch like a father over your Only Begotten Son,
who was conceived by the overshadowing of the Holy Spirit,
our Lord Jesus Christ.

Through him the Angels praise your majesty,
Dominions adore and Powers tremble before you.
Heaven and the Virtues of heaven and the blessed Seraphim
worship together with exultation.
May our voices, we pray, join with theirs
in humble praise, as we acclaim:

Holy, Holy, Holy Lord God of hosts . . .

PREFACE OF THE SOLEMNITY OF THE ANNUNCIATION
The mystery of the Incarnation

It is truly right and just, our duty and our salvation,
always and everywhere to give you thanks,
Lord, holy Father, almighty and eternal God,
through Christ our Lord.

For the Virgin Mary heard with faith
that the Christ was to be born among men and for men's
     sake
by the overshadowing power of the Holy Spirit.
Lovingly she bore him in her immaculate womb,
that the promises to the children of Israel might come about
and the hope of nations be accomplished beyond all telling.

Through him the host of Angels adores your majesty
and rejoices in your presence for ever.
May our voices, we pray, join with theirs
in one chorus of exultant praise, as we acclaim:

SANCTUS

Holy, Holy, Holy Lord God of hosts.
Heaven and earth are full of your glory.
Hosanna in the highest.
Blessed is he who comes in the name of the Lord.
Hosanna in the highest.

EUCHARISTIC PRAYER I (Roman Canon)

To you, therefore, most merciful Father,
we make humble prayer and petition
through Jesus Christ, your Son, our Lord:
that you accept
and bless ✛ these gifts, these offerings,
these holy and unblemished sacrifices,
which we offer you firstly
for your holy catholic Church.
Be pleased to grant her peace,
to guard, unite and govern her

throughout the whole world,
together with your servant N. our Pope
and N. our Bishop,
and all those who, holding to the truth,
hand on the catholic and apostolic faith.

Remember, Lord, your servants N. and N.
and all gathered here,
whose faith and devotion are known to you.
For them, we offer you this sacrifice of praise
or they offer it for themselves
and all who are dear to them:
for the redemption of their souls,
in hope of health and well-being,
and paying their homage to you,
the eternal God, living and true.

In communion with those whose memory we venerate,
especially the glorious ever-Virgin Mary,
Mother of our God and Lord, Jesus Christ,
† and blessed Joseph, her Spouse,
your blessed Apostles and Martyrs,
Peter and Paul, Andrew,
(James, John,
Thomas, James, Philip,
Bartholomew, Matthew,
Simon and Jude;
Linus, Cletus, Clement, Sixtus,
Cornelius, Cyprian,
Lawrence, Chrysogonus,
John and Paul,
Cosmas and Damian)
and all your Saints;
we ask that through their merits and prayers,
in all things we may be defended
by your protecting help.
(Through Christ our Lord. Amen.)

Therefore, Lord, we pray:
graciously accept this oblation of our service,
that of your whole family;
order our days in your peace,
and command that we be delivered from eternal damnation
and counted among the flock of those you have chosen.
(Through Christ our Lord. Amen.)

Be pleased, O God, we pray,
to bless, acknowledge,
and approve this offering in every respect;
make it spiritual and acceptable,
so that it may become for us
the Body and Blood of your most beloved Son,
our Lord Jesus Christ.

On the day before he was to suffer,
he took bread in his holy and venerable hands,
and with eyes raised to heaven
to you, O God, his almighty Father,
giving you thanks, he said the blessing,
broke the bread
and gave it to his disciples, saying:

TAKE THIS, ALL OF YOU, AND EAT OF IT,
FOR THIS IS MY BODY,
WHICH WILL BE GIVEN UP FOR YOU.

In a similar way, when supper was ended,
he took this precious chalice
in his holy and venerable hands,
and once more giving you thanks, he said the blessing
and gave the chalice to his disciples, saying:

TAKE THIS, ALL OF YOU, AND DRINK FROM IT,
FOR THIS IS THE CHALICE OF MY BLOOD,
THE BLOOD OF THE NEW AND ETERNAL COVENANT,

WHICH WILL BE POURED OUT FOR YOU AND FOR MANY
FOR THE FORGIVENESS OF SINS.

DO THIS IN MEMORY OF ME.

The mystery of faith.

A We proclaim your Death, O Lord,
and profess your Resurrection
until you come again.

B When we eat this Bread and drink this Cup,
we proclaim your Death, O Lord,
until you come again.

C Save us, Savior of the world,
for by your Cross and Resurrection
you have set us free.

Therefore, O Lord,
as we celebrate the memorial of the blessed Passion,
the Resurrection from the dead,
and the glorious Ascension into heaven
of Christ, your Son, our Lord,
we, your servants and your holy people,
offer to your glorious majesty
from the gifts that you have given us,
this pure victim,
this holy victim,
this spotless victim,
the holy Bread of eternal life
and the Chalice of everlasting salvation.

Be pleased to look upon these offerings
with a serene and kindly countenance,
and to accept them,
as once you were pleased to accept
the gifts of your servant Abel the just,
the sacrifice of Abraham, our father in faith,

and the offering of your high priest Melchizedek,
a holy sacrifice, a spotless victim.

In humble prayer we ask you, almighty God:
command that these gifts be borne
by the hands of your holy Angel
to your altar on high
in the sight of your divine majesty,
so that all of us, who through this participation at the altar
receive the most holy Body and Blood of your Son,
may be filled with every grace and heavenly blessing.
(Through Christ our Lord. Amen.)

Remember also, Lord, your servants N. and N.,
who have gone before us with the sign of faith
and rest in the sleep of peace.

Grant them, O Lord, we pray,
and all who sleep in Christ,
a place of refreshment, light and peace.
(Through Christ our Lord. Amen.)

To us, also, your servants, who, though sinners,
hope in your abundant mercies,
graciously grant some share
and fellowship with your holy Apostles and Martyrs:
with John the Baptist, Stephen,
Matthias, Barnabas,
(Ignatius, Alexander,
Marcellinus, Peter,
Felicity, Perpetua,
Agatha, Lucy,
Agnes, Cecilia, Anastasia)
and all your Saints;
admit us, we beseech you,
into their company,
not weighing our merits,

but granting us your pardon,
through Christ our Lord.

Through whom
you continue to make all these good things, O Lord;
you sanctify them, fill them with life,
bless them, and bestow them upon us.

Through him, and with him, and in him,
O God, almighty Father,
in the unity of the Holy Spirit,
all glory and honor is yours,
for ever and ever.

Amen.

The Lord's Prayer, p. 353.

EUCHARISTIC PRAYER II
Preface
It is truly right and just, our duty and our salvation,
always and everywhere to give you thanks, Father most holy,
through your beloved Son, Jesus Christ,
your Word through whom you made all things,
whom you sent as our Savior and Redeemer,
incarnate by the Holy Spirit and born of the Virgin.

Fulfilling your will and gaining for you a holy people,
he stretched out his hands as he endured his Passion,
so as to break the bonds of death and manifest the resurrection.

And so, with the Angels and all the Saints
we declare your glory,
as with one voice we acclaim:

Holy, Holy, Holy Lord God of hosts . . .

You are indeed Holy, O Lord,
the fount of all holiness.
Make holy, therefore, these gifts, we pray,

by sending down your Spirit upon them like the dewfall,
so that they may become for us
the Body and ✠ Blood of our Lord Jesus Christ.

At the time he was betrayed
and entered willingly into his Passion,
he took bread and, giving thanks, broke it,
and gave it to his disciples, saying:

TAKE THIS, ALL OF YOU, AND EAT OF IT,
FOR THIS IS MY BODY,
WHICH WILL BE GIVEN UP FOR YOU.

In a similar way, when supper was ended,
he took the chalice
and, once more giving thanks,
he gave it to his disciples, saying:

TAKE THIS, ALL OF YOU, AND DRINK FROM IT,
FOR THIS IS THE CHALICE OF MY BLOOD,
THE BLOOD OF THE NEW AND ETERNAL COVENANT,
WHICH WILL BE POURED OUT FOR YOU AND FOR MANY
FOR THE FORGIVENESS OF SINS.

DO THIS IN MEMORY OF ME.

The mystery of faith.

A We proclaim your Death, O Lord,
and profess your Resurrection
until you come again.

B When we eat this Bread and drink this Cup,
we proclaim your Death, O Lord,
until you come again.

C Save us, Savior of the world,
for by your Cross and Resurrection
you have set us free.

Therefore, as we celebrate
the memorial of his Death and Resurrection,
we offer you, Lord,
the Bread of life and the Chalice of salvation,
giving thanks that you have held us worthy
to be in your presence and minister to you.

Humbly we pray
that, partaking of the Body and Blood of Christ,
we may be gathered into one by the Holy Spirit.

Remember, Lord, your Church,
spread throughout the world,
and bring her to the fullness of charity,
together with N. our Pope and N. our Bishop
and all the clergy.

Remember also our brothers and sisters
who have fallen asleep in the hope of the resurrection,
and all who have died in your mercy:
welcome them into the light of your face.
Have mercy on us all, we pray,
that with the Blessed Virgin Mary, Mother of God,
with blessed Joseph, her Spouse,
with the blessed Apostles,
and all the Saints who have pleased you throughout the ages,
we may merit to be coheirs to eternal life,
and may praise and glorify you
through your Son, Jesus Christ.

Through him, and with him, and in him,
O God, almighty Father,
in the unity of the Holy Spirit,
all glory and honor is yours,
for ever and ever.

Amen.

The Lord's Prayer, p. 353.

Eucharistic Prayer III

You are indeed Holy, O Lord,
and all you have created
rightly gives you praise,
for through your Son our Lord Jesus Christ,
by the power and working of the Holy Spirit,
you give life to all things and make them holy,
and you never cease to gather a people to yourself,
so that from the rising of the sun to its setting
a pure sacrifice may be offered to your name.

Therefore, O Lord, we humbly implore you:
by the same Spirit graciously make holy
these gifts we have brought to you for consecration,
that they may become the Body and ✠ Blood
of your Son our Lord Jesus Christ,
at whose command we celebrate these mysteries.

For on the night he was betrayed
he himself took bread,
and, giving you thanks, he said the blessing,
broke the bread and gave it to his disciples, saying:

Take this, all of you, and eat of it,
for this is my Body,
which will be given up for you.

In a similar way, when supper was ended,
he took the chalice,
and, giving you thanks, he said the blessing,
and gave the chalice to his disciples, saying:

Take this, all of you, and drink from it,
for this is the chalice of my Blood,
the Blood of the new and eternal covenant,
which will be poured out for you and for many
for the forgiveness of sins.

Do this in memory of me.

The mystery of faith.

A We proclaim your Death, O Lord,
and profess your Resurrection
until you come again.

B When we eat this Bread and drink this Cup,
we proclaim your Death, O Lord,
until you come again.

C Save us, Savior of the world,
for by your Cross and Resurrection
you have set us free.

Therefore, O Lord, as we celebrate the memorial
of the saving Passion of your Son,
his wondrous Resurrection
and Ascension into heaven,
and as we look forward to his second coming,
we offer you in thanksgiving
this holy and living sacrifice.

Look, we pray, upon the oblation of your Church
and, recognizing the sacrificial Victim by whose death
you willed to reconcile us to yourself,
grant that we, who are nourished
by the Body and Blood of your Son
and filled with his Holy Spirit,
may become one body, one spirit in Christ.

May he make of us
an eternal offering to you,
so that we may obtain an inheritance with your elect,
especially with the most Blessed Virgin Mary, Mother of God,
with blessed Joseph, her Spouse,
with your blessed Apostles and glorious Martyrs
(with Saint N.: the Saint of the day or Patron Saint)
and with all the Saints,

on whose constant intercession in your presence
we rely for unfailing help.

May this Sacrifice of our reconciliation,
we pray, O Lord,
advance the peace and salvation of all the world.
Be pleased to confirm in faith and charity
your pilgrim Church on earth,
with your servant N. our Pope and N. our Bishop,
the Order of Bishops, all the clergy,
and the entire people you have gained for your own.

Listen graciously to the prayers of this family,
whom you have summoned before you:
in your compassion, O merciful Father,
gather to yourself all your children
scattered throughout the world.

† To our departed brothers and sisters
and to all who were pleasing to you
at their passing from this life,
give kind admittance to your kingdom.
There we hope to enjoy for ever the fullness of your glory
through Christ our Lord,
through whom you bestow on the world all that is good. †

Through him, and with him, and in him,
O God, almighty Father,
in the unity of the Holy Spirit,
all glory and honor is yours,
for ever and ever.

Amen.

The Lord's Prayer, p. 353.

EUCHARISTIC PRAYER IV
Preface
It is truly right to give you thanks,
truly just to give you glory, Father most holy,

for you are the one God living and true,
existing before all ages and abiding for all eternity,
dwelling in unapproachable light;
yet you, who alone are good, the source of life,
have made all that is,
so that you might fill your creatures with blessings
and bring joy to many of them by the glory of your light.

And so, in your presence are countless hosts of Angels,
who serve you day and night
and, gazing upon the glory of your face,
glorify you without ceasing.

With them we, too, confess your name in exultation,
giving voice to every creature under heaven,
as we acclaim:

Holy, Holy, Holy Lord God of hosts . . .

We give you praise, Father most holy,
for you are great
and you have fashioned all your works
in wisdom and in love.
You formed man in your own image
and entrusted the whole world to his care,
so that in serving you alone, the Creator,
he might have dominion over all creatures.
And when through disobedience he had lost your friendship,
you did not abandon him to the domain of death.
For you came in mercy to the aid of all,
so that those who seek might find you.
Time and again you offered them covenants
and through the prophets
taught them to look forward to salvation.

And you so loved the world, Father most holy,
that in the fullness of time

you sent your Only Begotten Son to be our Savior.
Made incarnate by the Holy Spirit
and born of the Virgin Mary,
he shared our human nature
in all things but sin.
To the poor he proclaimed the good news of salvation,
to prisoners, freedom,
and to the sorrowful of heart, joy.
To accomplish your plan,
he gave himself up to death,
and, rising from the dead,
he destroyed death and restored life.

And that we might live no longer for ourselves
but for him who died and rose again for us,
he sent the Holy Spirit from you, Father,
as the first fruits for those who believe,
so that, bringing to perfection his work in the world,
he might sanctify creation to the full.

Therefore, O Lord, we pray:
may this same Holy Spirit
graciously sanctify these offerings,
that they may become
the Body and ✠ Blood of our Lord Jesus Christ
for the celebration of this great mystery,
which he himself left us
as an eternal covenant.

For when the hour had come
for him to be glorified by you, Father most holy,
having loved his own who were in the world,
he loved them to the end:
and while they were at supper,
he took bread, blessed and broke it,
and gave it to his disciples, saying:

TAKE THIS, ALL OF YOU, AND EAT OF IT,
FOR THIS IS MY BODY,
WHICH WILL BE GIVEN UP FOR YOU.

In a similar way,
taking the chalice filled with the fruit of the vine,
he gave thanks,
and gave the chalice to his disciples, saying:

TAKE THIS, ALL OF YOU, AND DRINK FROM IT,
FOR THIS IS THE CHALICE OF MY BLOOD,
THE BLOOD OF THE NEW AND ETERNAL COVENANT,
WHICH WILL BE POURED OUT FOR YOU AND FOR MANY
FOR THE FORGIVENESS OF SINS.

DO THIS IN MEMORY OF ME.

The mystery of faith.

A We proclaim your Death, O Lord,
and profess your Resurrection
until you come again.

B When we eat this Bread and drink this Cup,
we proclaim your Death, O Lord,
until you come again.

C Save us, Savior of the world,
for by your Cross and Resurrection
you have set us free.

Therefore, O Lord,
as we now celebrate the memorial of our redemption,
we remember Christ's Death
and his descent to the realm of the dead,
we proclaim his Resurrection
and his Ascension to your right hand,
and, as we await his coming in glory,
we offer you his Body and Blood,

the sacrifice acceptable to you
which brings salvation to the whole world.

Look, O Lord, upon the Sacrifice
which you yourself have provided for your Church,
and grant in your loving kindness
to all who partake of this one Bread and one Chalice
that, gathered into one body by the Holy Spirit,
they may truly become a living sacrifice in Christ
to the praise of your glory.

Therefore, Lord, remember now
all for whom we offer this sacrifice:
especially your servant N. our Pope,
N. our Bishop, and the whole Order of Bishops,
all the clergy,
those who take part in this offering,
those gathered here before you,
your entire people,
and all who seek you with a sincere heart.

Remember also
those who have died in the peace of your Christ
and all the dead,
whose faith you alone have known.

To all of us, your children,
grant, O merciful Father,
that we may enter into a heavenly inheritance
with the Blessed Virgin Mary, Mother of God,
with blessed Joseph, her Spouse,
and with your Apostles and Saints in your kingdom.
There, with the whole of creation,
freed from the corruption of sin and death,
may we glorify you through Christ our Lord,
through whom you bestow on the world all that is good.

Through him, and with him, and in him,
O God, almighty Father,
in the unity of the Holy Spirit,
all glory and honor is yours,
for ever and ever.

Amen.

COMMUNION RITE
LORD'S PRAYER
At the Savior's command
and formed by divine teaching,
we dare to say:

**Our Father, who art in heaven,
hallowed be thy name;
thy kingdom come,
thy will be done
on earth as it is in heaven.
Give us this day our daily bread,
and forgive us our trespasses,
as we forgive those who trespass against us;
and lead us not into temptation,
but deliver us from evil.**

Deliver us, Lord, we pray, from every evil,
graciously grant peace in our days,
that, by the help of your mercy,
we may be always free from sin
and safe from all distress,
as we await the blessed hope
and the coming of our Savior, Jesus Christ.

**For the kingdom,
the power and the glory are yours
now and for ever.**

SIGN OF PEACE
Lord Jesus Christ,
who said to your Apostles:
Peace I leave you, my peace I give you,
look not on our sins,
but on the faith of your Church,
and graciously grant her peace and unity
in accordance with your will.
Who live and reign for ever and ever.
Amen.

The peace of the Lord be with you always.
And with your spirit.

Let us offer each other the sign of peace.

BREAKING OF THE BREAD
May this mingling of the Body and Blood
of our Lord Jesus Christ
bring eternal life to us who receive it.

Lamb of God, you take away the sins of the world,
   have mercy on us.
Lamb of God, you take away the sins of the world,
   have mercy on us.
Lamb of God, you take away the sins of the world,
   grant us peace.

Lord Jesus Christ, Son of the living God,
who, by the will of the Father
and the work of the Holy Spirit,
through your Death gave life to the world,
free me by this, your most holy Body and Blood,
from all my sins and from every evil;
keep me always faithful to your commandments,
and never let me be parted from you.

Or:

May the receiving of your Body and Blood,
Lord Jesus Christ,
not bring me to judgment and condemnation,
but through your loving mercy
be for me protection in mind and body
and a healing remedy.

INVITATION TO COMMUNION

Behold the Lamb of God,
behold him who takes away the sins of the world.
Blessed are those called to the supper of the Lamb.

**Lord, I am not worthy
that you should enter under my roof,
but only say the word
and my soul shall be healed.**

If there is no singing, the communion antiphon is recited.

PRAYER AFTER COMMUNION

CONCLUDING RITES

FINAL BLESSING

▌▌ The Lord be with you.

▌▌ **And with your spirit.**

▌▌ May almighty God bless you,
the Father, and the Son, ✠ and the Holy Spirit.

▌▌ **Amen.**

DISMISSAL

A Go forth, the Mass is ended.

B Go and announce the Gospel of the Lord.

C Go in peace, glorifying the Lord by your life.

D Go in peace.

Thanks be to God.

Celebration of the Liturgy of the Word
[With Holy Communion]

INTRODUCTORY RITES
INTRODUCTION
Deacon or lay leader:

We gather here to celebrate the Lord's Day.
Sunday has been called the Lord's Day because
  it was on this day
that Jesus conquered sin and death and rose to new life.
Unfortunately, we are not able to celebrate the Mass today
because we do not have a priest.
Let us be united in the spirit of Christ with
  the Church around the world
and celebrate our redemption in Christ's suffering,
  death, and resurrection.

SIGN OF THE CROSS
Deacon or lay leader:

▍▍ In the name of the Father, and of the Son, and of the
  Holy Spirit.
▍▍ **Amen.**

GREETING
Deacon or lay leader:

▍▍ Grace and peace to you from God our Father and from
  the Lord Jesus Christ. Blessed be God for ever.
▍▍ **Blessed be God for ever.**

COLLECT

LITURGY OF THE WORD
FIRST READING
RESPONSORIAL PSALM
SECOND READING
GOSPEL ACCLAMATION
GOSPEL
HOMILY OR REFLECTION ON THE READINGS

PERIOD OF SILENCE
PROFESSION OF FAITH
[The Nicene Creed can be found on p. 332]

Apostles' Creed
I believe in God,
the Father almighty,
Creator of heaven and earth,
and in Jesus Christ, his only Son, our Lord,

> At the words that follow, up to and including the Virgin Mary,
> all bow.

who was conceived by the Holy Spirit,
born of the Virgin Mary,
suffered under Pontius Pilate,
was crucified, died and was buried;
he descended into hell;
on the third day he rose again from the dead;
he ascended into heaven,
and is seated at the right hand of God the Father almighty;
from there he will come to judge the living and the dead.

I believe in the Holy Spirit,
the holy catholic Church,
the communion of saints,
the forgiveness of sins,
the resurrection of the body,
and life everlasting. Amen.

PRAYER OF THE FAITHFUL

COMMUNION RITE
LORD'S PRAYER
Deacon or lay leader:
The Father provides us with food for eternal life.
At the Savior's command
and formed by divine teaching,
we dare to say:

Our Father, who art in heaven,
hallowed be thy name;
thy kingdom come,
thy will be done
on earth as it is in heaven.
Give us this day our daily bread,
and forgive us our trespasses,
as we forgive those who trespass against us;
and lead us not into temptation,
but deliver us from evil.
Amen.

INVITATION TO COMMUNION
Deacon or lay leader:

Behold the Lamb of God,
behold him who takes away the sins of the world.
Blessed are those called to the supper of the Lamb.

Lord, I am not worthy
that you should enter under my roof,
but only say the word
and my soul shall be healed.

COMMUNION

ACT OF THANKSGIVING

CONCLUDING RITE

INVITATION TO PRAY FOR VOCATIONS TO THE PRIESTHOOD
Deacon or lay leader:

Mindful of our Lord's word, "Ask the Master of the harvest
to send out laborers for the harvest," let us pray for an
increase of vocations to the priesthood. May our prayer
hasten the day when we will be able to take part in the
celebration of the Holy Eucharist every Sunday.

BLESSING

SIGN OF PEACE

Guide to *Lectio Divina*

Choose a word or phrase of the Scriptures you wish to pray. It makes no difference which text is chosen, as long as you have no set goal of "covering" a certain amount of text. The amount of text covered is in God's hands, not yours.

Read. Turn to the text and read it slowly, gently. Savor each portion of the reading, constantly listening for the "still, small voice" of a word or phrase that somehow says, "I am for you today." Do not expect lightning or ecstasies. In *lectio divina*, God is teaching us to listen, to seek him in silence. God does not reach out and grab us but gently invites us ever more deeply into his presence.

Ponder. Take the word or phrase into yourself. Memorize it and slowly repeat it to yourself, allowing it to interact with your inner world of concerns, memories, and ideas. Do not be afraid of distractions. Memories or thoughts are simply parts of yourself that, when they rise up during *lectio divina*, are asking to be given to God along with the rest of your inner self. Allow this inner pondering, this rumination, to invite you into dialogue with God.

Pray. Whether you use words, ideas, or images—or all three—is not important. Interact with God as you would with one who you know loves and accepts you. Give to God what you have discovered during your experience of meditation. Give to God what you have found within your heart.

It is not necessary to assess the quality of your *lectio divina*, as if you were "performing" or seeking some goal. *Lectio divina* has no goal other than that of being in the presence of God by praying the Scriptures.

—Fr. Luke Dysinger

Luke Dysinger, OSB, is a Benedictine monk of Saint Andrew's Abbey, Valyermo, California.

O God of Faith, by You We Live

Lent—AM
Familiar Tune: On Jordan's Bank

1. O God of faith, by you we live;
2. A - rise be - neath the morn - ing skies,
3. May your re - demp - tion set us free

un - fail - ing is the hope you give.
O Lamb pre - pared for sac - ri - fice.
to fol - low you to Cal - va - ry.

Of your for - give - ness let us sing,
We bear the cross a - long the way
So help us ban - ish death and sin

and hearts of pen - ance let us bring.
that leads to life from day to day.
that you, O Lord, may dwell with - in.

Text: Unknown.
Music: WINCHESTER NEW, 88 88; adapt. from *Musikalisches Handbuch*, Hamburg, 1690.

O Merciful Redeemer, Hear

Lent—AM/PM
Familiar Tune: O Radiant Light, O Sun Divine

1. O mer - ci - ful Re - deem - er, hear:
2. Our hearts are o - pen, Lord, to thee
3. O, grant most ho - ly Trin - i - ty,

in pit - y now in - cline your ear;
and know - ing our in - iq - ui - ty,
in un - di - vid - ed u - ni - ty,

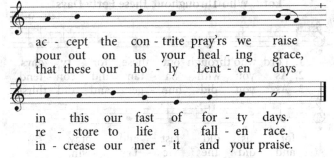

ac - cept the con - trite pray'rs we raise
pour out on us your heal - ing grace,
that these our ho - ly Lent - en days

in this our fast of for - ty days.
re - store to life a fall - en race.
in - crease our mer - it and your praise.

Text: Irvin Udulutsch, OFM, Cap., b. 1920, © 1959, 1977, Order of Saint Benedict,
administered by Liturgical Press, Collegeville, MN 56321. All rights reserved.
Music: JESU DULCIS MEMORIA, 88 88; Plainchant, Mode I.

The Glory of These Forty Days

Lent—AM/PM

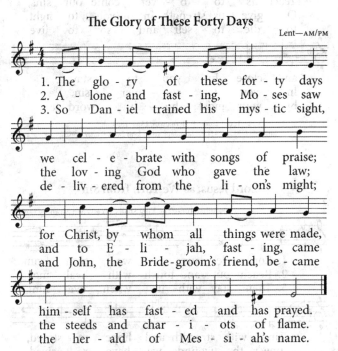

1. The glo - ry of these for - ty days
2. A - lone and fast - ing, Mo - ses saw
3. So Dan - iel trained his mys - tic sight,

we cel - e - brate with songs of praise;
the lov - ing God who gave the law;
de - liv - ered from the li - on's might;

for Christ, by whom all things were made,
and to E - li - jah, fast - ing, came
and John, the Bride-groom's friend, be - came

him - self has fast - ed and has prayed.
the steeds and char - i - ots of flame.
the her - ald of Mes - si - ah's name.

Text: *Clarum decus jejunii*; ascr. to Gregory the Great, c. 540–604; tr. Maurice F. Bell, 1862–1931.
Music: ERHALT UNS HERR, LM, Klug's *Geistliche Lieder*, 1543.

Lord, Who Throughout These Forty Days

Lent—AM/PM

1. Lord, who through-out these for-ty days, for us did fast and pray. Teach us to o-ver-come our sins, and close by you to stay.
2. As you with Sa-tan did con-tend and did the vic-t'ry win, O give us strength in you to fight, in you to con-quer sin.
3. As you did hun-ger and did thirst, so teach us, gra-cious Lord, to die to self and so to live by your most ho-ly word.

Text: Claudia F. Hernaman, 1838–1898, alt.
Music: ST. FLAVIAN, 86 86, adapt. from *John Day's Psalter*, 1562.

Lord Jesus, as We Turn from Sin

Lent—AM/PM
Familiar Tune: The King Shall Come When Morning Dawns

1. Lord Je-sus, as we turn from sin with strength and hope re-stored,
2. Reach out and touch with heal-ing pow'r the wounds we have re-ceived,
3. Then stay with us when eve-ning comes and dark-ness makes us blind,

re - ceive the hom - age that we
that in for - give - ness we may
O stay un - til the light of

bring to you, our ris - en Lord.
love and may no long - er grieve.
dawn may fill both heart and mind.

Text: Ralph Wright, O.S.B. © 1980, International Commission on English in the
Liturgy Corporation (ICEL). All rights reserved. Used with permission.
Music: MORNING SONG, 86 86, *Kentucky Harmony*, 1816.

Forty Days and Forty Nights

Lent—PM

1. For - ty days and for - ty nights
2. Shall not we, your sor - row share
3. And if Sa - tan on us press,

you were fast - ing in the wild;
and from world - ly joys ab - stain,
flesh or spir - it to as - sail,

for - ty days and for - ty nights
fast - ing with un - ceas - ing prayer,
vic - tor in the wil - der - ness,

tempt - ed and yet un - de - filed.
strong with you to suf - fer pain?
grant we may not faint or fail!

Text: George Hunt Smyttan, 1822–1890; tr. Francis Pott, 1832–1909, alt.
Music: HEINLEIN, 77 77, Martin Herbst, 1654–1681, attr.

All Creation Was Renewed

Marian—AM
Familiar Tune: Savior of the Nations, Come

1. All cre - a - tion was re - newed
2. By the Ho - ly Spir - it's love
3. Mo - ment of un - e - qualed faith,
4. Christ, the ho - ly one of God,

by the pow'r of God most high,
God pro-nounced his sav - ing Word,
here in an - y time or place:
Son of Da - vid, light from light,

when his pro - mise was ful - filled
then with free con - sent and trust
thus did God put on our flesh
dwells on earth, his glo - ry dimmed

Ad - am's race to jus - ti - fy.
Ma - ry bore cre - a - tion's Lord.
in his Vir - gin full of grace.
till he comes a - gain with might.

Music: NUN KOMM, DER HEIDEN HEILAND, 77 77; Erfurt *Enchiridia*, Wittenberg, 1524.

O Mary of Graces

Marian—AM/PM
Familiar Tune: How Firm a Foundation

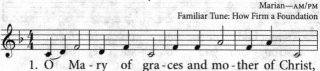

1. O Ma - ry of gra - ces and mo - ther of Christ,
2. O may you pro - tect us by land and by sea,

O may you di-rect us and guide us a-right.
and may you pro-tect us from sor-rows to be;

O may you pro-tect us from Sa-tan's con-trol,
a strong guard of an-gels a-bove us pro-vide;

and may you pro-tect us in bo-dy and soul.
may God walk be-fore us and stay at our side.

Text: Traditional Irish, alt.
Music: FOUNDATION, 11 11 11 11; Funk's *Compilation of Genuine Church Music*, 1832.

Great Temple of the Paraclete

Marian—AM/PM
Familiar Tune: Jerusalem, My Happy Home

1. Great tem-ple of the Par-a-clete, the
2. She crushed the anc-ient ser-pent's head, her
3. We come be-fore her, sin-ners all, con-
4. May we be spared from sud-den death, from

Ho-ly Spir-it's guest! O cit-y of the
splen-dor as the sun! She tri-umphs ov-er
fess our sins and say: O ho-ly Mar-y,
sick-ness and from ill, and share your glo-ry

glor-'ous God, of wo-man-kind the best!
moon and stars, more spot-less than the dawn!
ho-ly Queen, a mo-ther's care we pray.
meant for us, by God's e-ter-nal will.

Text: Bernard Mischke, OSC, 1926-2012, © 1965, Crosier Fathers and Brothers, Phoenix, AZ.
All rights reserved. Used with permission.
Music: LAND OF REST, CM, American.

Acknowledgments

Walter J. Burghardt, excerpt from *Sir, We Would Like to See Jesus: Homilies from a Hilltop* by Walter J. Burghardt, SJ. Copyright © 1982 by Walter J. Burghardt, SJ. Paulist Press, Inc., New York/Mahwah, NJ. Reprinted by permission of Paulist Press, Inc. www.paulistpress.com.

Luke Dysinger, "Guide to Lectio Divina," adapted from "Accepting the Embrace of God: The Ancient Art of *Lectio Divina*." Used with permission.

Cardinal Basil Hume, adapted from *A Turning to God* (Collegeville, MN: Liturgical Press, 2007), 20–21. Used with permission.

John J. McIlhon, adapted from *Forty Days Plus Three: Daily Reflections for Lent and Holy Week* (Collegeville, MN: Liturgical Press, 1989), 20–21. Used with permission.

Chiara Lubich, in *Essential Writings: Spirituality, Dialogue, Culture* (Hyde Park, NY: New City Press, 2007). Kindle edition. Used with permission.

Megan McKenna, *Lent: Reflections and Stories on the Daily Readings* (Maryknoll, NY: Orbis Books, 1996), 98–99. Used with permission of the author.

Irene Nowell, adapted from *Pleading, Cursing, Praising: Conversing with God through the Psalms* (Collegeville, MN: Liturgical Press, 2013), 25–26. Used with permission.

"O Cross, more worthy than cedar . . .," in *Days of the Lord: The Liturgical Year, Volume 3, Easter Triduum/Easter Season* (Collegeville, MN: Liturgical Press, 1993), 34–35. Used with permission.

"On the Solemnity of the Annunciation," in *Proclaiming All Your Wonders: Prayers for a Pilgrim People* (Collegeville, MN: Liturgical Press, 1991), 139. Used with permission.

Pope Francis, *General Audience*, May 11, 2016, www.vatican.va. © 2016 Libreria Editrice Vaticana. Used with permission.

"Prayer to Saint Joseph," from *Blessings and Prayers for Home and Family*, copyright © Concacan Inc., 2004. All rights reserved. Reproduced with permission of the Canadian Conference of Catholic Bishops. Visit cccbpublications.ca.

Mark A. Villano, adapted from *Journey to Jerusalem: Steps on the Road to Your Soul* (Collegeville, MN: Liturgical Press, 2020), 113–14. Used with permission.

Art Credits

Front cover: *The Annunciation* by Olga Shalamova. © Olga Shalamova. www.sacredmurals.com. Used with permission.

Carpet pages and calendar: Door design, Sleepy Hollow Cemetery, Sleepy Hollow, New York. Photo by Kendra Richards Ohmann. Used with permission.

Pages 23, 59, 119, 213, 233, 326: Illustrations by Frank Kacmarcik, OblSB, Saint John's Abbey, Collegeville, Minnesota. Used with permission.

Pages 40, 98, 192, 253, 275: Illustrations by Br. Martin Erspamer, OSB, a monk of Saint Meinrad Archabbey, Indiana. Used with permission.

Page 52: *Transfiguration of Jesus* by Lucinda Naylor. © Lucinda Naylor. www.lucindanaylor.com. Used with permission.

Page 122: *Jesus and the Samaritan Woman at the Well*, gold leaf, paint, and etching on glass, ca. 1420, German. Collection of the Metropolitan Museum of Art, New York. Gift of J. Pierpont Morgan, 1917. Public domain.

Page 153: Illustration by Fr. Emmanuel Franco, O. Carm., a friar of Our Lady of Mount Carmel Priory, Tucson, Arizona. Used with permission.

Page 266: *St. Lazarus of Bethany* by Nikola Sarić. © Nikola Sarić. www.nikolasaric.de. Used with permission.

Back cover: *Raising of Lazarus* by Brian Whelan. © Brian Whelan. www.brianwhelanart.com. Used with permission.

About the Cover

Later this month, we pause our Lenten journey to celebrate the Annunciation of the Lord. The angel's appearance to the Blessed Virgin represents the beginning of the message of the Incarnation of the Savior. Images of the Annunciation are among the oldest in Christian art—the earliest example is in the Catacombs of Priscilla in Rome. Olga Shalamova's cover icon represents a modern take on a Byzantine-inspired interpretation (www.sacredmurals.com).

The figures in Shalamova's icon display little emotion in their facial features, but true to the Byzantine style, their posture and gestures provide insight. Archangel Gabriel, hovering in front of the Blessed Virgin, holds a staff—symbol of the angel's role as divine messenger—and extends his other hand in a gesture of address used by orators of the classical period. The Italian title above the image identifies it as a depiction of the Annunciation, and the angel's greeting is written within the two panels: *Hail, O full of grace; the Lord is with you.*

The Virgin is in a standing position as she faces the angel, showing proper respect for her heavenly visitor, though she holds up her right hand with the palm facing out, a gesture indicating her initial question and hesitation: *How can this be?* In her other hand, she holds what may be a bobbin of thread. In iconography of the Byzantine tradition, Mary is often depicted spinning the thread that will be used to make the veil of the Temple. Lilies in the right-hand panel symbolize the purity of the Virgin and may also hint at the coincidence of the Annunciation with the coming of spring. Springtime's splendor is a fitting reminder of the true meaning behind our current liturgical season . . . and the one to follow.

—Br. Ælred Senna

Ælred Senna, OSB, is a monk of Saint John's Abbey in Collegeville, Minnesota, and publisher of Give Us This Day.

Give Us ThisDay®
DAILY PRAYER FOR TODAY'S CATHOLIC

Mary Stommes, *Editor*

Ælred Senna, OSB, *Publisher*

Catherine Donovan, *Associate Publisher*

Regina Scaringella, OP, *Assistant Editor*

Kendra Richards Ohmann, *Publishing Assistant*

Colleen Stiller, *Production Manager*

Julie Surma and Mark Warzecha, *Desktop Publishers*

Tara Wiese, *Art Design*

Robert Ellsberg, *"Blessed Among Us" Author*

Susan Barber, OSB, *Intercessions*

Therese L. Ratliff, *Liturgical Press Director*

Editorial Advisors
James Martin, SJ ♦ Irene Nowell, OSB
Carolyn Y. Woo ♦ Timothy Radcliffe, OP
Kathleen Norris ♦ Ronald Rolheiser, OMI

www.giveusthisday.org
Give Us This Day, Liturgical Press
PO Box 7500, Collegeville, MN 56321-7500
Customer Service: 888-259-8470, subscriptions@giveusthisday.org

Give Us This Day® (March 2023/Vol. 13, No. 3. ISSN 2159-2136, print; 2166-0654, large print; 2159-2128, online) is published monthly by Liturgical Press, an apostolate of Saint John's Abbey, 2950 Saint John's Road, Collegeville, Minnesota. Rev. John Klassen, OSB, *Abbot*. Periodicals postage paid at Collegeville, MN 56321 and other mailing offices. The annual standard subscription rate is $46.95; single copy price is $5.95. POSTMASTER: Send all UAA to CFS. (See DMM 507.1.5.2): NON-POSTAL AND MILITARY FACILITIES: Send address changes to *Give Us This Day*, PO Box 417, Congers, NY 10920-9984.